GREEN LONDON

Exploring London's
Parks & Gardens

Nana Ocran

GREEN LONDON

Exploring London's
Parks & Gardens

Nana Ocran

Acknowledgements

There are too many friends to mention who were sources of fun and inspiration while I was working on this new edition– many of them recommending their favourite parks or landmarks and a good few coming along with me for some urban green inspiration.

Once again I'd like to thank my family for their enthusiasm, and all those readers of the book who have contacted me over the years with recommendations and kind words.

I'd like to also thank the London boroughs whose staff were a huge help to the research of the book. Stand outs were Lambeth Borough Council, Islington Borough Council, City of London Corporation, Redbridge Borough Council, and Hackney Borough Council. I'd also like to thank the staff at the parks and gardens that I visited, and in particular those at Walworth Garden Farm, West Square Garden, Brockwell Park, Valentine's Park and Queen Elizabeth Olympic Park for their patience while I snooped around and threw questions at them.

Dedicated to my family

Queen Elizabeth Olympic Park

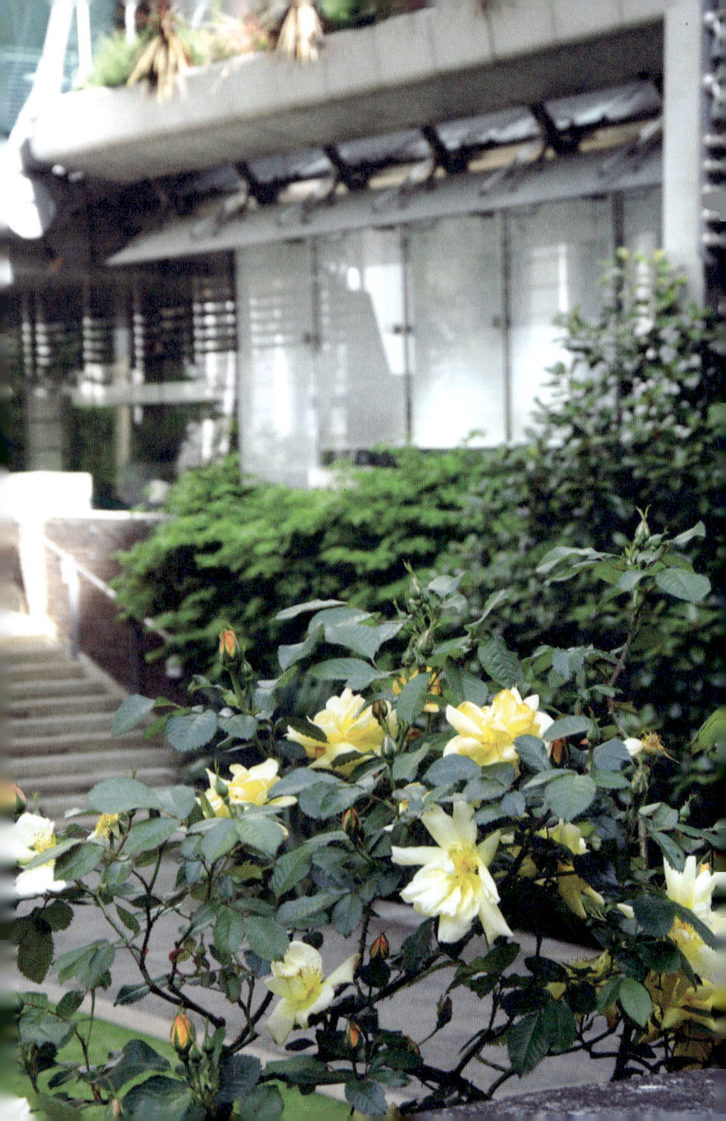

Contents

Introduction 1

Parks
- Area Map 6
- Central 8
- North 40
- West 76
- South-west 98
- South-east 118
- East 174
- Outer London 208

Gardens & Squares
- Area Map 228
- Central 234
- North 254
- West 255
- South 258
- East 261

Other Green Spaces
- Gated Parks & Gardens 264
- Commons 282
- Roof Gardens 294

Landmarks 300

Park Life
- Cafés 316
- Park Events 326

Index 334

London Fields

Introduction

Strangely enough, I've pretty much always thought of a park as just a park. A convenient green space to chill out in the absence of a garden, or to escape from the confines of an office, which has always meant latching on to whichever park is nearest to where I live or work.

However, in writing this book, I wanted to venture out to the four corners of London. This has meant viewing the capital in a more expansive way, unearthing London's character through some of the stories that have been generated by centuries of use of its outdoor spaces.

It's not just buildings that give London its character. The city's open spaces are a world within a world with the various strands of park life being particularly active during the summer months, when cyclists, runners, picnickers, sunbathers et al pack out London's avenues, woodlands, lawns and meadows. Often the bigger the park, or the better the facilities, the larger the crowds, but with each individual green space there often comes a particular type of visitor. It's lovely to see people practicing yoga or Tai Chi in Lincoln's Inn Fields, seasoned kite flyers on Hampstead Heath, lunchtime office workers scrutinising the hand-lettered tiles in Postman's Park, or earnest walkers heading into or out of Queen's Wood, Epping Forest or the woodland areas of Osterley Park. Sports grounds, boating lakes and even seasonally-filled paddling pools help generate a fleeting al fresco culture, and there's a huge pleasure in hearing the yelps of excitable children in places such as Priory Park's children's pool, or seeing young visitors' delight in getting drenched in the fountains at Bishop's Park.

But then again, it's not all about the spring and summer months or the sunshine. Autumn and winter bring a completely new vibe to London's green spaces, which although more sparsely populated in cold weather, are still oases of escapism. My September visit to Green Park meant stepping through blankets of autumn leaves on the extensive tree-dotted lawns, while a little later, a pre-Christmas frost on the vast hills of Alexandra Palace Park in the north was dramatically mirrored by the crisp white hilly mounds of Greenwich Park to the south.

With such a broad spectrum of park locations and sizes, it was a pleasure but also a challenge to negotiate the multiple acres. Bijou parks or little-known gardens were often tucked away behind lofty hedges or hidden down inconspicuously-signed side roads, which meant a certain persistence was needed to discover the jewels of particular green spaces – even with given postcodes or the help of a decent map.

However, whether tricky or easy to find, London's parks and green spaces all have fascinating stories to tell. Back histories of royal hunts, executions, demonstrations, film shoots, Victorian zoos or literary fantasies, offer much more than the chance to simply walk and talk in the open air.

Whatever the season or size of the park some things remain constant. Sadly in some of the larger or medium sized places I visited, the familiar bandstands – a feature of many open green spaces – were clearly unused. These faded theatrical landmarks were sometimes fenced or scaffolded off, although a few in parks such as Greenwich Park, Hyde Park, Kensington Gardens, Regent's Park, West Ham Park and Queen's Park offer live music or children's shows during the summer months.

Aside from the picturesque and calming tree-lined avenues, lush shrubberies and borders to be found in many parks, it was the unique character of some of the working green spaces that alerted my green-fingered sensibilities. A new gem for me was Kennington's Walworth Garden Farm, whose abundant public garden is a hive of horticultural activities, from vegetable growing to bee-keeping – all a short walk from the traffic-lined Kennington tube station.

The parkland treasures of London are such an intrinsic part of the life of this metropolis, that in fact, whichever corner of the capital you happen to be in, you can pretty much chose your own green experience.

Map Key

- Footpath
- Main path/road
- Bridlepath
- Cycle path
- Athletics track
- Swimming
- Fountain
- Bandstand
- Tennis courts
- Sports' pitches
- National Rail
- Overground
- Tube
- DLR
- War memorial
- Viewpoint
- Parking
- Toilets
- Refreshments
- Children's playground

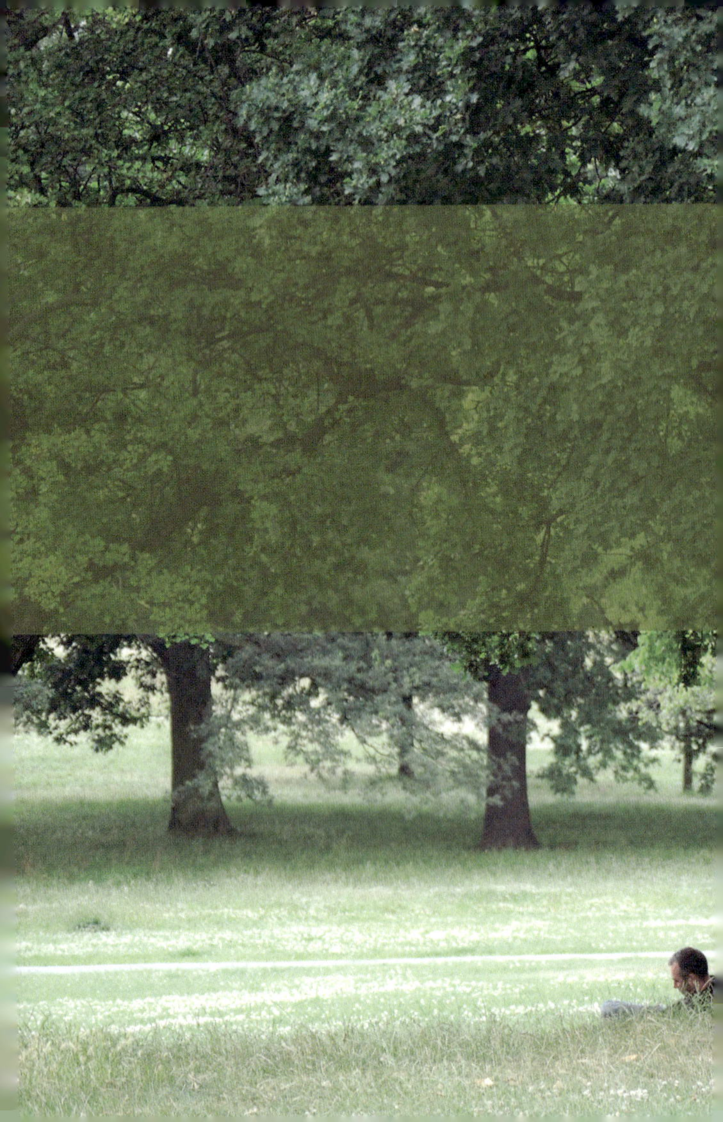

PARKS

MAP OF LONDON'S PARKS

London Parks Map

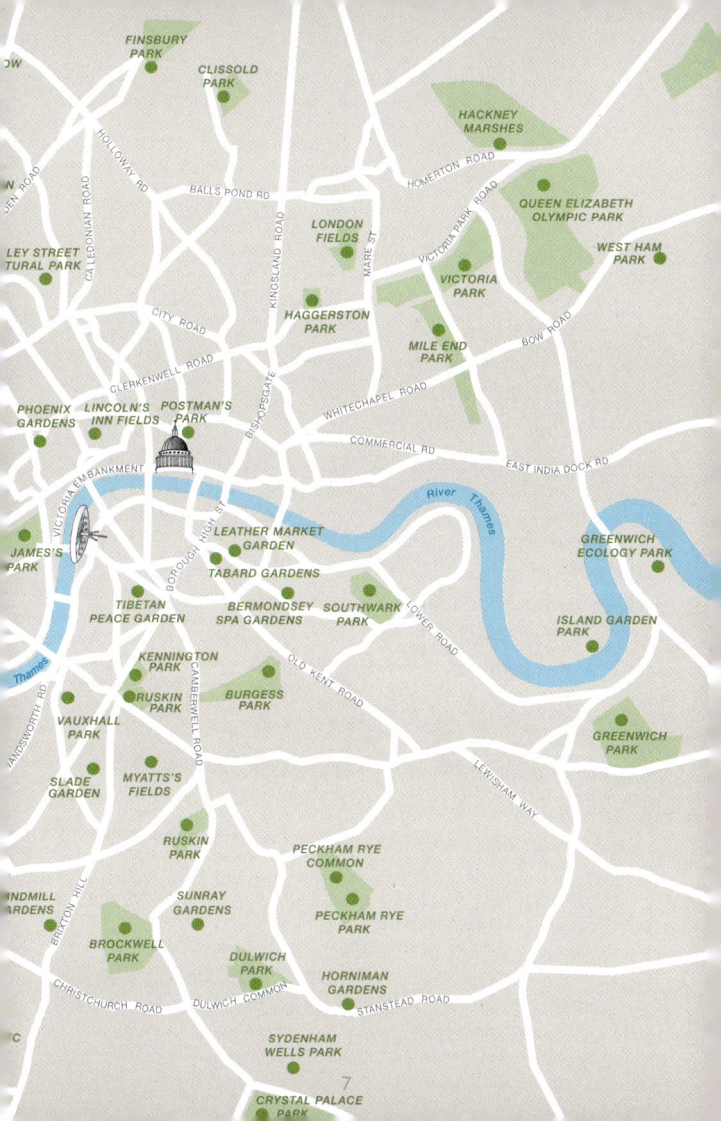

- FINSBURY PARK
- CLISSOLD PARK
- HACKNEY MARSHES
- QUEEN ELIZABETH OLYMPIC PARK
- WEST HAM PARK
- LONDON FIELDS
- VICTORIA PARK
- HAGGERSTON PARK
- MILE END PARK
- LEY STREET TURAL PARK
- PHOENIX GARDENS
- LINCOLN'S INN FIELDS
- POSTMAN'S PARK
- JAMES'S PARK
- LEATHER MARKET GARDEN
- TABARD GARDENS
- TIBETAN PEACE GARDEN
- BERMONDSEY SPA GARDENS
- SOUTHWARK PARK
- GREENWICH ECOLOGY PARK
- ISLAND GARDEN PARK
- KENNINGTON PARK
- RUSKIN PARK
- BURGESS PARK
- VAUXHALL PARK
- GREENWICH PARK
- SLADE GARDEN
- MYATT'S FIELDS
- RUSKIN PARK
- PECKHAM RYE COMMON
- SUNRAY GARDENS
- PECKHAM RYE PARK
- BROCKWELL PARK
- DULWICH PARK
- HORNIMAN GARDENS
- NDMILL ARDENS
- SYDENHAM WELLS PARK
- CRYSTAL PALACE PARK

Roads
- HOLLOWAY RD
- CALEDONIAN ROAD
- BALLS POND RD
- KINGSLAND ROAD
- MARE ST
- HOMERTON ROAD
- VICTORIA PARK ROAD
- CITY ROAD
- BOW ROAD
- CLERKENWELL ROAD
- BISHOPSGATE
- WHITECHAPEL ROAD
- COMMERCIAL RD
- EAST INDIA DOCK RD
- VICTORIA EMBANKMENT
- BOROUGH HIGH ST
- LOWER ROAD
- OLD KENT ROAD
- CAMBERWELL ROAD
- LEWISHAM WAY
- WANDSWORTH RD
- BRIXTON HILL
- CHRISTCHURCH ROAD
- DULWICH COMMON
- STANSTEAD ROAD

River Thames

7

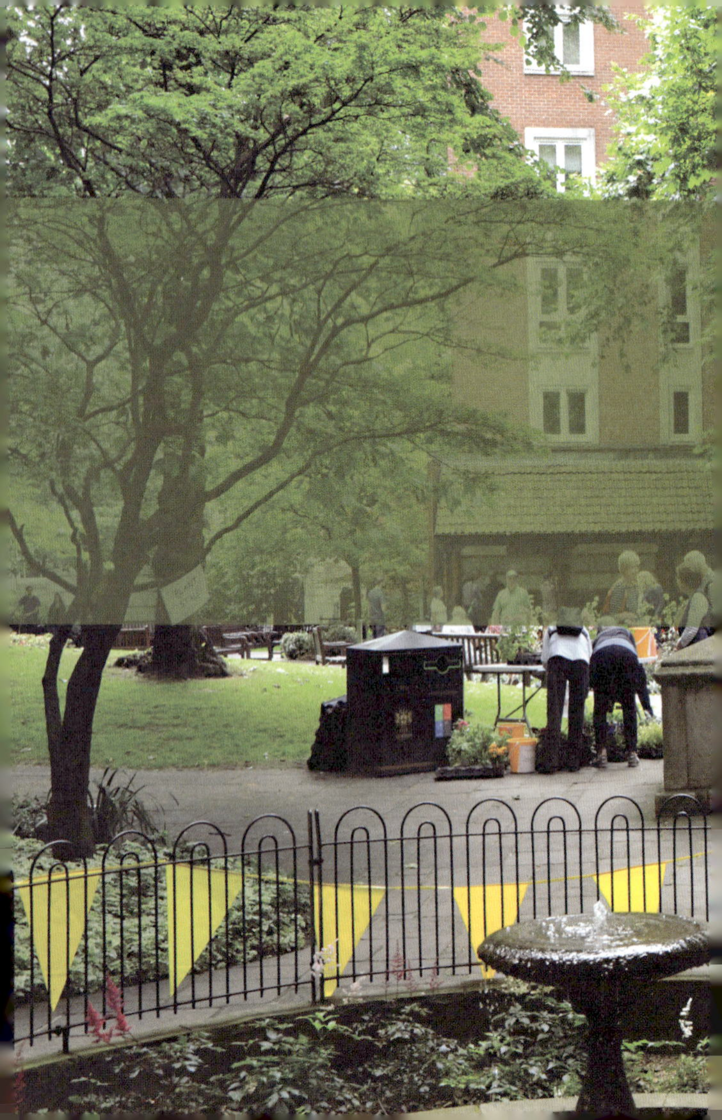

CENTRAL

Postman's Park

CENTRAL

Coram's Fields... 13
Green Park.. 15
Kensington Gardens............................18
Hyde Park..19
Lincoln's Inn Fields 27
Phoenix Gardens 28
Postman's Park....................................31
Regent's Park & Primrose Hill.........33
St James's Park...................................37

Kensington Gardens

Statue of Thomas Coram outside the Foundling Museum

Coram's Fields

93 Guilford Street, WC1 1DN
Daily 9:00-19:00 (May-Aug) & 9:00-16:30 (Sep-Apr)
020 7837 6138
www.coramsfields.org
Travel: Russell Square LU
Area: 7 acres
Facilities: Football pitch, basketball courts, paddling pool, playground, café

London's famous children's park in WC1 caters to all those up to nineteen years – with signs warning adults against entry, unless accompanied by children under 16. Formerly the Foundling Hospital for abandoned children, the site was the brainchild of philanthropist Thomas Coram, who set up the charity in 1739. The hospital was demolished in the 1920's but, it wasn't until 1936 that the site became a children's play area.

Enclosed by a high white wall and an L-shaped terraced building (used for occasional corporate functions), the Fields are well obscured from the road, so that the internal seven acres, which include a paddling pool, playground, climbing equipment and café can all be enjoyed in safety. The Astro Turf football pitch and basketball court are popular with older children.

You'll often spot sheep from Spitalfields City Farm, who like to graze the grass beyond their enclosure. Signs warn children to contain their energy when it comes to the park's fountain, which has endured its fair share of repair work due to their persistent standing on the water jets. Along with lone adults, dogs are also denied access to the park, and thanks to these precautions, this is a lively, safe and thriving area throughout the year, where children can take advantage of the play equipment, turn their hands to gardening in an ongoing wildlife project, or enjoy visiting bands and circus acts in the summer.

London's Parks – Central

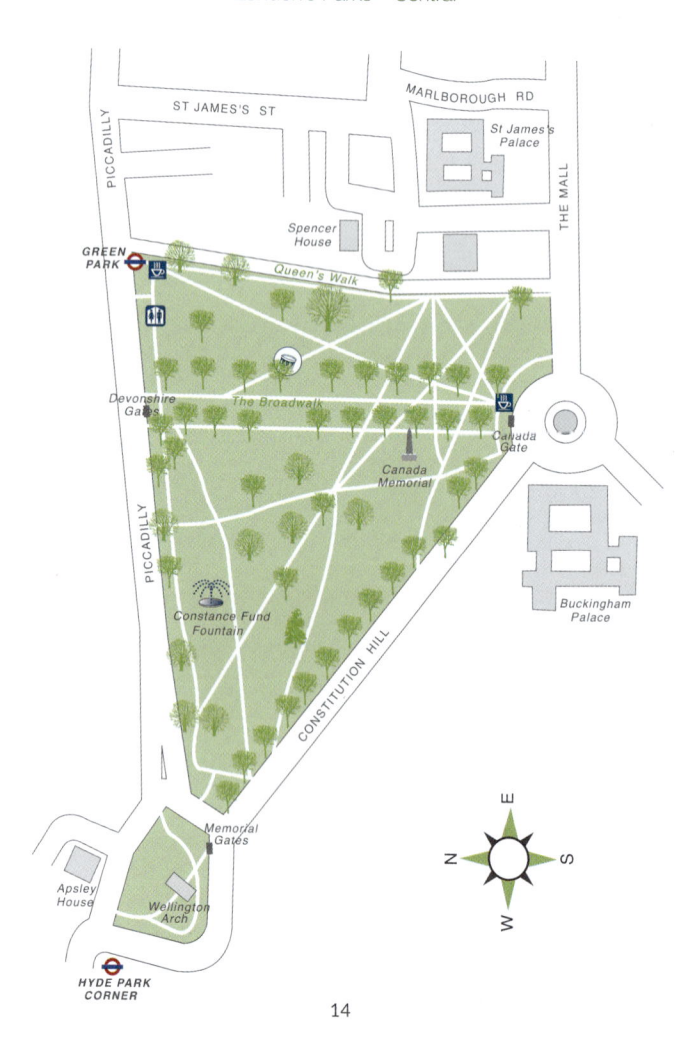

The Green Park

SW1A 1BW
Daily 5:00-0:00
020 7930 1793
www.royalparks.org.uk/parks/green-park
Travel: Green Park LU
Facilities: Deck chairs available for hire (Mar-Oct)

Not quite as fabulous as the adjacent St James's Park with its lake, swans and flowerbeds, Green Park has nonetheless come a long way since its days as a 16th-century plague pit. The place was known for its duels and highwaymen in the 18th century, but nowadays nature supplies the wow factor. Blankets of daffodils carpet the park in spring and drifts of copper coloured leaves cover the lawns in autumn. Flanked by Piccadilly and Constitution Hill, Green Park is separated from the larger St James's Park by the Mall, and although it has a general absence of fancy flowerbeds, it's a peaceful haven for walks as well as being popular with joggers for its many paths lined with London planes, limes and silver maples. It's also a good central London link to the far larger Hyde Park.

Formerly known as Upper St James's Park, Green Park once had families of deer, a ranger's house, ice house and two temples (both of which burnt down in the 18th and 19th centuries respectively). There's nothing in the way of landmark buildings left, (apart from the backdrop of Buckingham Palace) but the park does have the Canada Memorial at its Constitution Hill entrance. The memorial was erected in 1992 and consists of two triangular slabs of polished granite with shallow cascades of water and bronze maple leaves embedded in the stone. In front of Buckingham Palace, there's also the awesome gold-topped monument to Queen Victoria, which can be spotted from as far back as the park's north entrance by the Ritz Hotel.

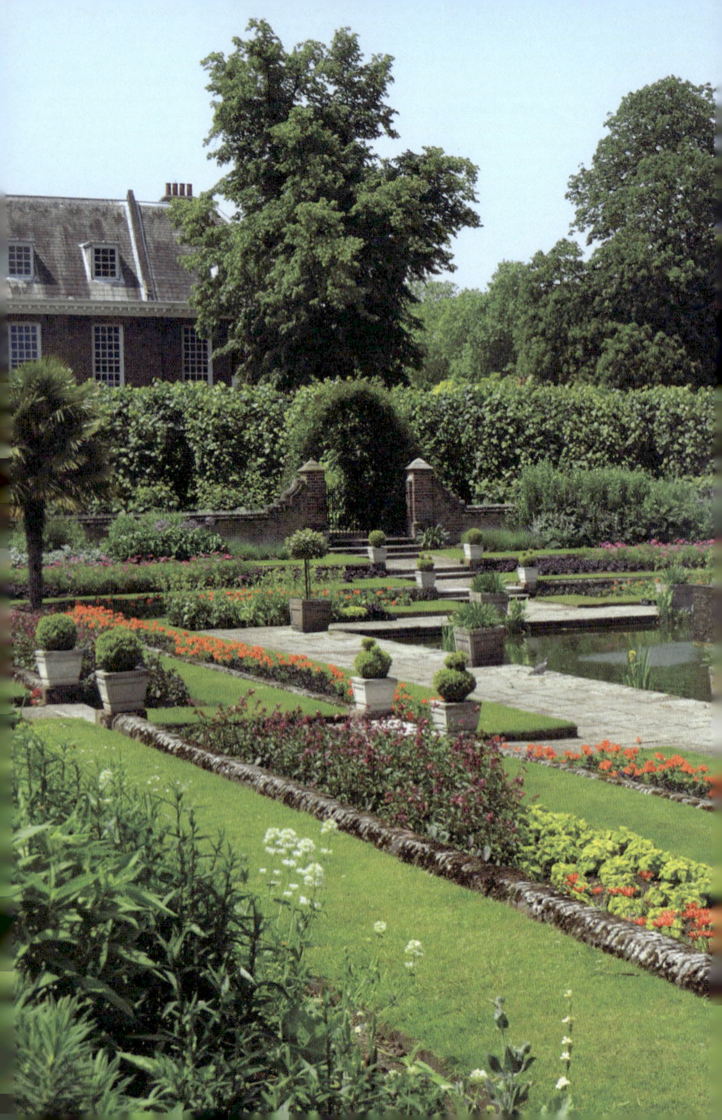

Kensington Gardens

Central

Kensington Gardens

W2 2UH
Daily 6:00 until dusk
0300 061 2000
www.royalparks.org.uk/parks/kensington-gardens
Travel: Queensway LU
Area: 242 acres
Facilities: Children's playground, deck chairs available for hire (Mar-Oct), gallery, café

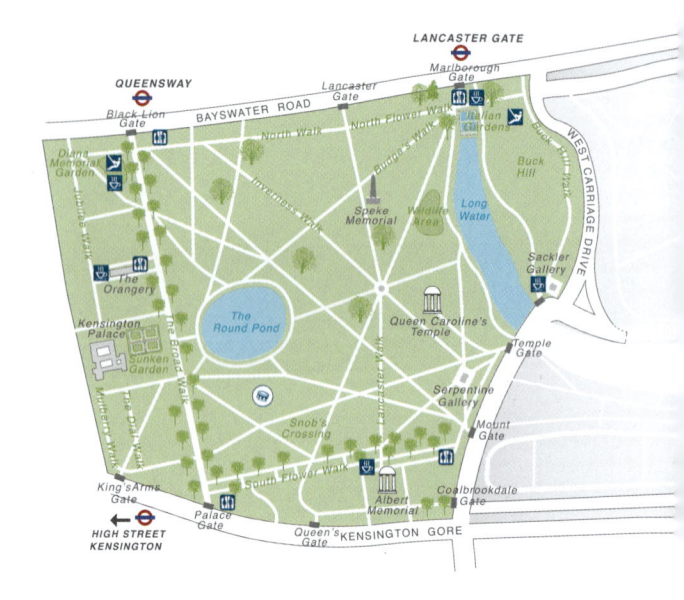

Central

Hyde Park

W2 2UH
Daily 5:00 until dusk
0300 061 2000
www.royalparks.org.uk/parks/hyde-park
Travel: Hyde Park Corner LU
Area: 350 acres
Facilities: Lido, paddling pool, sports centre (tennis, football netball and lawn bowling), horse riding arenas, boating lake, deck chairs available for hire (Mar-Oct), senior playground, café, restaurant

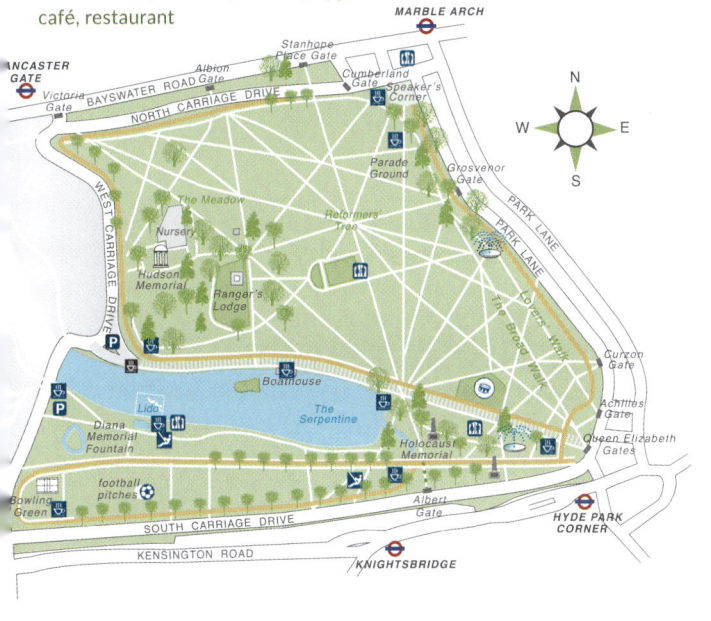

Central

Hyde Park's sprawling 350 acres of green space incorporate Kensington Gardens as well as being home to a beguiling mix of lawns, gardens, sculpture and horse tracks. Once an exclusive hunting ground for Henry VIII, this Royal Park is today a venue for some of London's most distinctive annual events such as the Swim Serpentine, a race which raises money for royal parks and the music festival BST. A popular site for protest marches, it is also the home of Speakers' Corner, at the Marble Arch end of the park. On Sundays since the mid 19th century agitated speakers and often equally animated hecklers have exercised their right to speak publicly concerning anything that takes their fancy.

The Serpentine lake runs between Hyde Park and Kensington Gardens and is straddled by a bridge that divides the lake's southern end from the narrower Long Water section, beyond which lie the extravagant Italian Gardens. This ornate terrace has carved water nymphs, Neptune-like bearded males, four pools, spurting fountains, benches and overlooking the scene, a statue of Edward Jenner by William Calder Marshall. A renowned doctor in his lifetime, Jenner discovered the vaccine for smallpox in 1806. His statue, which had a brief stay in Trafalgar Square (1858-1862) was the first to be erected in Kensington Gardens in 1862. Down at the lake's southern end is Rotten Row, a four mile sandy track for horse riders who can book in for lessons at the Hyde Park Stables (020 7723 2813). Classes run for groups, individuals and there are even hen night options.

The Serpentine is popular for boating and sailing and also has its fair share of wildfowl. The Serpentine Swimming Club (www.serpentineswimmingclub.com), which has been going since 1864, also puts this lake on the map. Swimmers can roll up to the water's edge at 8am every Saturday, even during the worst winters when the layers of ice get enthusiastically broken by some of the most determined dippers. One long-running tradition is the 100-yard race, which is held every Christmas morning, with the winner picking up the Peter Pan cup – which used to be presented by the character's creator, JM Barrie. If you're after a more serene swimming experience, the Serpentine Lido is a 30 x 100 metre pool that opens from May to September for swimming and children's paddling. Conveniently attached to a busy restaurant and café, it's also within easy reach of the Diana, Princess of Wales Memorial Fountain. Attracting around a million visitors each year, the structure has three bridges that allow visitors to cross the swirling water to get to the heart of the fountain. Within a copse of trees beside the fountain complex can be found the Isis Education Centre (also known as the Lookout) where discovery rooms, indoor and outdoor workspaces and nature gardens are available for all ages. Towards Bayswater is the Princess Diana, Princess of Wales Memorial Playground, a sanctuary for youngsters from 9:00 daily (closing times change seasonally), with adults allowed only rationed access to the area's pirate ship, water fountain, sensory trail, teepees, music area and storytelling space.

Popular landmarks within Kensington Gardens include the Albert Memorial which was unveiled in 1875 and is a grand expression of Queen Victoria's grief at the loss of her husband in 1861. The monument is 180 feet high with a gold-encrusted spire and cost the then grand sum of £120,000. Further into the park is the monument to Peter Pan which was erected overnight in 1912, Kensington Gardens being one of the inspirations for J.M. Barrie's stories. The Serpentine Galleries are another major feature of the gardens (see page 306) hosting regular exhibitions and a temporary pavilion each summer. Further allegiance to Princess Diana's memory comes with the seven-mile Memorial Walk, which meanders through Kensington Gardens, Hyde Park, St James's Park and Green Park. Seventy plaques mark a number of locations that were important in the Princess's life, including Kensington Palace, where the offices and private apartments of members of the Royal Family are found, Clarence House which was the official London home of Prince Charles before becoming King and the private mansion of Spencer House in the heart of St James's.

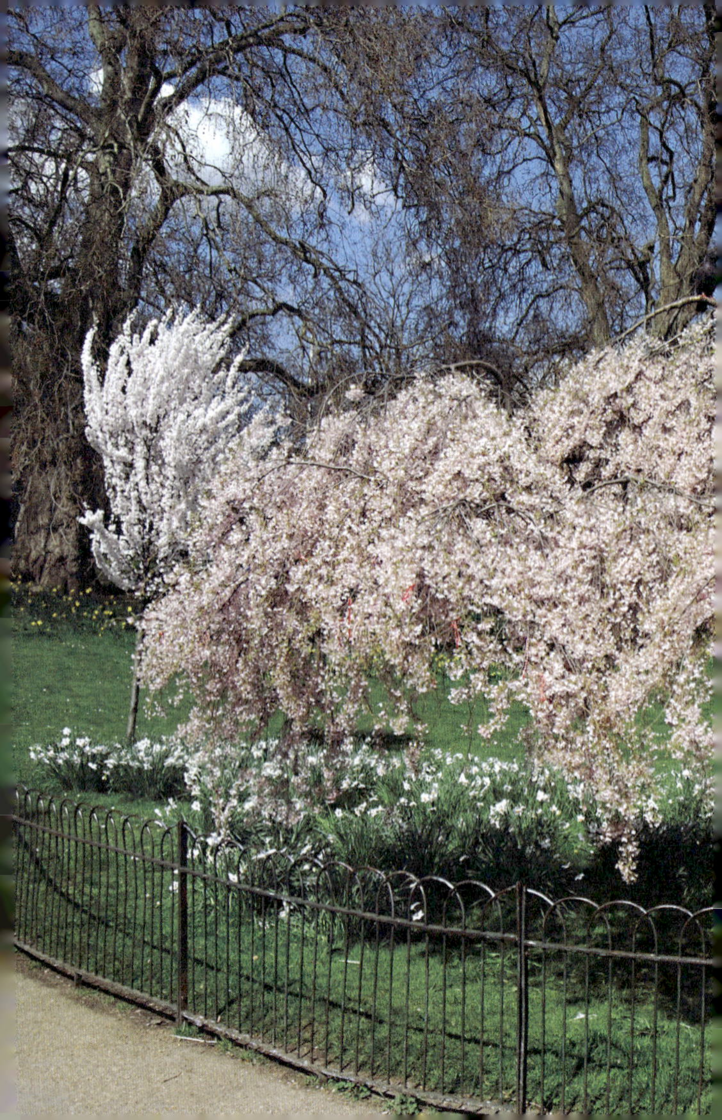

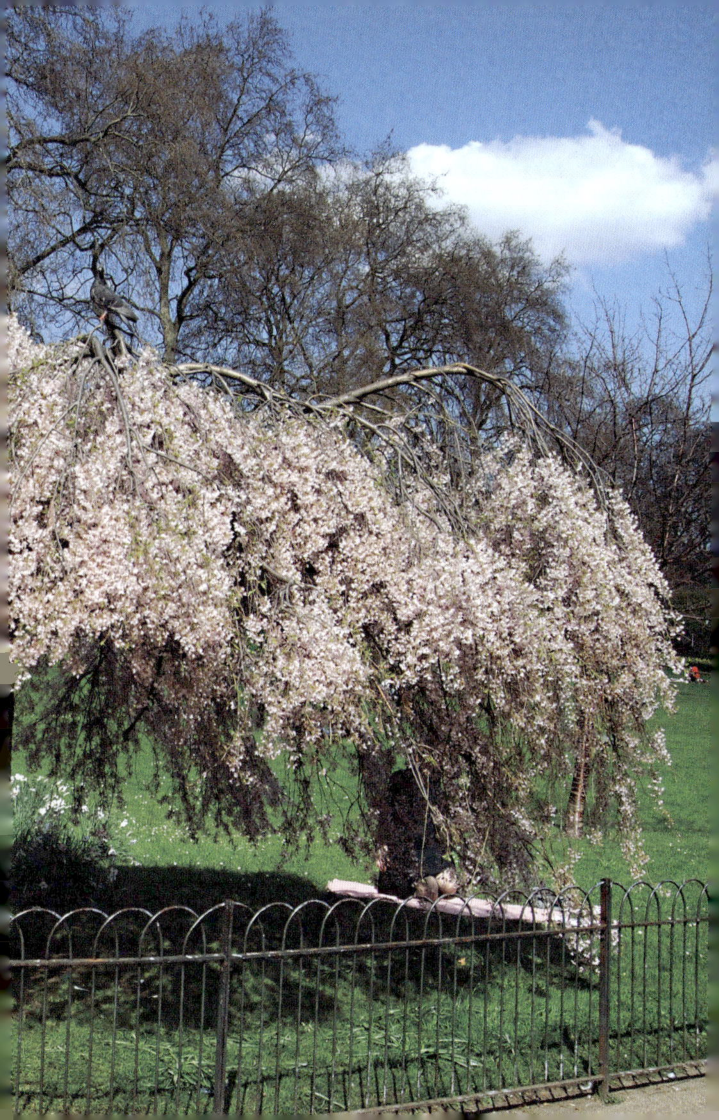

Central

- The Speaker's Corner location was once the infamous place of execution known as Tyburn. In 1661 Oliver Cromwell's exhumed body was hung there in a cage for public display, as a warning to others who might wish to abolish the monarchy.

- In 1724 200,000 people flocked to Hyde Park to see the petty thief Jack Sheppard hung from the Tyburn Tree, which was also known as the Tyburn Gallows.

- In 1816, Harriet Westbrook, the pregnant wife of poet Percy Bysshe Shelley, drowned herself in the Serpentine in Kensington Gardens, after learning that her husband had eloped with his 16-year-old mistress Mary Godwin. Mary went on to become Mrs Shelley and the author of the novel *Frankenstein*.

- The Albert Memorial in Kensington Gardens was constructed as a national memorial to Queen Victoria's husband, the Prince Consort. The book in his hand represents the catalogue of the 1851 Great Exhibition which was his inspiration and took place in Hyde Park.

- In the 1820s, a man with a shirt marked with 'S.T. Coleridge' was found hanging from a tree in Hyde Park. The papers reported that the poet Samuel Taylor Coleridge had died, much to the poet's surprise, who heard two men discussing his death in a coffee house. It turned out that the shirt did belong to Coleridge, who'd lost it a few years before.

- Two assassination attempts were made on Queen Victoria in the early 1840s as she drove through Hyde Park. Firstly, by barman Edward Oxford, who was sent to an asylum, and secondly by John Francis, who was transported for life.

- In the summer of 1855, crowds gathered at Hyde Park to protest against the Sunday Trading Bill – designed to end shopping on Sundays. The protest helped persuade the government of the time and the bill never became law.

Central

- In the 1860s, Catherine Walters was one of the best known society prostitutes. She made her name by posing in Hyde Park for a Mayfair livery stable to advertise its horses. She wore a 'skin tight outfit with no underwear'.

- Photographer Robert Freeman did a photo shoot with The Beatles in Hyde Park in 1964. Two of the images were used on the cover of the *Beatles For Sale* album, which was released in December of that year.

- On 29 June 1968, Pink Floyd gave Hyde Park's first free concert to promote their new album *A Saucerful of Secrets*. Around 15,000 people attended this landmark event.

- On 5 July 1969, The Rolling Stones played a free concert for over 250,000 people by the Serpentine in Hyde Park, just three days after the death of their former guitarist, Brian Jones.

- On 15 Dec 1969, John Lennon and Yoko Ono turned up at Speakers' Corner in Hyde Park in a white Rolls-Royce. Both of them huddled inside a sealed white bag with the label 'A Silent Protest for James Hanratty' (who was convicted of the A6 murder) attached to it.

- In July 1982, a massive IRA explosion killed a mounted group of the Household Cavalry as they rode through Hyde Park. Two hours later, six bandsmen of the Royal Green Jackets were killed in a bomb explosion as they played in Regent's Park.

- In 2003, over one million people marched to Hyde Park to demonstrate against the war in Iraq.

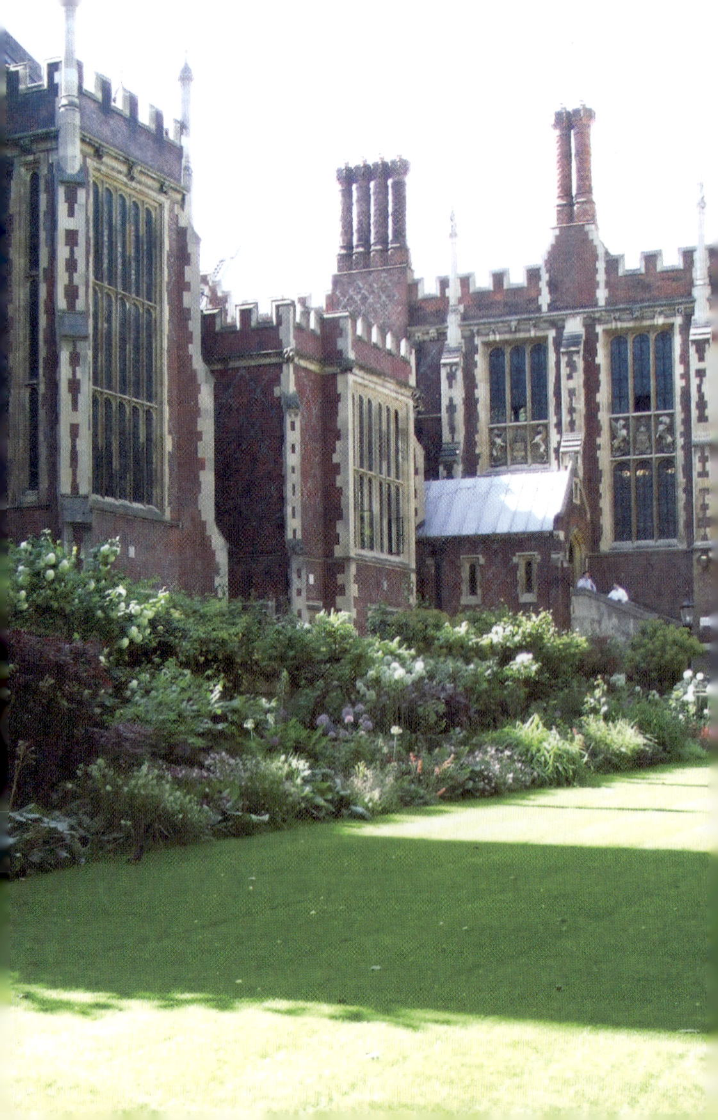

Lincoln's Inn Fields

Newman's Row, London WC2A 3TL
Daily 7:00 until dusk
020 7974 1693
www.camden.gov.uk
Travel: Chancery Lane LU
Area: 11 acres
Facilities: Tennis and netball courts, bandstand

This huge public square, the largest in London, has a history of executions including those of Anthony Babington (1586) who was accused of plotting to kill Queen Elizabeth I, Catholic martyrs Robert Morton and Hugh More (1588), and Lord Russell who was executed in 1683 near the current bandstand for his involvement in the Rye House Plot to assassinate King Charles II. Nowadays, you're more likely to see circuit training or Tai Chi sessions taking place within the grounds, or picnickers luxuriating on the well-kept lawns of this circular park. Because of its location near the Inns of Court, this is a barristers' lunchtime haunt although the popular café that once stood here has now closed and people are obliged to bring their own food to this tranquil spot. Sir John Soane's Museum is to be found nearby at 13 Lincoln's Inn Fields and is well worth a visit.

Did you know?

- During the 1980s Lincoln's Inn Fields was a popular sleeping area for the homeless. In the early 1990s fences were raised to discourage this. Now, during the month of Ramadan, Muslims visit the Fields at sunset to feed any homeless there.

Central

Phoenix Gardens

21 Stacey Street, WC2 8DG
Daily 9:00 until dusk
07716 480049
www.thephoenixgarden.org
Travel: Tottenham Court Road LU
Area: 0.5 acres

This peaceful community garden still manages to get a great deal of sunlight despite being dwarfed by the surrounding shops, offices and apartments. This part of London was once one of the most squalid in the capital as a site of WWII bombing and the gardens are located within the site of the 12th-century leper hospital of St. Giles-in-the-Fields. In more recent times it was a car park until the Covent Garden Open Spaces Association took over in 1984. A fine job they've done too. The high railing that encloses this site forms a decorative framework for this small park with its erratic bricked pathways that start confidently and often tail off to nowhere. Other features include shrubs, flowerbeds, arbours, wooden benches, sturdy log seating and a raised grassland area. The garden also boasts a population of frogs (apparently the only ones in the West End) which have made the small grill-covered pond their home. Fruit trees and honeysuckle attract a wide variety of insects including various species of bees and butterflies. A wildlife pond was added to the gardens a couple of years ago.

Although small and little known, Phoenix Gardens is very popular with local office workers who come here to eat and relax on fine days – away from the traffic and crowds of nearby Charing Cross Road and Shaftesbury Avenue.

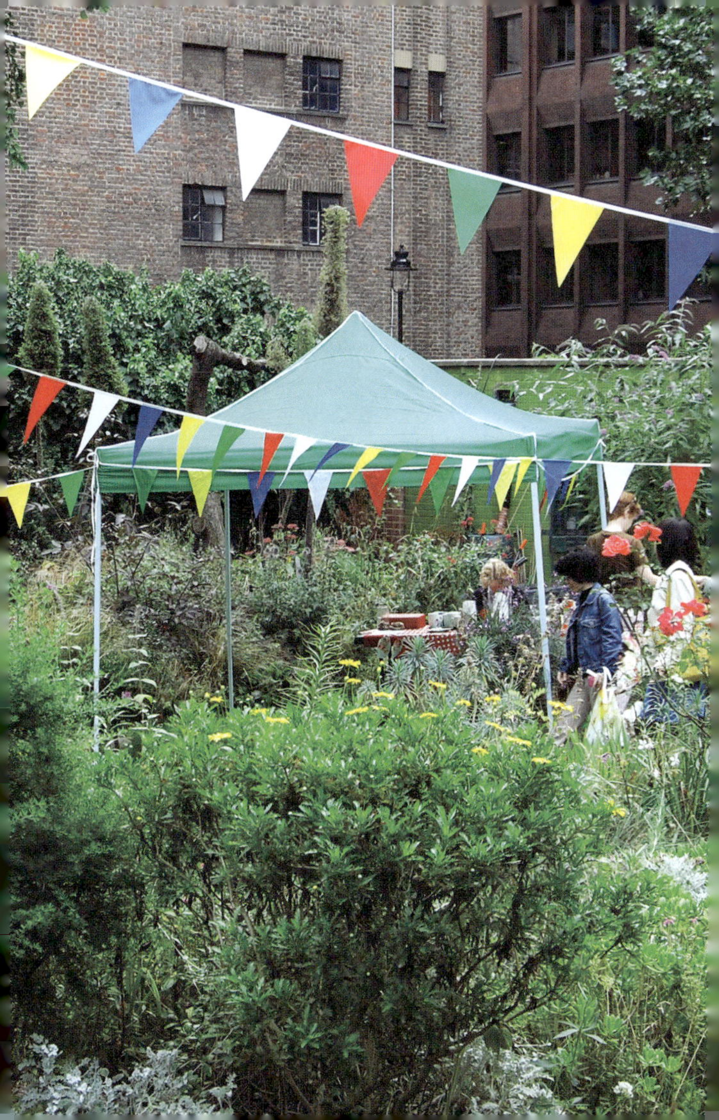

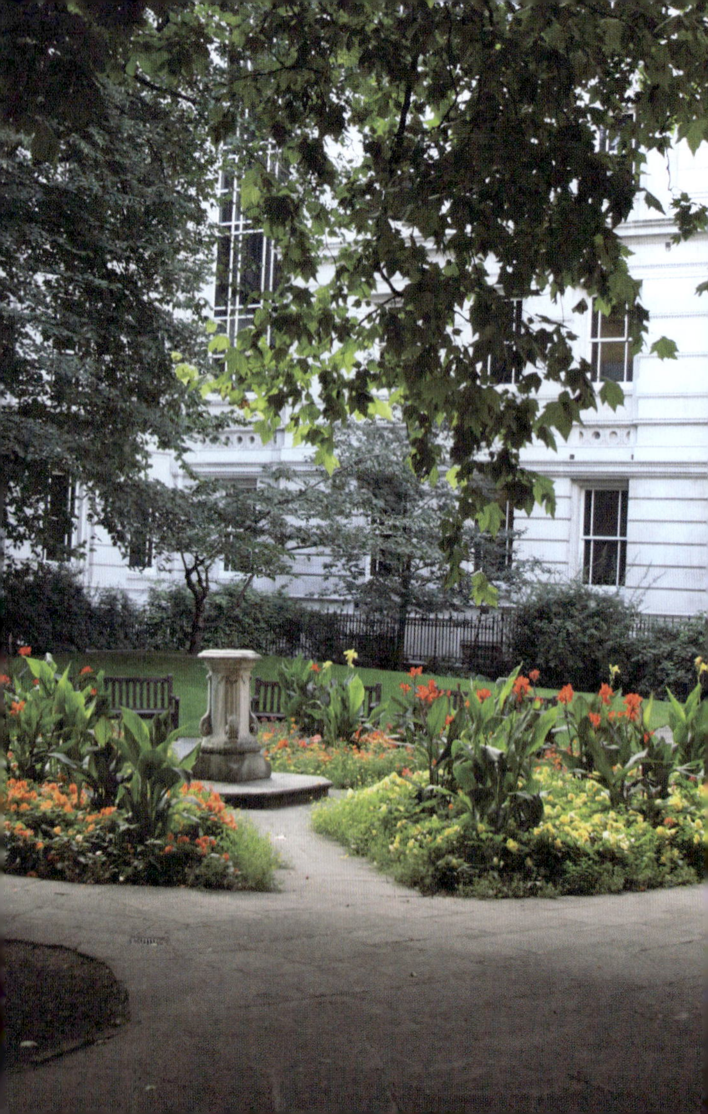

Central

Postman's Park

EC1 4AS
Daily 8:00 until dusk
020 7374 4127
www.cityoflondon.gov.uk
Travel: St Paul's LU
Area: 0.5 acres

It is the altruistic spirit of Victorian painter and philanthropist G F Watts we have to thank for this commemorative green space in the heart of the City. Watt's sympathy towards the urban poor and his disdain for the upper classes led him to petition The Times newspaper in 1887 for a site marking the lives of ordinary 'heroic men and women', who had lost their lives saving others. This idea fell on deaf ears, so he took up the project himself and created a 50 feet Heroes' Wall within this former churchyard. The park gets its name from the nearby, but long-demolished, postal sorting office.

These stories of selfless courage are told on hand-lettered ceramic tiles with decorative borders. Unfortunately the florid Victorian prose of some of the fifty or so obituaries, in a more cynical age, read with unintentional comedy. Cases in point are inscriptions like that of 'Sarah Smith, pantomime artiste. At Prince's Theatre died of terrible injuries received when attempting in her flammable dress to extinguish the flames which had enveloped her companion. January 24 1863', or 'Ernest Bening, compositor, aged 22. Upset from a boat one dark night off Pimlico Pier grasped an oar with one hand supporting a woman with the other but sank as she was rescued. August 25 1883'. These people are heroes nonetheless, and their tales of selfless sacrifice add a particular resonance to the park.

The rest of the garden is designed with bright flowerbeds and a small fountain greeting visitors at the entrance. The office workers that enjoy the park at lunchtime share the space with stag beetles, bees, butterflies and ladybirds.

Central

Central

The Regent's Park and Primrose Hill

The Store Yard, Inner Circle, Regent's Park, NW1 4NR
Daily 5:00 until dusk
020 7486 7905
www.royalparks.org.uk/parks/the-regents-park
Travel: Regent's Park LU
Area: 395 acres
Facilities: Open Air Theatre, boating lake, football fields, tennis courts, golf course, athletics track, rugby pitch, cricket pitch, cafés, restaurants, kiosks

Depending on where you enter, Regent's Park is either close to Madame Tussaud's in Marylebone on its southern edge, the gold-covered dome of the London Central Mosque to the east, and at the northern tip, Primrose Hill, which although found across the intersecting Prince Albert Road, is still included within the boundaries of the park. Primrose Hill famously offers far-reaching views over London's landscape, taking in the London Eye on the South Bank, and the TV mast of Crystal Palace, way over in SE19.

Originally known as Marylebone Park, Regent's Park was yet another acquisition by Henry VIII for his beloved Royal Hunt. It wasn't until 1845 that Queen Victoria opened the grounds to the public, but only for two days a week.

Made up of an inner and outer circle, Regent's Park contains Queen Mary's Gardens, with wide herbaceous beds, sunken gardens, a pretty lake, rock features, waterfall and a rose garden planted with over 12,000 roses. Next door, the Open Air Theatre kicks into action every summer, and features selected Shakespeare plays or more contemporary classics such as *Porgy and Bess* or *To Kill a Mockingbird*. Just off the Inner Circle, a secret garden (St John's Lodge Garden) is a perfect retreat if you want a quiet stroll, as not many people use it. An arboured walkway leads to a beautifully manicured area with flowerbeds, a dramatic fountain sculpture showing Hylas being abducted by a mermaid, and the grand St John's Lodge, one of the first villas to be built in the park.

The Outer Circle, the main road that runs around the park, is two miles long and frames the larger section of the park, which includes a section of the Grand Union Canal and the 36-acre London Zoo towards Primrose Hill. Entry to the Zoo is expensive (£21-£33), but it's more a conservation area than a traditional zoo, with landscaped gardens, over 600 species of animals, reptiles, birds and invertebrates, and a range of art and educational activities for children. The rest of the outer circle features a large boating lake with herons and other fine wildfowl and wide open green areas that are dotted with deck chairs in the summer.

Regent's Park is also graced with an impressive number of sports facilities and is home to 'The Hub' – the largest outdoor sports facility in London. Tennis and netball courts, an athletics track, cricket, football, rugby and hockey pitches are all available, along with changing rooms and showers. The park also has four playgrounds for children – one at the foot of Primrose Hill, another by the Camden Town entrance, one by Marylebone Road, and the last close to the London Central Mosque.

Did you know?

- In the 19th century, Primrose Hill was a favourite spot for the fighting of duels.

- Pop band Madness had their photo taken on Primrose Hill for their 1982 album *The Rise and Fall*. The Rolling Stones were photographed for the cover of their *Between the Buttons* album on Primrose Hill in 1966.

- In January 1867, forty people drowned when the ice cracked on the lake in Regent's Park. Some time afterwards, the lake was lowered and skating forbidden.

- In 1940, Prime Minister Neville Chamberlain supported a scheme to build a mosque in London. Eventually a piece of land on the western edge of Regent's Park was handed over, although the project wasn't finished until 1978.

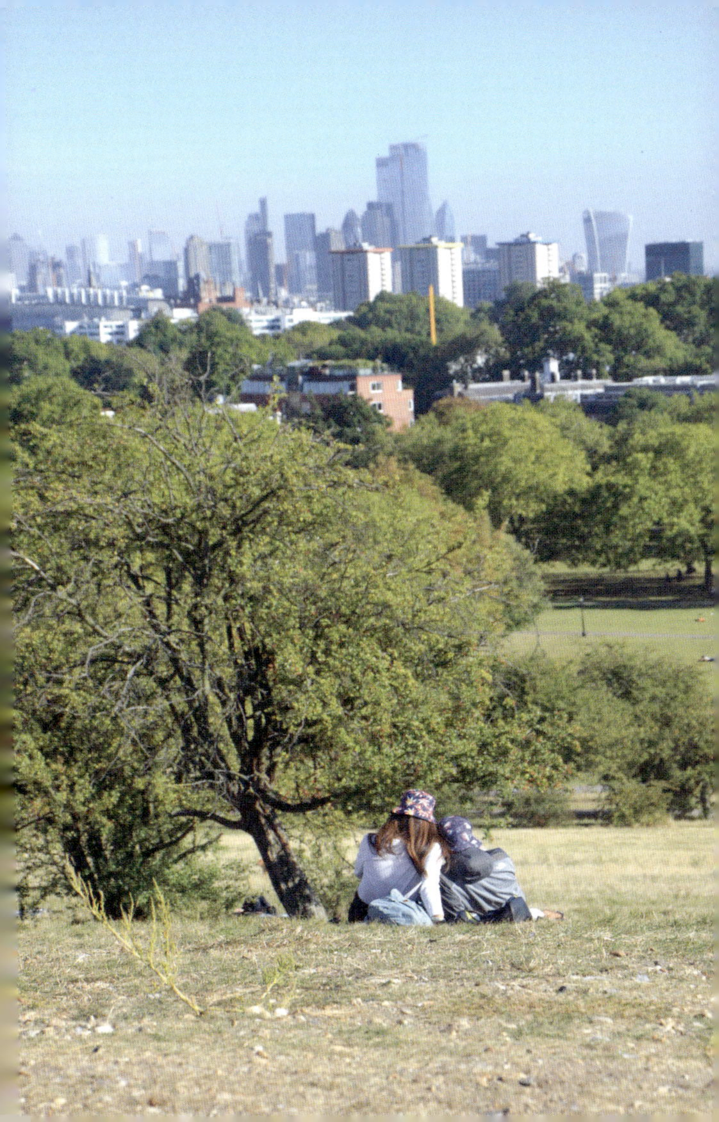

Central

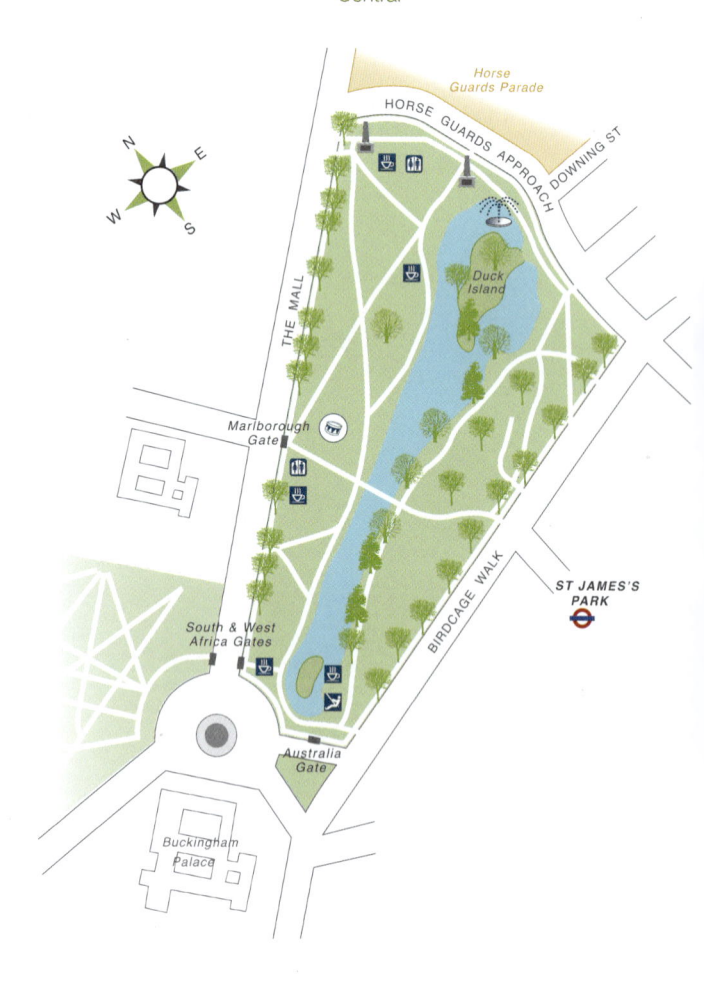

St James's Park

SW1A 2BJ
Daily 5:00-0:00
0300 061 2350
www.royalparks.org.uk/parks/st-jamess-park
Travel: St James's Park LU
Area: 58 acres
Facilities: Children's playground, deck chairs available for hire (Mar-Oct), restaurant

Escaping from the hustle and bustle of Whitehall through Horse Guard's Parade and into this peaceful park in the heart of London is always a treat. Next door to the less elaborate Green Park, St James's Park is surrounded by three palaces. Westminster (now the Houses of Parliament) is the oldest one, then there's St James's Palace, and of course Buckingham Palace on St James's west side. At the heart of the Park is the lake with its hump-backed bridge that offers views of Whitehall to the east. Swans, geese and ducks often wander from the water and waddle across the perfectly groomed lawns and around the flowerbeds. Signs warn visitors not to feed the pelicans, as there's a bit of a side show each afternoon at 14:30 when park staff take to the lawns to feed these large-billed birds. Deckchairs are available for hire from Park Deckchair (www.parkdeckchairs.co.uk – 020 7486 8117) who supply chairs at £3 for up to an hour to £11 for the day to this park as well as Hyde Park, Kensington Gardens, Regent's Park and Green Park.

Once an expanse of marsh and meadowland, St James's Park has been through substantial changes since its establishment. The 13th century saw the land being used for a lepers hospital, which was founded by 'four leprous maidens'. In the 15th century Henry VIII acquired the land, along with Hyde Park, for the less philanthropic activity of deer hunting. In the mid 17th century Charles II, fresh from his exile in France, landscaped St James's in the formal French style. Even though today's park is more casual, its royal status still means cautionary signs warn against ball games, and the park is tended by an army of park rangers who weave in and out of the orderly troops of pedestrian tourists in their motorised green buggies. They are kept particularly busy maintaining the grand paths leading towards Buckingham Palace.

The Changing of the Guard, Trooping the Colour and Beating the Retreat are some of the royal ceremonies that draw the crowds at Horse Guards Parade. If you want to take a bit of a break from the pomp and circumstance, there's the state-of-the-art St James's Café situated towards The Mall. It's an eco-friendly building made of wood, with a turf roof and terrace which offers contemporary British cuisine, and a large self-service café for children's packed lunches, cakes and pastries.

Did you know?

- In 1649, Charles I was led through St James's Park to his execution.

- At one time there was a tradition that no one could be arrested in St James's Park unless the crime was very serious; but in 1677 a man called Richard Harris was sent to Bedlam for throwing an orange at King William III. Six months later, a woman called Deborah Lydall was sent to the same place for threatening to throw a stone at the Queen.

- In the 18th century, cows were kept tethered in St. James's Park and visitors could buy mugs of fresh warm milk for a penny.

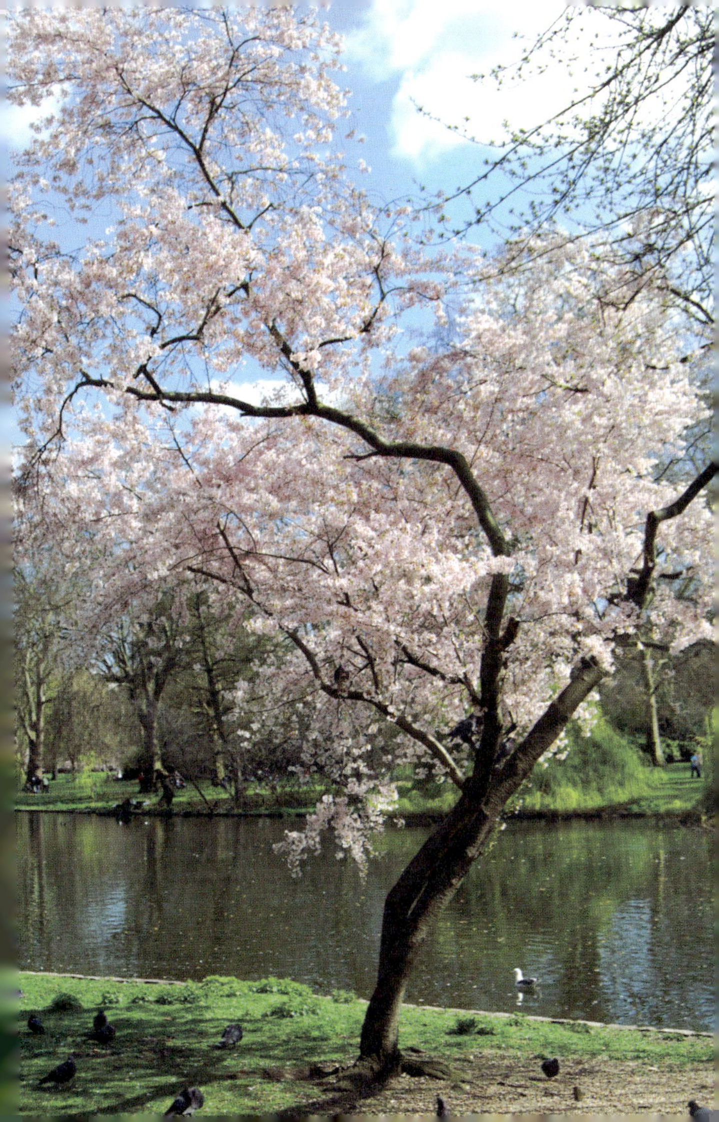

Hampstead Heath

NORTH

NORTH LONDON

Abney Park Cemetery.......................44
Alexandra Palace Park......................47
Barnsbury Wood................................48
Bruce Castle Park...............................49
Camley Street Natural Park............50
Clissold Park.......................................53
Finsbury Park.....................................54
Gladstone Park..................................56
Hampstead Heath.............................63
Highgate Wood &
Queen's Wood...................................67
Kentish Town City Farm...................70
Paradise Park.....................................70
Priory Park..71
Waterlow Park...................................72
Queen's Park......................................75

Waterlow Park

North

Abney Park Cemetery

Stoke Newington High Street, N16 0LH
Daily 8:00 until dusk
020 7275 7557
www.abneypark.org
Travel: Stoke Newington Rail
Area: 31 acres

This Victorian memorial park and cemetery were laid out in 1840 as one of seven plots built to alleviate the overcrowding of inner-city graveyards that were struggling to cope with London's escalating population. Because the grounds were unconsecrated, the area became a favourite final resting place for Nonconformists, and eventually a thriving haven for wildlife. The park stands between what was once an ancient ridgeway track – now Stoke Newington High Street – and the Hackney Brook, a stream that once ran down to the River Lea. Long gone are the 17th-century Fleetwood and Abney Houses that once stood within the grounds, although the decorative ironwork over the Church Street entrance to the cemetery is a remnant from Abney House. There's more ironwork over the Stoke Newington High Street entrance where the grand Egyptian gates incorporate an old lodge. A cobbled path leads to a sundial, which marks the start of the cemetery. From here the woodland is split three ways leading to what initially looks like a gothic mess of tombstones and overgrown foliage. Amid the chaos, shrubs and trees including elms, oaks, ashes and sycamores are labelled. Those interested in fauna will find a wonderful array of butterflies, moths and birds – particularly in the warmer months. Paths lead to historical treasures like the raised war memorial with panels etched with the names of those who lost their lives in the two world wars. Nearby are the ruins of an old chapel. Locked up to prevent further damage, it's a weather-beaten shell that serves as a makeshift climbing frame for inquisitive children, or a landmark for others who crane their necks at the padlocked gate to admire the central spire. Guided walks and regular craft and nature activities take place in the grounds and the Abney Park Cemetery

North

Trust offers lots of information about the cemetery's Victorian past. Events at Abney Park include botanical drawing workshops, fungi identification walk, bird watching walks and a monthly history walk. The Park is a popular spot for plaques and memorials, and the Abney Park Trust (020 7275 7557) offers guidance on personal designs for memorials on trees or benches within the grounds, and information on workshops for carved plaque designs.

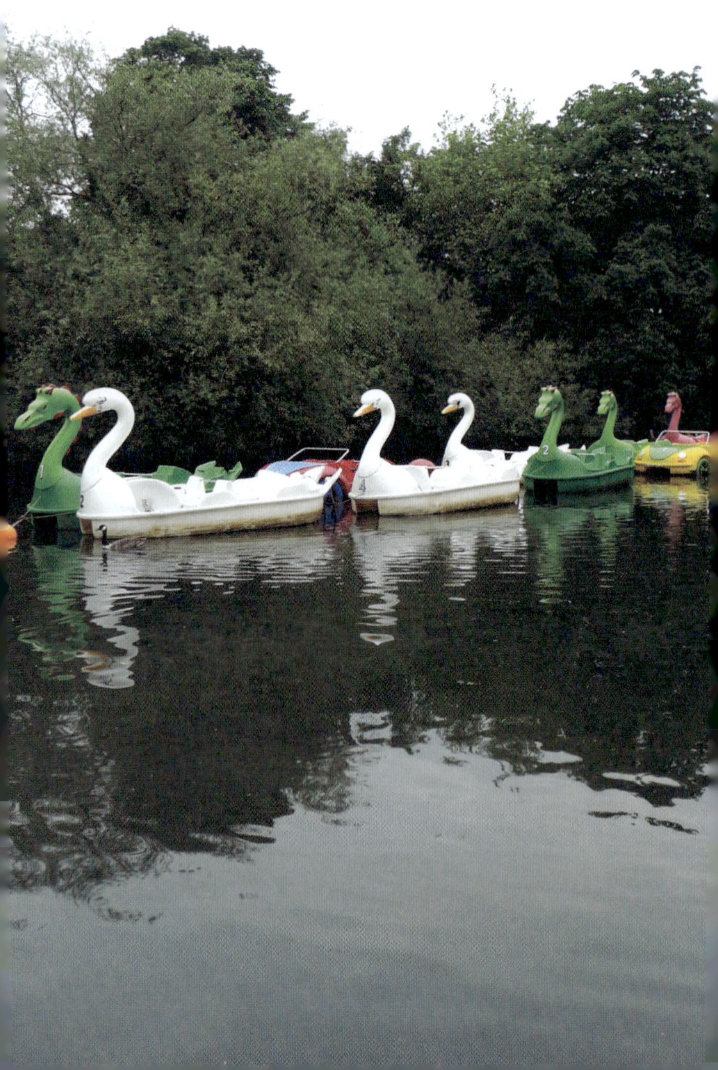

North

Alexandra Palace Park

Alexandra Palace Way, N22 7AY
Daily 24 hours
020 8365 2121
www.alexandrapalace.com/park
Travel: Wood Green LU, Alexandra Palace LO
Area: 196 acres
Facilities: Alexandra Palace with indoor skating rink, children's playground, boating lake, deer enclosure, garden centre, cafés

Above Muswell Hill, Alexandra Palace has soldiered on despite burning down in 1873 and again in 1980. Ironically, it was built as a mini replica of the Crystal Palace, which succumbed to fire in 1936. Despite such disasters, the hillside parkland that dominates the front of the building continues to thrive.

To the east of the grounds is the New River, Wood Green Reservoir and the railway line. The conservation area at the southeast entrance near Wood Green tube station was formerly used as a rifle range, and also once made up part of an old racecourse. It's now a five acre area of meadow and woodland, with a large number of oaks, some dating back three hundred years to when Tottenham Wood was still in existence. Elms, holly and chestnut trees also stake out their territory here. The start of the Parkland Walk Footpath is over on the west side of the grounds. The route leads to Finsbury Park, taking in Queen's Wood and Highgate Wood along the way.

Behind the Palace, the boating lake is open all year round and caters for those who want to enjoy fishing or pedal boat rides. Beside the lake is the deer enclosure where the park's herd of fallow deer graze the vegetation. There are two play areas, on the east and west side of the park. On the east side, the Little Dinosaurs is a soft play area with a café that opens daily.

Barnsbury Wood

N1 1BT
Tue 14:00-16:00
020 7527 4374
www.islington.gov.uk
Travel: Caledonian Road LU & LO
Area: 0.84 acres

Barnsbury Wood holds the crown as London's smallest nature reserve at just under an acre in size. A dog-free enclave, it's a popular place for spotting stag beetles, toads and ladybirds. Despite its size it has the biggest area of woodland in Islington, which comes into its own in the spring when the woody areas become blanketed with bluebells. While opening hours are limited, Barnsbury Wood is well worth a visit.

North

Bruce Castle Park

Lordship Lane, N17 8NU
Daily 24 hours
020 8808 8772
www.new.haringey.gov.uk
Travel: White Hart Lane LO
Facilities: Children's playground, tennis and basketball courts, bowling green, paddling pool, museum, café, multi-use games area

Bruce Castle Park surrounds the Bruce Castle Museum, a former 16th-century manor house at the eastern end of Lordship Lane. The name comes from the House of Bruce, a Scottish clan who once owned the land on which it sits. During the 19th century the building was converted into a school, but it now operates as a free museum focusing on the history of the Borough of Haringey.

A central point of interest is the magnificent ancient oak – said to be around 500 years old – near the children's playground. The playground has two noticable dips in the ground that are said to be the remnants of a medieval fishpond, which also hints at the area's past. Just beyond the main entrance on Lordship Lane, a turreted redbrick tower dates from the early 1500's. There's a sealed entrance to its basement, and a window high up on the south side, which can be better seen from inside the park. An octagonal stone slab just north of the museum marks the spot where a drinking fountain was placed in 1893 by the Temperance Association to encourage people to keep off the beer.

Well-manicured lawns and flowerbeds next to the bowling green have surely contributed to the park's Green Flag award, although the enclosed Holocaust Garden of Remembrance stands out as a poignant addition to the grounds. Opened in January 2001, this circular garden, with its benches, rock features and tall hedges, was created in honour of all victims of the Holocaust and genocide. A memorial sculpture designed by a team of young offenders was added in 2013, consisting of six upright wooden sleepers on a base of a Star of David.

Camley Street Natural Park

12 Camley Street, NC1 4PW
Daily 10:00-17:00
020 7833 2311
www.wildlondon.org.uk
Travel: King's Cross LU & LO
Area: 2 acres
Facilities: Visitor centre, café

A welcome green space in the heart of the King's Cross area, Camley Street Natural Park offers a haven for Londoners. The entrance is through an ornate metal gate on Camley Street, the reserve running parallel with a section of the Regent's Canal. Once a derelict site, it was originally used for coal storage during the Victorian era. Following an extensive redevelopment, it opened its doors in 1985, offering a visitor centre with a workshop area for children and a patchwork of meadow, coppice, woodland and pond areas – most of which are wheelchair accessible.

A rich variety of plant life exists throughout, with trees including silver birch, hazel and rowan obscuring most of the urban surroundings. It's only at the upper point of the woodland paths that you get a reminder of the gritty NC1 landscape. Otherwise, this is a perfect retreat for spotting frogs, newts and toads in the damp marshy areas, and grasshoppers and butterflies in the wildflower meadow. Children are fascinated by the 'mini beast hotel' that attracts everything from ladybirds to grubs and spiders. Special education programmes can be booked during term time for schools and groups.

A recent addition to the park has been the viewpoint structure – called 'Habitat Island'. This floating platform is moored on the Regent's Canal and offers great views across the park and further afield.

Environmentally themed activities run throughout the year, with donations suggested for events like Tree Dressing days, Wildlife Watches and hands-on conservation workshops.

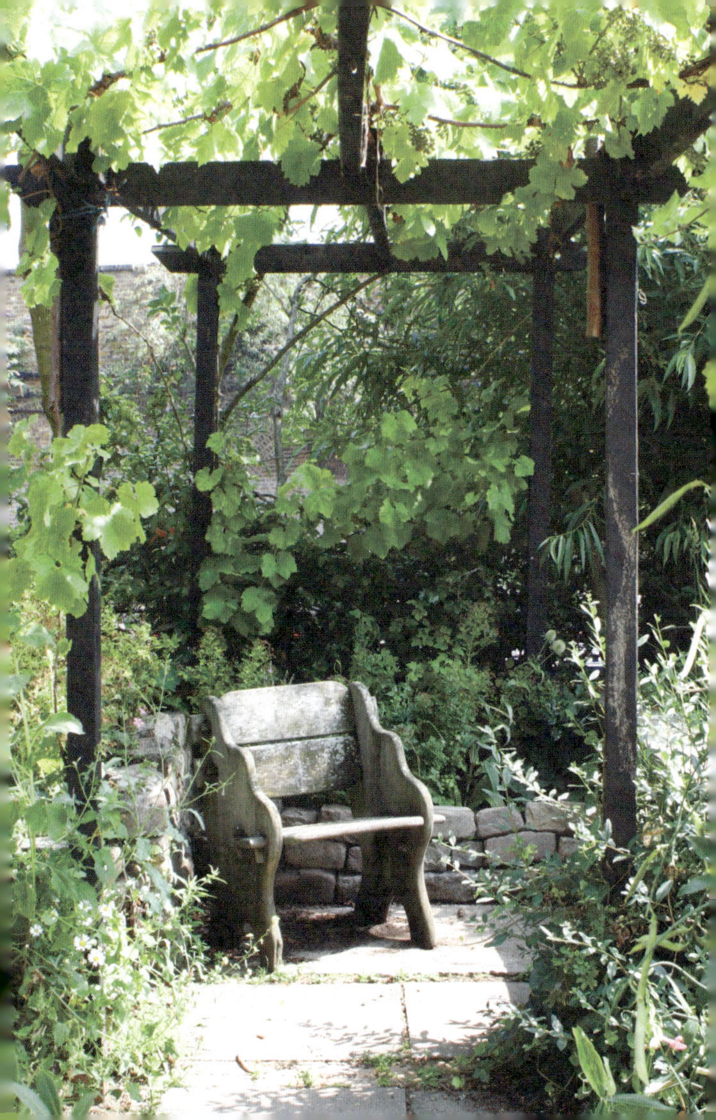

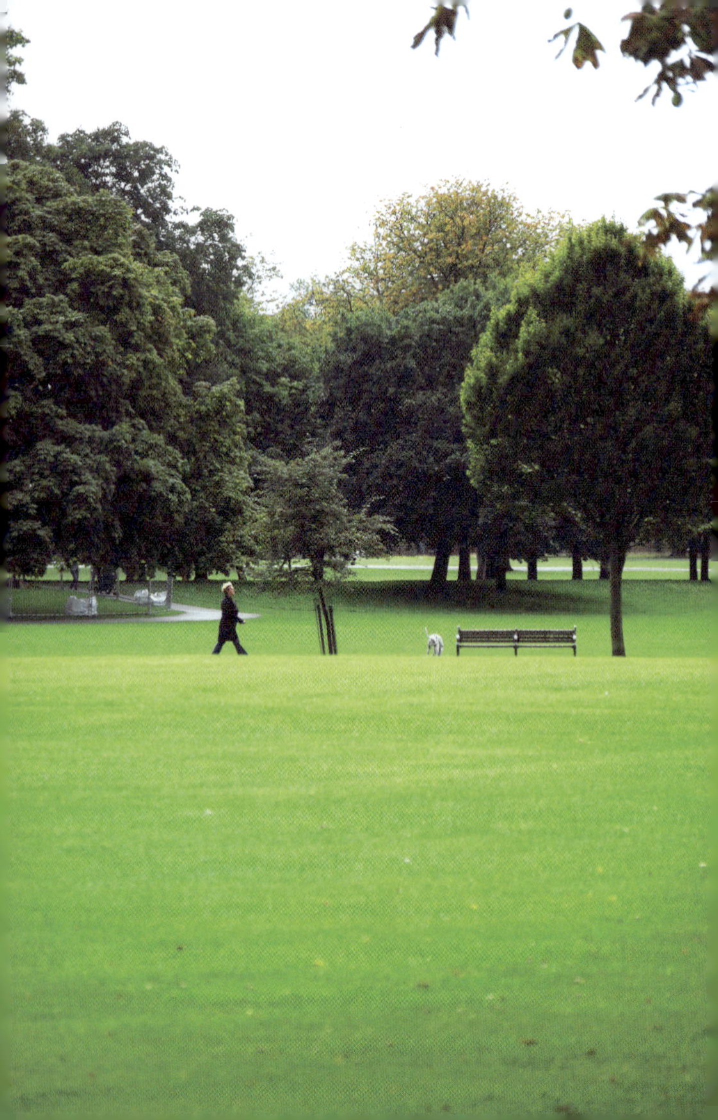

Clissold Park

Stoke Newington Church Street, N16 9HJ
Daily 7:00 until dusk
020 8356 3000
www.clissoldpark.com
Travel: Stoke Newington LO
Area: 53 acres
Facilities: Children's playground, paddling pool, multi-use games area, aviary and animal enclosures, skate park, café, kiosk

Along with Hackney's two other historical parks (Abney Park Cemetery and Springfield Park), Clissold has been awarded Grade II* listed status. Set in the grounds of an 18th-century house, it was once known as Crawshaw Farm before opening as a public space in 1889. Its 53 acres stretch from Green Lanes to the west, Queen Elizabeth's Close to the north and Stoke Newington Church Street to the southeast.

A two-year restoration programme started in 2010, and now the park's two lakes, animal enclosures with deer, goats and chickens and play area have all been nicely spruced up. The famous Clissold House also benefitted from financial attention. An 18th-century Grade II* listed building, the house now boasts beautifully restored historic interiors and terrace seating overlooking the grounds. While only available as a venue for weddings and events, it has a café that is open seven days a week.

The park's other features include avenues of ash, lime, oak and plane trees, as well as two ponds (with terrapins) and a resting island for herons, swans, kestrels and ducks.

A children's playground, summer paddling pool and cricket and football pitches and tennis courts provide facilities for active types.

North

Finsbury Park
Endymion Road, N4 2NQ
Daily 24 hours
020 8489 1000
www.haringey.gov.uk
Travel: Finsbury Park LU & LO
Facilities: Children's playground, athletics track, gym, cricket pitch, basketball, boating lake, tennis court, skate park, art gallery, zip wire

Perhaps best known for hosting big events including Wireless London, the sprawl of green land that makes up Finsbury Park has a long history. The park was officially opened in 1869, but it lies on the site of the ancient forest of Middlesex and shares some of the original boundaries. Features from the mid-19th century are the grand gated entrances, the lake and island, and a modest number of willows, poplars, and oaks.

The southern entrance to the park from Finsbury Park station slopes up from Manor House and Seven Sisters. It's all a bit sparse until you reach the lake and boathouse where you can hire boat.

A £5m regeneration programme ensured Green Flag status for the Grade II listed park since 2007. Improved facilities include the re-landscaping of the historic American Gardens and the flower gardens, a free open-air gym with 14 pieces of cardiovascular equipment, an enclosed, dog-free play area and a water feature designed by children. There's also a redesigned café building with public toilets, which opens all year round, as well as two Victorian-style seating shelters.

At the heart of the park, the Furtherfield Gallery (www.furtherfield.org) is a contemporary art space that programmes online and physical exhibitions and pop-up events.

The path of the New River aqueduct also runs alongside the park. Opened in 1613 to bring fresh water from Hertfordshire to London, it is still used by Thames Water as a source for London's drinking water. The course of the river provides a 28-mile-long footpath which starts at its source near Hertford and extends to its terminus at New River Head in Islington. There's no public access to the river from the park, but you can gain access from other points in Stoke Newington if this vast park has not exhausted your need for exploration.

Gladstone Park

52 Mulgrave Road, NW10 1JG
Daily 24 hours
020 8937 1234
www.gladstonepark.org.uk
Travel: Dollis Hill LU
Facilities: Two play areas, bowling green, tennis courts, English wilderness woodland, rose terrace, walled garden, gallery, café

Gladstone Park may not seem like the prettiest green space if you enter from the Kendal Road entrance. Essentially it is an open meadow with a basic football pitch and old tree trunks that have been levelled and are now used as seating logs. You have to go well beyond the busy road before the sound of the city begins to dull.

The further away from the road you are, the more beautiful the park gets. A hillier section towards the north of the park is split by a beautiful path lined by tall trees. This area is dotted with huge carved tree trunks that look almost talismanic.

Overall, the park is well kept and feels peaceful, despite some slightly disconcerting signs asking visitors to keep their eyes peeled for aggressive dogs being trained for fighting.

The biggest draw at Gladstone Park, is the walled garden at the top of the park. At the front of the red-bricked entrance are rows of well-trimmed rose beds. The garden inside offers a joyful burst of colour with flowerbeds, cobbled paths and benched seating. The gardens are also the vibrant home of the Stables Café where fresh juices, hot drinks and cakes can be enjoyed in a courtyard setting. It's this hilliest area of the park that offers great views of London on a clear day, including Wembley Stadium and the Shard.

Did you know?

- Dollis Hill House (the remains of which sit within the park) was built as a farmhouse in 1825, when the area was still rural. By the 1990s it had been destroyed by a fire but in its glory days –during the 1880s – its owner, the 1st Baron of Tweedmouth often had high profile friends to stay. These included Lord Randolph Churchill (Winston's dad), the politician and statesman Joseph Chamberlain and Prime Minister William Ewart Gladstone, after whom Gladstone Park was named in 1899. The Dollis Hill House building had been earmarked for renovation for years but was finally demolished in 2012.

The remains of Dollis Hill House

View from Hampstead Heath

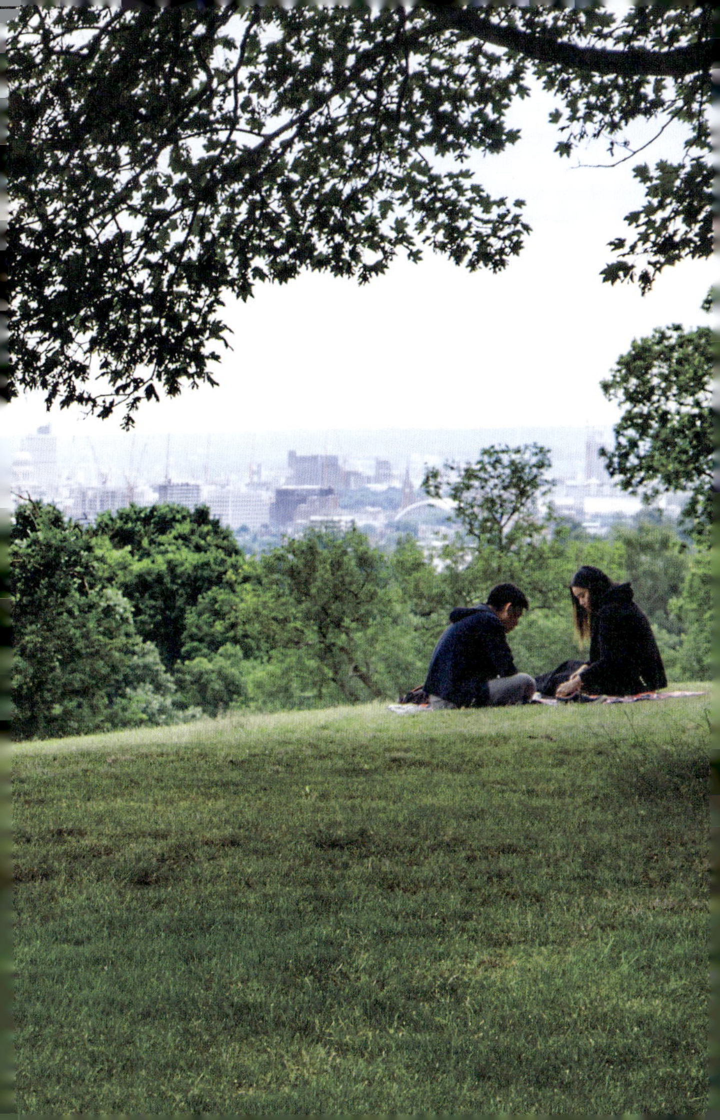

North
Sports Pitches
HAMPSTEAD WAY
WILDWOOD RD
GOLDERS GREEN
NORTH END RD
WEST HEATH AV
Spaniards Inn
Bull & Bush
Tennis
Golders Hill Park
Deer Enclosure
The Elms
Sandy Heath
SPANIARDS RD
Hill Garden
NORTH END WAY
Pergola
Inverforth House
Heath House
West Heath
East He
Pond
Vale of Heath
WEST HEATH RD
EAST HE
LOWER TER
HEATH ST
BRANCH HILL
NEW END SQ
WELL WLK
W
FLASK WLK
HAMPSTEAD
HAMPSTEAD HIGH ST

Hampstead Heath Map

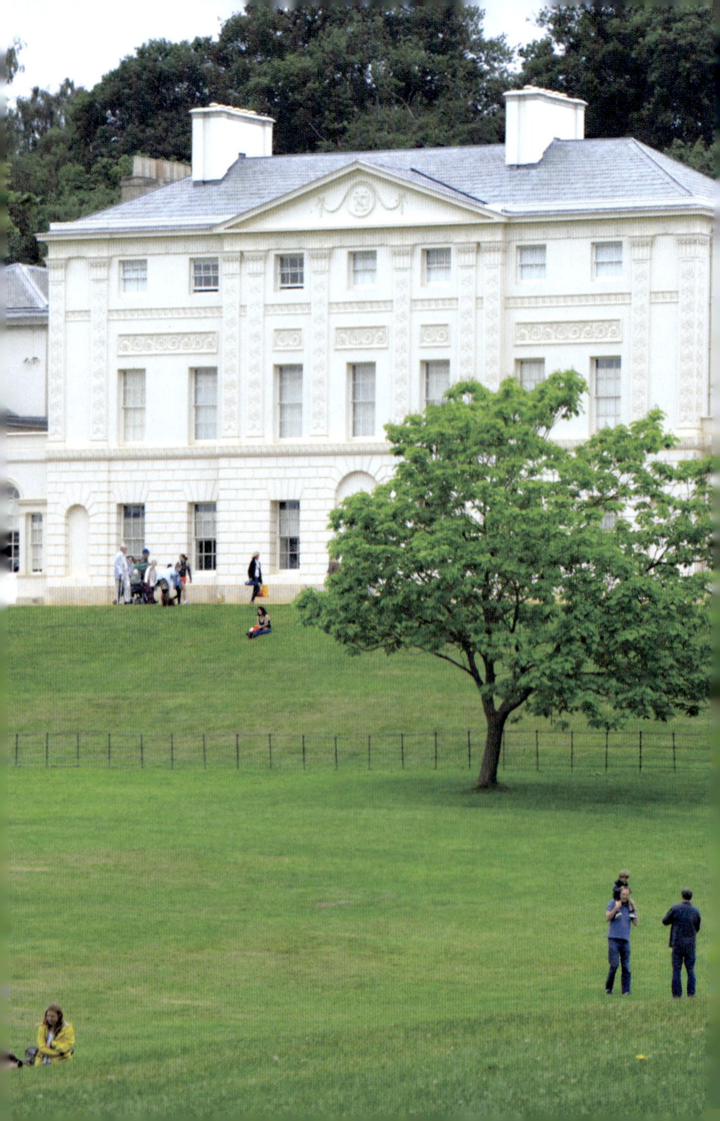

North

Hampstead Heath

NW5 1QR
Daily 24 hours
020 7332 3322
www.hampsteadheath.net
Travel: Hampstead Heath & Gospel Oak LO
Area: 320 acres
Facilities: Swimming ponds, lido, fishing ponds, cricket pitches, football and rugby pitches, golf putting greens, horse-riding circuit, model boating lake, tennis courts, bowling green cafés and restaurant, historic house

Depending on which part of Hampstead Heath you pitch up in, the vast area can feel like a forest inside London. It is however a wonderfully diverse space. Take your pick to explore the meadow, lawns, valleys, flowerbeds and woodlands that are all found within this 800 acre site on the hill above Hampstead Heath station. The heath is famous for its ponds – there are around 30 of them in total, the best-known ones being the three swimming ponds (two of which are restricted to single sex bathing). With a loyal community of swimmers made up both Hampstead residents and non-residents, the ladies' ponds in particular is so adored it has even inspired multiple books, including *At the Pond* by Margaret Drabble. Since the pandemic its previously laissez-faire approach has become stricter with their woodland entrance now shut and a ticket office opened (£4.50 adults, £2.70 concessions). During the summer months the hours between 12:00 and 16:45 are via pre-booking only, with tickets for the coming week released each Monday.

Stretching across two boroughs (Camden and Barnet), Hampstead Heath is run by the City of London and hosts regular large scale events including cross country runs of heath-based groups such as the Highgate Harriers, who train at the Parliament Hill Athletics track. The Hampstead Rugby Football Club and the London Orienteering Klubb (LOK) both use the heath for training, and Parliament Hill is also a favourite location for kite flyers, who can catch the best winds and also take in the excellent views of

Canary Wharf and the yawning miles of the capital. Down towards Gospel Oak railway station, there are tennis courts, a running track, bandstand and bowling green.

Much used as a location for film shoots (including *Les Bicyclettes de Belsize* 1968 and *Scenes of a Sexual Nature* 2006) and the inspiration for novels, paintings and poetry, Hampstead Heath's connections with art and literature go far back. Keats House, (which opens from Tuesday to Sunday) in Keats Grove, close to the heath, is where the poet lived from 1818 to 1820. Originally called Wentworth House, the dwelling is now a museum hosting poetry and literary events to keep the work of Keats alive. Around the same time that the poet was writing his famous odes, the painter John Constable was committing the heath to canvas, with dramatic paintings that were created during his annual visits to the area, starting in 1819. So enamoured was Constable with the heath as a respite and as a creative source of his work, by 1827 he'd leased a house in nearby Well Walk where he lived with his wife Maria.

Today, the northern edge of the heath is a good place for picnickers who can lounge in the grounds of the elegant Robert Adam designed Kenwood House. It's from here that the valley slopes down to the ponds. The Kenwood open air stage has summer concerts, and the house offers tours of the Iveagh Bequest – a collection of paintings by artists including Van Dyck, Reynolds and Rembrandt.

At the tip of the West Heath, the delightful Hill Garden and Pergola are well worth a visit. This section of the heath can feel like a secret enclave, particularly if you've trekked across the park's other expanses and points of interest to find it. The well-kept Hill Garden sits at the back of Inverforth House, an Edwardian-style mansion that's now a gated block of luxury homes. Walking around the Pergola you'll get an expansive view of the West Heath as well as a long view of London. The long Pergola walkway has a spiral staircase that leads down into the Italianate Hill Garden, which is a cool haven in the summer and hauntingly beautiful in the winter.

Children and families swarm to Golders Hill Park on the far western edge of the heath, where the café selling excellent ice-cream does a roaring trade during the summer months. This is the only area of the Heath that is closed at night. Its other landmarks include a deer area and a free zoo with lemurs, donkeys and Patagonian maras, large rabbit-like rodents which, despite their name, hail from Argentina.

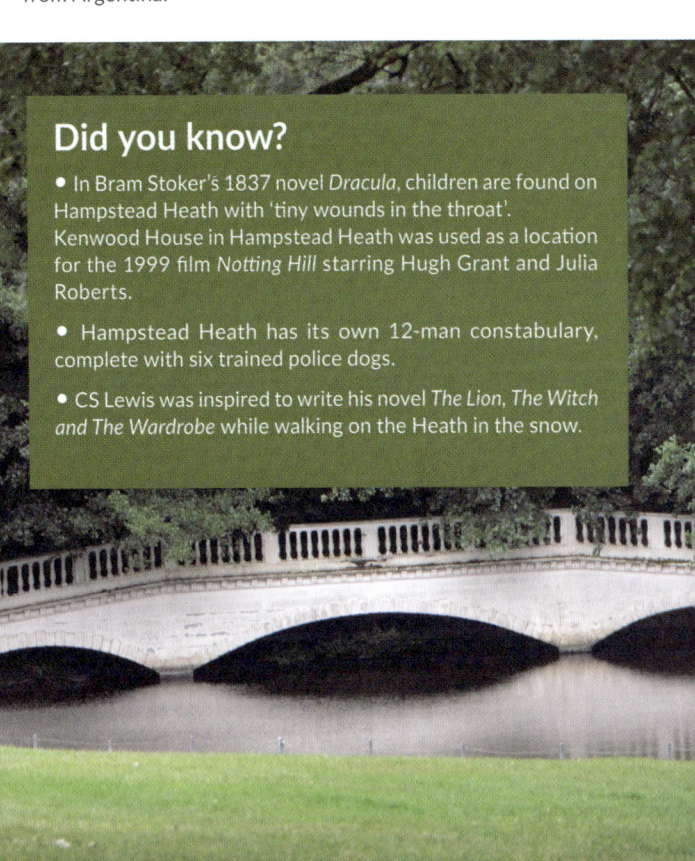

Did you know?

- In Bram Stoker's 1837 novel *Dracula*, children are found on Hampstead Heath with 'tiny wounds in the throat'. Kenwood House in Hampstead Heath was used as a location for the 1999 film *Notting Hill* starring Hugh Grant and Julia Roberts.

- Hampstead Heath has its own 12-man constabulary, complete with six trained police dogs.

- CS Lewis was inspired to write his novel *The Lion, The Witch and The Wardrobe* while walking on the Heath in the snow.

North
WOODSIDE AVE
LANCHESTER RD
Cranley Gate
Keeper's Cottage
Bridge Gate
The Hollies (bird sanctuary)
MUSWELL HILL RD
Onslow Gate
Disused railway line
Pavillion Café
Keeper's Cottage
Lodge Gate
Cricket Pitches
Sports Pitches
Wildlife Info Hut
New Gate
Keeper's Cottage
ARCHWAY RD
Archway Gate
Gypsy Gate
TALBOT RD
CHURCH RD
BISHOPS RD
HIGHGATE

North

Highgate Wood and Queen's Wood

Muswell Hill Road, N10 3JN
Daily 24 hours
020 8444 6129
www.cityoflondon.gov.uk
Travel: Highgate LU
Area: 70 acres
Facilities: Football & cricket pitches, playground, information centre, café

The seventy acres of Highgate Wood were once part of the ancient forest of Middlesex, and were part of the Bishop of London's hunting park in medieval times. Located north of Highgate station, the woods today are generally an area of conservation with nature trails, a children's playground and spaces for picnics and ballgames. This is also a popular destination for those looking for great food as the Pavillion Café serves delicious organic fare in a pretty garden setting framed by rhododendron bushes and rosebeds (open every day except Christmas Day).

Owned by the Corporation of London, the woods have been generally well tended since 1886 and have been recipients of The Green Flag Award for over a decade. Vast oaks and hornbeams are the most common trees within the grounds, but there's also ample eye-candy by way of the swathes of bluebells that cover much of the ground during the spring. Some parts of the wood are fenced off to allow for further growth of the shrublands, and visitors with a deeper yearning for nature can take part in organised wildlife walks or trails that reveal numerous species, including over 900 invertebrate species, 338 moth species and 353 types of fungi to date.

Highgate Wood is a busy place throughout the year with seasonal activities including bat watch walks, Christmas tree recycling at the beginning of every year, and insect safaris which focus on the hundreds of spottable species here. Children can have fun in the award-winning playground, whose bridge and tower features are both wheelchair and buggy accessible.

Across Muswell Hill Road is the 52 acre Queen's Wood, which has also been awarded for its landscape. Less manicured than Highgate Wood, it's a denser option that preserves a far more natural woodland than its larger neighbour, with over 100 species of spiders thriving its wilderness. Back in the 19th century, it was known as Churchyard Bottom Wood, due to the unearthing of a human burial pit from the Great Plague of 1665. Its current name refers to Queen Victoria. These days, thanks to the natural felling of trees in the huge storm of 1987, a tad more sunlight is able to penetrate the woodland. There's a stream at the northern end of the grounds, and visitors can join the Parkland Walk Footpath – a four mile route that runs along north London's disused railway lines from Finsbury Park to Alexandra Palace via Highgate.

Highgate Wood

Kentish Town City Farm

1 Cressfield Close, NW5 4BN
Daily 9:00-17:00
020 7916 5421
www.ktcityfarm.org.uk
Travel: Gospel Oak LO & Chalk Farm LU
Area: 4.5 acres

The first city farm in the UK celebrated its 50th birthday in 2022 and it's still going strong since a local action group first rented and transformed what were originally a house, a cottage and an abandoned timber yard. A fun and educational space, the farm runs a well-respected series of riding programmes for young people including therapeutic riding for children with special needs. Events include 'Garden Explorers' every Tuesday, a gardening workshop for children aged 2 and above and an annual sheep shearing day.

Paradise Park

51 Lough Road, N7 8BZ
Daily 8:00 until dusk
020 7527 2000
www.islington.gov.uk
Travel: Caledonian Road, Highbury & Islington LU
Area: 5 acres
Facilities: Children's playground, play centre, astroturf football pitch, water play feature, meadow, table tennis tables

This small local park is a favourite with children and families who flock here for the well-run children's play centre which offers a range of activities for adults and toddlers as well as health services and baby massage. All visitors can turn up and work out for free in the park's open area, where an outdoor gym boasts bright green cardiovascular equipment. It's part of the Great Outdoor Gym Company's ethos of encouraging health and wellbeing in various open spaces in the UK – with Paradise Park being just one of them.

Priory Park

Middle Lane, N8 8LN
Daily 24 hours
020 8489 1000
www.haringey.gov.uk
Travel: Hornsey Rail
Area: 16 acres
Facilities: Paddling pool, tennis courts, playground, basketball courts, café, table tennis tables, a petanque court

Previously known as the Middle Lane Pleasure Grounds, the land for today's Priory Park was bought by Hornsey Local Board in 1891, although it took until the early to mid 1920s for the park to come into full existence. The huge stone fountain was installed in 1909 and was previously sited in St Paul's Cathedral churchyard. Jets of water once shot from its 50-tonnes of granite but the structure is now used as a decorative planter. The prettiest sections of Priory Park are on its east side where shrubberies, tall silver birches, plane trees and flowerbeds are well looked after. At one time, a debating society used to meet in the park. The last remnants of this are an area in the west side of the park called the Philosopher's Garden, which is now a dog-free picnic area.

North

Waterlow Park

Dartmouth Park Hill, N19 5JF
Daily 7:00 until dusk
020 7974 4444
www.waterlowpark.org.uk
Travel: Archway LU
Area: 29 acres
Facilities: Tennis courts, exhibition space, children's playground, café, historic house

Waterlow Park is situated just south of Highgate Village and directly connects to Highgate Cemetery. The park is a wonderful place to relax either before or after a visit to the cemetery whose famous permanent residents include Karl Marx, novelist George Eliot, pop artist Patrick Caulfield and, more recently, punk impresario Malcolm McLaren.

A beautifully hilly green space, Waterlow Park is well-known for the Lauderdale House café that sits near the steep Highgate Hill entrance if you approach from Archway station. The bright café offers a great menu of breakfasts, lunches and snacks. The house is also a venue for exhibitions, concerts, workshops and weddings. Outdoor tables look out over the downward slopes of the park where tree-lined walkways, meadow and nature areas are all gorgeously arranged. Long views from wooden benches at the highest point of the park reveal the Shard and much of the city, which can be glimpsed through the tips of a mass of tall trees. Features within the park include a herb-planted kitchen garden and also a bush-obstructed gravel pathway leading to an expansive pond (one of three) that can seem wonderfully secret on quiet days.

Did you know?

- Sir Sidney Waterlow inherited the family printing business and went on to become a successful banker, Member of Parliament and Lord Mayor of London. Waterlow gave this land to London County Council in 1889, so that it might serve as a 'garden for the gardenless'. A fine bronze monument to the man can be found within the park that bears his name.

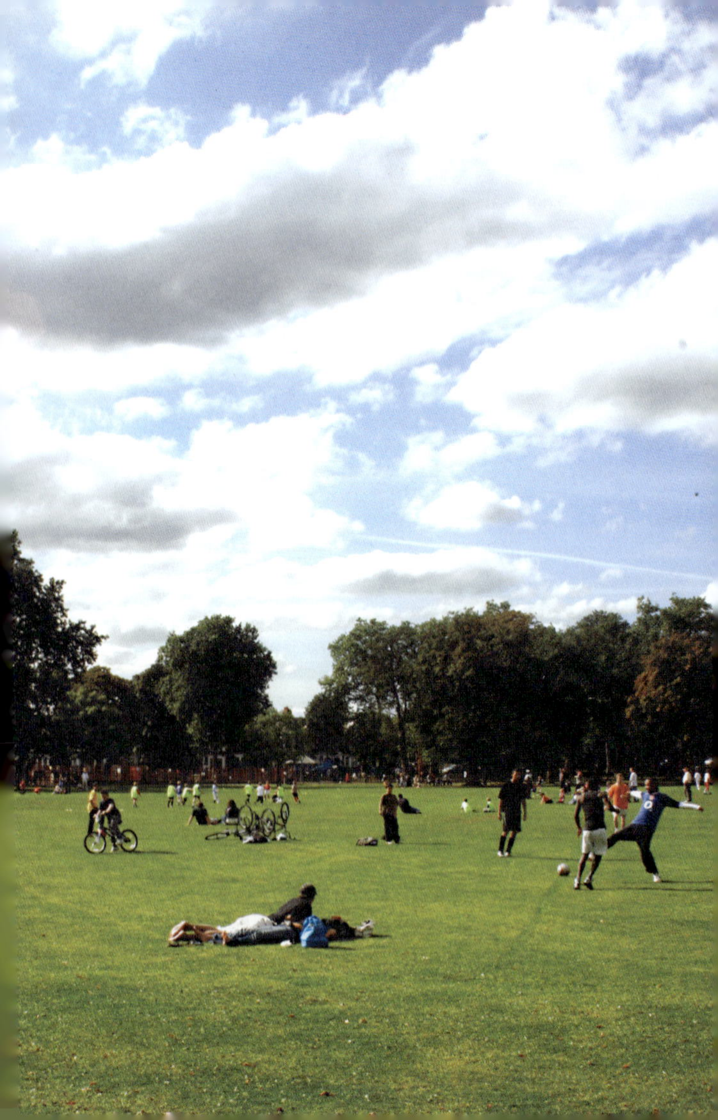

Queen's Park

Kingswood Avenue, NW6 6SG
Daily 7:00 until dusk
020 8969 5661
www.cityoflondon.gov.uk
Travel: Queen's Park LU
Area: 30 acres
Facilities: Farm, tennis courts, playground, pitch and putt course, café

This Victorian park comes as a quiet antidote to the bustling Kilburn High Road. One of the Corporation of London's portfolio of well-maintained green spaces, the park was used as part of the 1879 Royal Kilburn Agricultural Show, attended by Queen Victoria. Her title was attached to the park in honour of her Golden Jubilee. Today, the park's 30 acres are designed to give visitors a space in which to exercise, play or relax. The Quiet Garden at the Queen's Park station entrance on Harvist Road is designated as a restful area and is a bit more formal than the rest of the park with manicured lawns skilfully interspersed with vivid flowerbeds, bushes, hedgerows and a bench-lined path. Next to this garden is a small farm (or Pet's Corner) where children are always happy to look at (and handle) the chickens, turkeys, rabbits and goats. The area has a fox-proof fence to keep its residents safe. For more raucous activity, there's a children's playground over on the park's west side.

At the park's centre is a water feature, windchimes and fragrant plants for further peaceful contemplation. Sports are available on the tennis courts and the pitch and putt field, and a listed bandstand offers a summer programme of music events.

Nature calls in the Woodland Walk area, which has fairly recently had its pathways relaid. It's located in the park's northeast corner, where wildflowers, frogs, toads, insects, foxes and hedgehogs can all be spotted. There are numbered posts throughout the area to help explain all the different features.

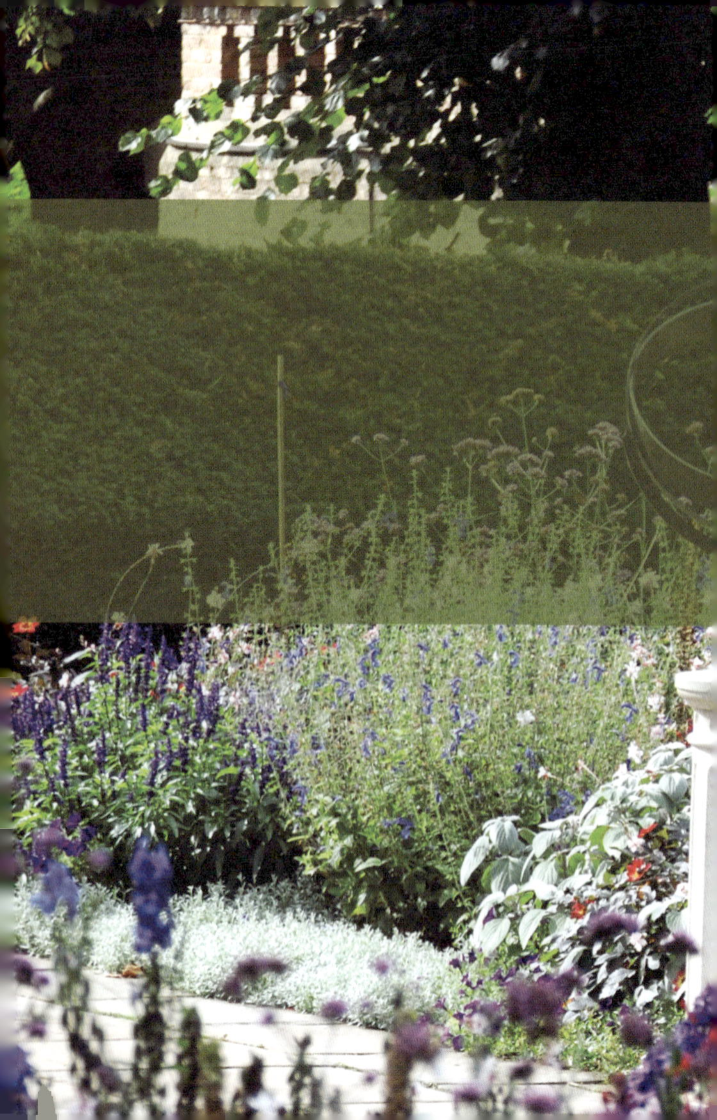

WEST

WEST

Bishop's Park..**81**
Emslie Horniman Pleasance 82
Fulham Palace Gardens **85**
Gunnersbury Park................................. 86
Hammersmith Park **89**
Holland Park 90
Meanwhile Gardens **94**
Ravenscourt Park................................. 96
Wormwood Scrubs........................... **97**

京都庭園

Kyoto Garden In Holland Park

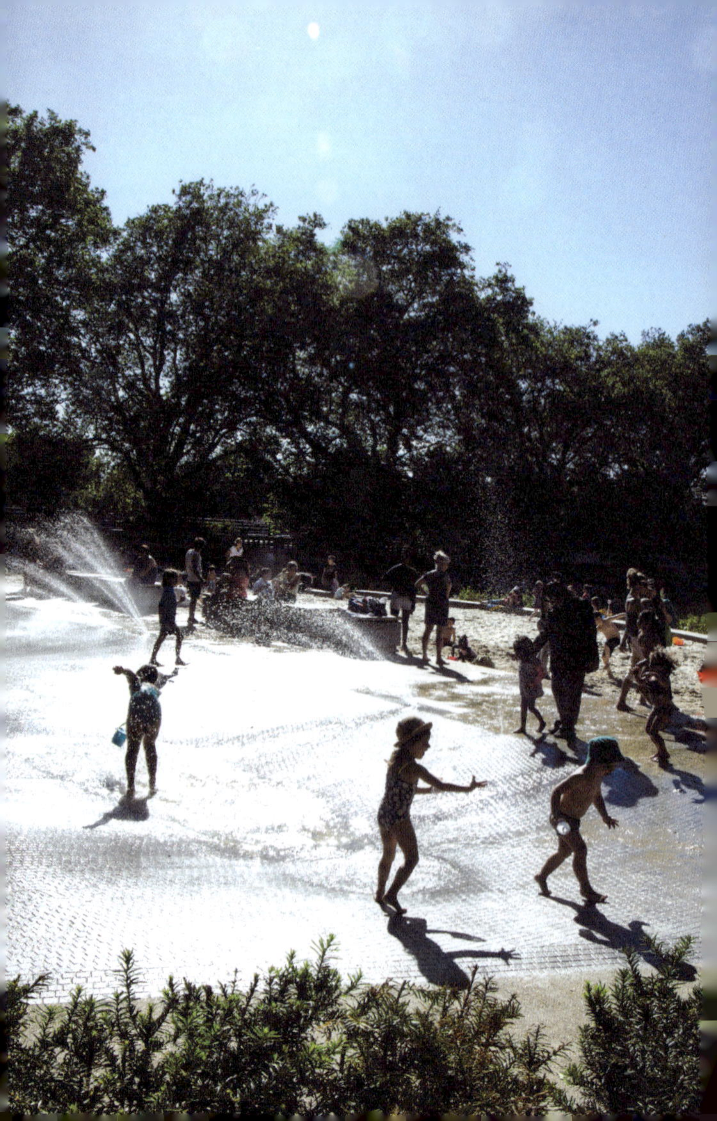

Bishop's Park

Bishop's Avenue, SW6 6EA
Daily dawn until dusk
020 7736 3854
www.friendsofbishopspark.com
Travel: Putney Bridge, East Putney LU
Area: 27 acres
Facilities: Waterplay area, urban beach, bowling greens, tennis courts, playground, table tennis tables, basketball, outdoor gym, café

Grade II* listed by English Heritage as being of special historic interest, Bishop's Park is a much-loved favourite in Hammersmith and Fulham. The park opened to the public in 1893 and its recreational facilities include playgrounds, meadows and a sculpture garden as well as a unique 'urban beach'. The park runs alongside a section of the Thames Path overlooking Putney Bridge making it a perfect vantage point for the annual Oxford vs Cambridge boat race. A firework display has take place in the park every November for years but there are now plans to make this into an environmentally friendly laser display.

The park contains the ancient site of Fulham Palace and its beautiful grounds, once enclosed by a moat, are still partly visible today (see page 305). Over the last few years, most of these areas have been refurbished, resulting in elements like the tarmac paths leading to the ornamental lake, which was given terracotta perimeter walls. In the 1960s there was an open-air theatre in the park but now events include pop up cinema screenings in the summer and a regular Sunday farmers' market.

Did you know?

- Bishop's Park was one of the locations for the 1976 film *The Omen*, starring Gregory Peck. The actor shot a scene in the park in which he meets the priest. The priest's death scene was shot nearby in the graveyard at All Saints Church.

West

Emslie Horniman Pleasance

Bosworth Road, W10 5EG
Daily 7:30 until dusk
020 7361 3003
www.rbkc.gov.uk
Travel: Westbourne Park LU/Rail
Area: 13 acres
Facilities: Shops, museum, toilets, café

This west London park opened in 1914, on land donated by Emslie John Horniman, MP for Chelsea. The park was designed by architect Charles Voyse, working with landscape designer Madeline Agar, although it is Voysey's name that lives on in the enclosed, Spanish-style Voysey Garden in the park's far corner. This white-walled area with a mini sunken moat, herb borders, flowerbeds and a pergola for climbing plants is only accessible with the permission of the park warden. The park has a large and traditional adventure playground, while all other areas display an excellent use of diverse contemporary materials in a natural setting. Bright metal pillars and artworks, raised and cobbled flowerbeds, a floodlit hard play area and a large multicoloured enclosed children's playground are all found here, with the whole park being overlooked by the high-rise Trellick Tower.

A nice touch within Emslie Horniman Pleasance is the circular and peaceful sunken 'Quiet Garden' designed by the artist Avtarjeet Dhanjal. Here you'll find heavy-duty stone and wooden benches, stone seating and cobblestones etched with moralistic missives like 'loving words are more powerful than a big stick'. Although the park is relatively small, it has been lovingly preserved for the local community and is also used for annual events – most notably the Notting Hill Carnival which uses the park as the starting point for the festivities.

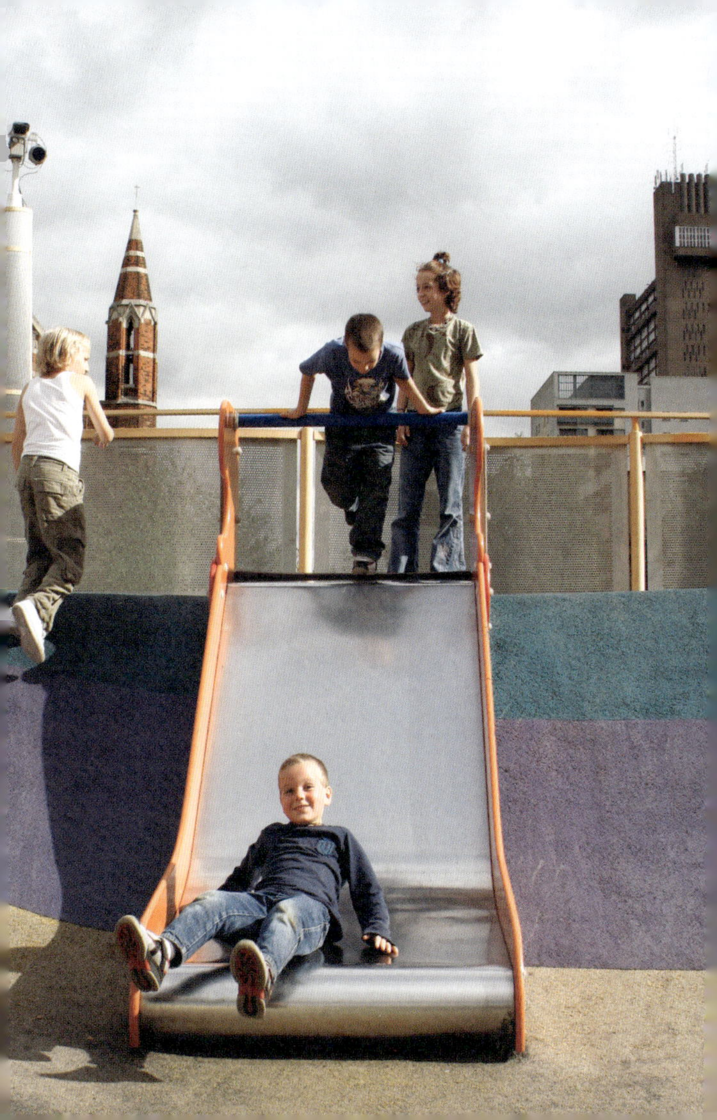

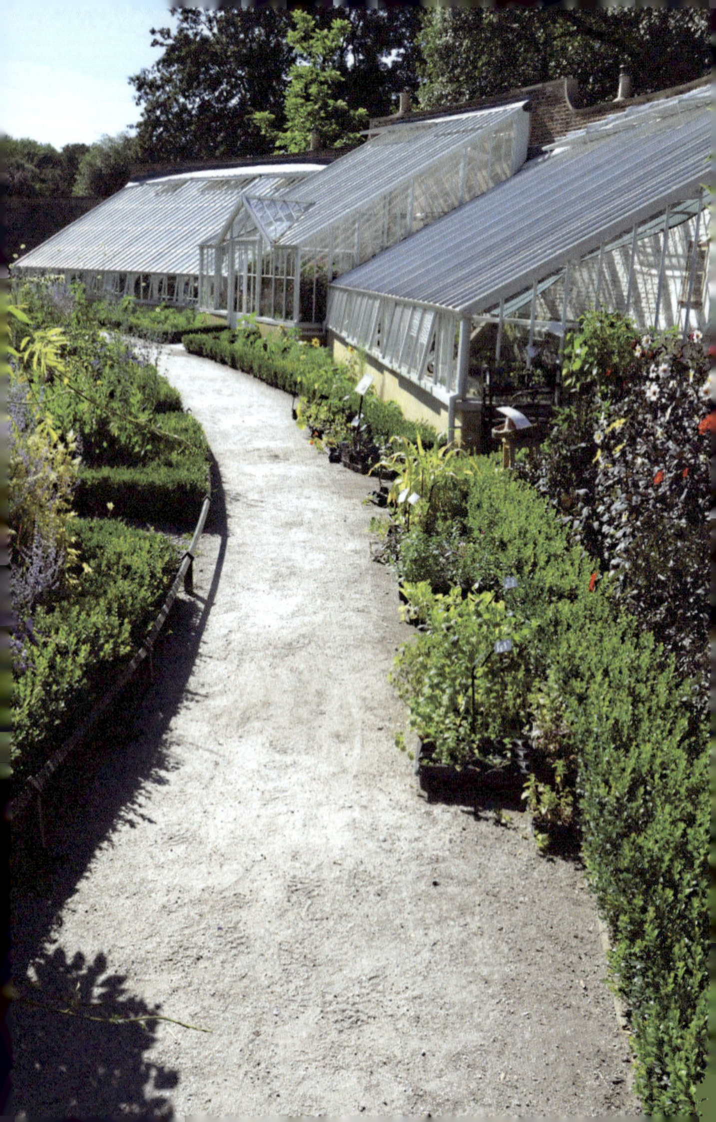

Fulham Palace Gardens

Bishop's Avenue, SW6 6EA
Daily 10:30-17:30
020 7736 3233
www.fulhampalace.org
Travel: Hammersmith or Putney Bridge LU
Area: 13 acre
Facilities: Museum, café

Fulham Palace has 13 acres of gardens that are set within the surrounding grounds of Bishop's Park (see page 81), although they were separated from the larger grounds in the late 19th century. The gardens form an attractive enclosure for the Palace, and are historically significant, having at one time been home to the important botanical collections of Bishop Compton (1675- 1713). The Fulham Palace site is a Scheduled Ancient Monument, while the surrounding park area is Grade II English Heritage listed – the only such green space in the borough. There are usually tours of the grounds by the Palace curator, with times and days for these sessions outlined in the garden section of the website.

The garden consists of an open lawn at the back of the Palace building and is edged by magnolias, shrubs and woodland paths. In a far corner is the evergreen holm oak (Quercus Ilex), that is now over 450 years old and considered to be a Great Tree of London.

The old walled kitchen garden at the far end of the lawn has recently been restored and the 19th-century knot garden replanted to its original design. This plot can be entered through a small Tudor gate, or from an alternative side entrance beyond the refurbished Victorian gardeners' bothies. A small productive vegetable area has been re-established and this, along with a peaceful meadow and fruit trees, make this a quiet spot for a picnic. In the far distance towards the south, you can see the flag-topped turrets of the medieval tower of All Saint's Church, which sits at the Putney Bridge end of Bishop's Park.

West

Gunnersbury Park

Popes Lane, Acton, W3 8LQ
Daily 7:00 until dusk
020 3961 0280
www.visitgunnersbury.org
Travel: Acton Town LU, Kew Bridge Rail
Area: 186 acres
Facilities: Children's playgrounds, museum, miniature golf, boating and fishing lake, bowling green, tennis courts, football and rugby pitches, café

Gunnersbury Park Museum

Gunnersbury Park was for many centuries part of the estate of the Bishops of London, before falling into private ownership. A grand house was built here in the mid-17th century, designed by architect John Webb – a pupil of fellow architect and theatre designer Inigo Jones. Gunnersbury House served as the home of Princess Amelia – George II's favourite daughter – between 1763 and her death in 1786. Although the original house was destroyed in 1801, much of the park's current landscaping and several of its features date from Princess Amelia's residency. The house and grounds went through several owners before Alexander Copland bought the land and built the large Georgian house that stands here today. It in turn was acquired by Nathan Rothschild in 1835 and remained as a family estate until it was sold to the boroughs of Ealing and Acton in 1925.

The large and leafy park that stands here today has been in existence since 1926 but has lost little of its former glory with many original features such as a boating lake, several ponds, orangery, Italian gardens, mock-Gothic ruin and a neo-classical temple. These ornate features are complemented by acres of open space with plenty of mature trees. Those looking for sport rather than relaxation will also find plenty to do here from a gentle game of bowls to the physical demands of football and rugby. In the winter, the park is able to accommodate 20 football pitches. There are also two playgrounds for those seeking to keep kids entertained. Gunnersbury Park has the usual selection of park wildlife but has a particularly varied selection of wildfowl. The large white stucco house within the park was used in the 1951 comedy film *The Lavender Hill Mob* made by Ealing Studios and is now a local history museum.

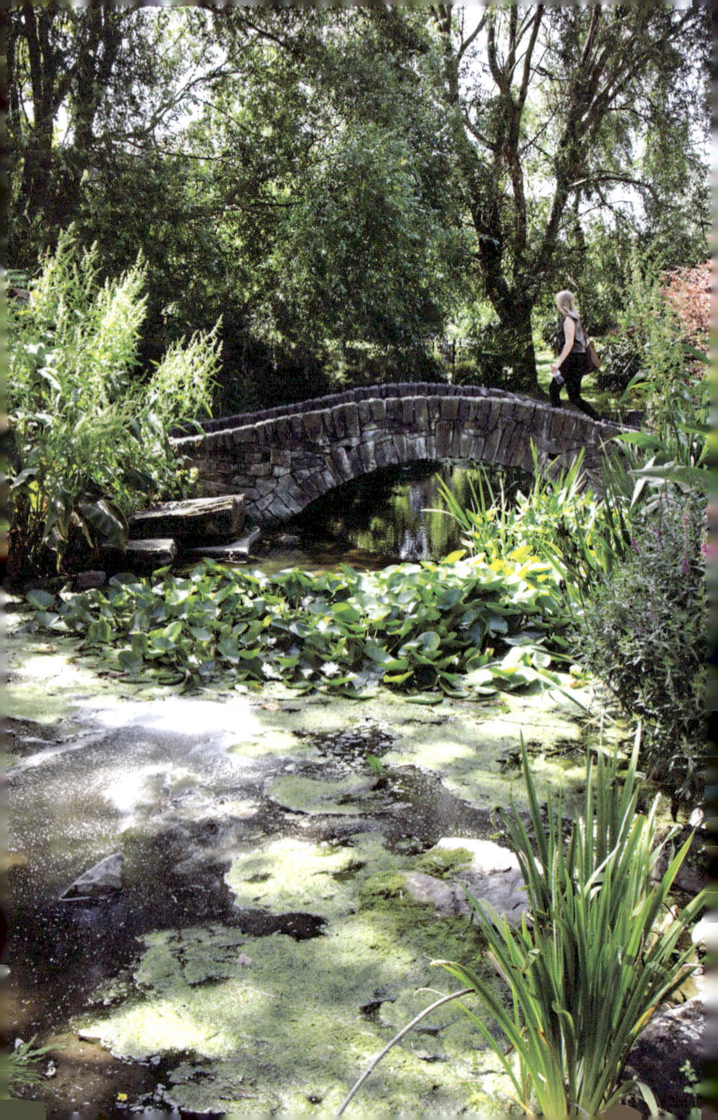

West

Hammersmith Park

South Africa Road, W12 7NU
Daily 7:30 dusk
020 8748 3020
www.lbhf.gov.uk
Travel: Shepherd's Bush & White City LU
Area: 7 acres
Facilities: Bowling green, sandpit and paddling pool, playground, tennis and basketball courts, pond and football pitch

A neat and tidy neighbourhood park behind the White City Estate and close to the grounds of Queen's Park Rangers Football Club. The biggest draw of this linear landscape is its central garden and lake. The main entrance at South Africa Road offers a picturesque promenade of benches and rosebeds, as well as a gated paddling pool, tennis courts and play area. This area leads on to the central garden, which is designed in a Japanese style, complete with stone lanterns, a stone basin and a cobbled path. Rugged steps lead up to the two stone viewing benches at its highest point, which overlook a humpbacked bridge over the pond. Just north of this is a rock garden which is used as a play area for children. The lush surroundings include lovingly planted bushes, trees, bamboo grasses, azaleas, Japanese holly, a hedge maze and a climbing forest.

    The park lies on land that is one of the few remaining remnants of the great White City Franco-British Exhibition of 1907. This was a dazzling 140 acre stretch of pavilions, courts and decorative domes all adorned in white stucco. The site was later used for the fourth Olympic Games of 1908 and later for the Anglo-Japanese exhibition of 1910, of which the park's Japanese garden is a surviving feature.

West

Holland Park
Ilchester Place, W8 6LU
Daily 7:30 until dusk
020 7602 2226
www.rbkc.gov.uk
Travel: Holland Park LU
Area: 54 acres
Facilities: Cricket pitch, youth hostel, theatre, tennis courts, football pitch, play-facilities, netball court, ecology centre, café

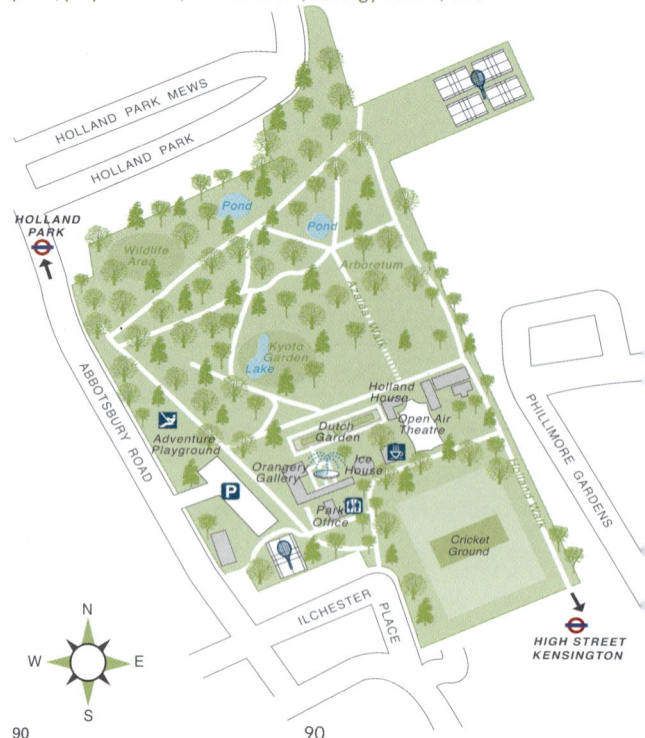

Holland Park is the largest green space in the well-heeled Royal Borough of Kensington and Chelsea and is surrounded by grand residential mansion houses. There are several landmark buildings in the area that are open to the public for guided tours such as the house of Victorian cartoonist Linley Sambourne, and Leighton House – the former home of artist Frederic Lord Leighton. Central to the park are the murals and terraces that are all that remains of Holland House, which was destroyed by bombing during the Second World War. The house was originally named after a former owner, the Earl of Holland, whose wife is said to have introduced the dahlia to England. The site is now used as the venue for open-air theatre during the summer.

Most people tend to flock to the Japanese-style Kyoto Garden with its Koi carp-filled pond and central waterfall. The sloping woodlands that surround the park are good for spotting squirrels, peacocks, and a further fifty or so species of birds that have been found here over the last decade. Crows, jays, robins and magpies are regular visitors, and long-eared bats can be seen near the ponds during dusk, or hovering around the slightly forlorn statue of a seated Lord Holland who surveys his own pond at the edge of a woodland path. The Ecology Centre in the Old Stableyard has maps, nets for pond dipping and is a great source of wildlife information.

The park has an excellent café and a conservatory-style Orangery which is used for weddings, parties and exhibitions. The numerous Parks Police and special dog toilets show how seriously the maintenance of the lawns and gardens are taken.

Sports activities include football, tennis and cricket, as well as five-week jogging programmes for beginners. The netball course for those nostalgic for their schooldays, and sessions at their sport faciltiies can all be booked by calling 020 7602 2226.

Kyoto Garden in Holland Park

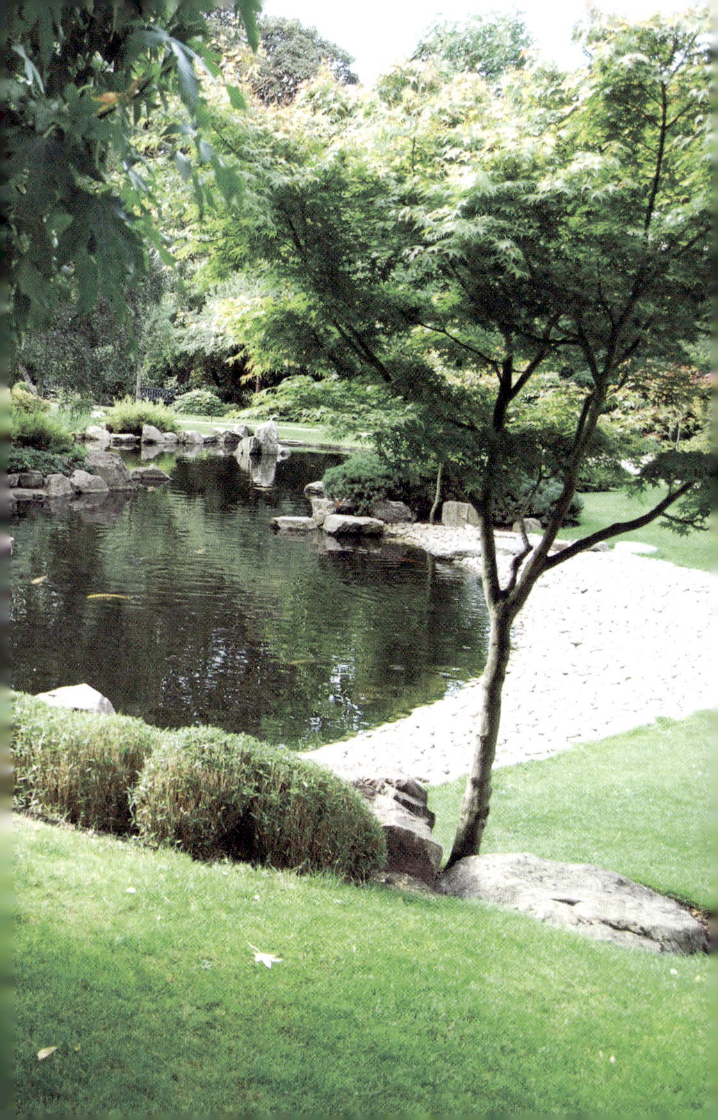

West

Meanwhile Gardens

156-158 Kensal Road, W10 5BN
Daily 24 hours
020 8960 4600
www.meanwhile-gardens.org.uk
Travel: Westbourne Park or Westbourne Grove LU & Rail
Area: 4 acres
Facilities: Skate bowl, community centre

This community garden was set up in the 1970s to offset the urban surrounds of W10 and the then recently built Westway. Overshadowed by Trellick Tower, it's a linear strip of land running from the residential estates of Kensal Road to the Carlton Bridge steps leading up to Westbourne Park Road. The garden extends along a section of the Grand Union Canal, where cyclists and walkers share the open pathway, and residents can be seen enjoying their gardens on the opposite side. Inside Meanwhile Gardens, features include the wildlife garden, allotment area, herb-scented courtyard and duck pond, which are all at the Kensal Road end. The path towards Westbourne Park includes cobbled walkways, meadowland, and a free play hut for under-6s. The park is also the site of one of London's oldest skateparks. With three interlocking bowls, it's a popular alternative to the skate areas at Kennington Park, Stockwell and the South Bank Centre. Despite some obvious wear and tear, it's been pretty well looked after over the years. Nearby is another skatepark called Royal Oak (or Meanwhile 2) that sits under the cover of the concrete Westway.

Did you know?

- Meanwhile Gardens took its name from the fact that back in the 1970s, Westminster local authority gave local sculptor Jamie McCullough temporary permission to turn what was then a derelict wasteland into a community garden. Meanwhile has become a permanent part of the landscape but the name has remained.

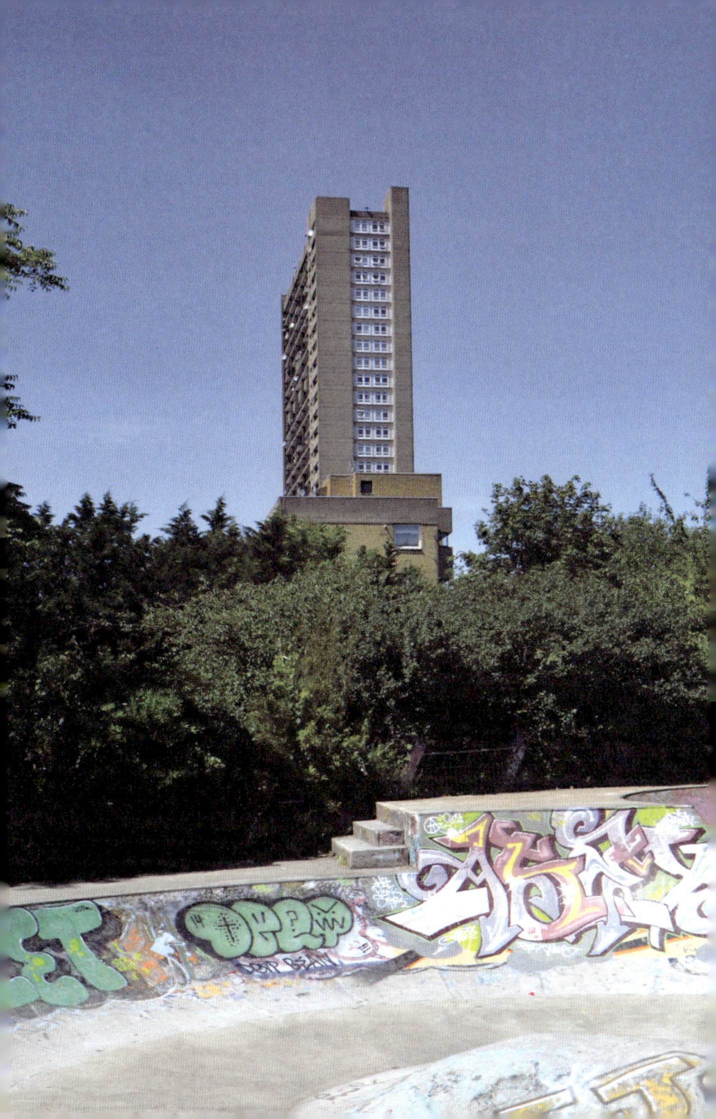

Ravenscourt Park

Paddenswick Road, W6 0UA
Opens at dawn daily, closing time varies monthly
020 8748 3020
www.lbhf.gov.uk
Travel: Ravenscourt Park LU
Area: 30 acres
Facilities: Children's playgrounds, basketball nets, tennis courts, bowling green, football pitch, café

An ordered expanse of open land in a fairly well-heeled area of London, Ravenscourt Park has a history that goes back to 1888. When the park was established, Ravenscourt House (at the Paddenswick Road entrance) rivalled the grand pile of Fulham Palace and provided a second residence for the Bishop of London. The building crumbled under bombing in 1941, and now a scented walled garden blossoms in its place. Neatly-sculpted topiary, lively flowerbeds and serene communal seating are all beautifully arranged here, thanks to the green-fingered hard work of local volunteers. In the other areas of the main park, the prettiest spot is beside the tree-lined lake, which is best viewed from the small humpbacked bridge. Framed by pristine flowerbeds, willows and bushes, the lake is populated by ducks, coots, swans and mallards. Children are also well catered for with a large playground, complete with a wooden climbing frame, and several paddling pools.

West

Wormwood Scrubs Park

Scrubs Lane, W12 0DF
Daily 24 hours
020 8748 3020
www.scrubs-online.org.uk
Travel: White City & East Acton LU
Area: 200 acres
Facilities: Linford Christie Outdoor Sports Centre, football pitches, rugby pitch, Gaelic football pitch, outdoor gym

Lesser known than the prison, Wormwood Scrubs Park is the largest open green space in the area and a peaceful respite from the noise and pace of West London. The park contains a 33-acre nature reserve, which attracts a range of mammals and reptiles to its woodlands, hedgerows and grasslands. If you're keen eyed you may well see rabbits, field and bank voles, brown rats and foxes as well as frogs, toads and lizards. There are over 100 species of birds in the park and the nature reserve, including blackcaps, chiffchaffs, kestrels and song thrushes. The Scrubs is also home to over 250 species of wildflower and throughout the park's 200 acres, you'll find trees that include hawthorn, Norway maple and English oak.

For sports lovers, the Linford Christie Outdoor Sports Centre inside Wormwood Scrubs main park is packed with facilities including an 11-a-side football and hockey pitch, a 400-metre track, field areas for long jump, triple jump, shot put, discus and hammer and floodlit training facilities.

Scrubs Lane separates the main park from Little Wormwood Scrubs over to the east. This smaller open space is a Site of Nature Conservation Importance, and in 2008 was one of ten London parks awarded a grant (after a public vote) for a new playground and other improvements.

Battersea Park

SOUTH-WEST

SOUTH-WEST

Battersea Park **102**
Streatham Rookery 106
Vauxhall City Farm **111**
Vauxhall Park 112
Vauxhall Pleasure Gardens **114**
Windmill Gardens 117

Battersea Park

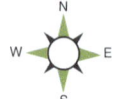

South-west

Battersea Park

SW11 4NJ
Daily 6:30 until dusk
020 8871 7530
www.batterseapark.org
Travel: Battersea Power Station LU
Area: 200 acres
Facilities: Sports pitch and grounds, pump house gallery, children's zoo, playground, café

South-west

There are a multitude of attractions in this inner city park, which features a series of circular carriageways around a grand central bandstand. With 200 acres of land split into lush gardens (Old English, Herb, Rose, Sub-Tropical and Winter), well-designed flowerbeds, exotic trees, open lawns and playgrounds; there's something for everyone here. A key attraction is the large fishing lake which offers rowing during the summer months. A Barbara Hepworth sculpture called *Single Form* is situated between the lake and the South Carriage Drive. Henry Moore also gets a look in with his *Three Standing Figures*, which overlooks the lake's north side, south of the central carriageway. At the eastern end of the lake is the fabulous Pear Tree Café which is one of the best park eateries in London (see p.321).

Peace Pagoda

Battersea Park was the site of the 1951 Festival of Britain Pleasure Gardens, which had a permanent funfair that rolled along until the early 1970s, by which time the park seemed to lose its lustre. Large-scale renovations took place throughout 2003, resulting in new features, including the fountain area just below the North Carriage Drive. The fountain is impressive with jets of up to fifteen feet high and low metal barriers to keep excitable children from diving in. The adjacent Rose Garden is a well-landscaped area that seems to inspire visitors with yoga mats, or those practising Tai Chi. On North Carriage Drive itself, the huge Thameside Peace Pagoda is perhaps the park's best-known landmark. Three tiers tall, with panels variously showing a preaching, sleeping or contemplating Buddha, the Pagoda can be climbed to access panoramic views of the Thames and both Chelsea and Albert bridges. The structure was built in 1985 by Japanese monks and nuns in memory of Hiroshima Day, and to encourage world peace. The park's Battersea Park Children's Zoo is run by the Heap family who saved it from closure. Resident animals include wallabies, ring-tailed lemurs and the ever-popular meerkats. There is also an adventure playground within the zoo.

Did you know?

- Battersea Park was featured in singer Petula Clark's 1954 single *Meet Me in Battersea Park*. In the 1960s the park featured in the films *The Long Arm of the Law*, starring Peter Sellers and a British sci-fi movie, *The Day the Earth Caught Fire*. It was also featured in a 1991 episode of *Mr Bean*, called *Mr Bean to Town*.

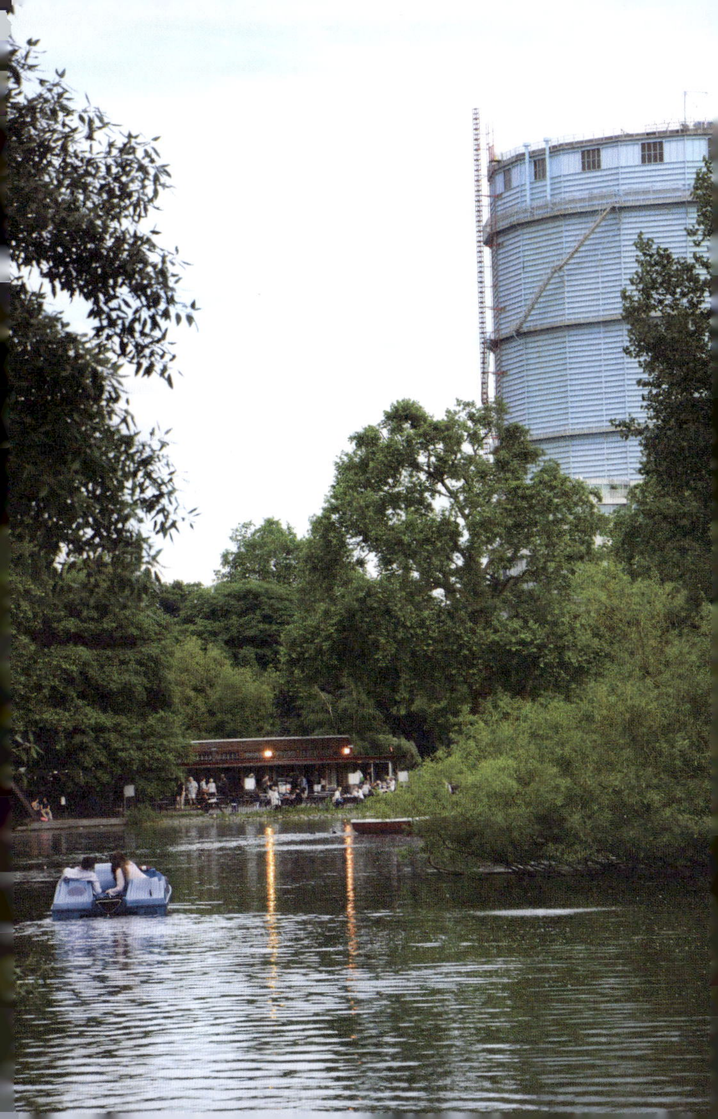

South-west

Streatham Rookery

Covington Way, Streatham Common, SW16 3BX
Daily 7:30 until dusk
020 7926 9000
www.lambeth.gov.uk/parks/rookery-streatham
Travel: Streatham Common LU & Streatham Rail
Area: 4 acres
Facilities: Tennis court, basketball court, football pitch, café

Streatham is a designated conservation area with 70 acres of green space that includes Streatham Common (see page 288), which stretches from the main high street and up towards Norwood. However, many people in and around SW16 are unaware of the walled Rookery, a peaceful and well-kept series of circular gardens found within the highest point of the common. Two entrances next to the main car park reveal the four-acre gardens, where the main bench-lined path offers an expansive view beyond the gardens and over towards Norwood Grove. Steps within the Rookery lead down to each separate 'garden room', which includes an Old English Garden, Ornamental Garden, tennis court, picnic area and orchard and the White Garden – an oblong-shaped space with six white benches, and all-white flowering plants.

The gardens are framed by narrow sloping paths, either cobbled or smooth, with surrounding bushes. The arboured walkways look particularly good in the summer, and even during hot weather the Rookery never gets overcrowded, which adds to its sense of being a secret garden. Features include a sundial, a mini pond and water fountain, large cedars, fern trees and even the occasional outdoor theatre event. One particular point of interest is a central wishing well – originally one of three – which marks the site of the ancient mineral wells that Streatham was famous for in the 17th and 18th centuries.

The Rookery opened as a public park in 1913 and was created from the grounds of a large house that had previously been demolished. However its history, which is very much linked with

Streatham's waters, goes back to 1659 when agricultural labourers freshened up at the spring here, and made elaborate claims for the effects of the waters that were said to cure everything from rheumatism to gout and blindness. No wonder then, that the site was developed as a medicinal spa with coaches and crowds often queuing for a mile along Streatham High Road to get into the grounds. The phenomenon sparked quite an enterprise, with the water packaged and sold at St Paul's Churchyard, Temple Bar and Royal Exchange, with each dose comprising around three cups, which was estimated to be the equivalent of nine cups of Epsom water. Even Queen Victoria got in on the action when she came to take the waters at Streatham Spa.

Nearby local nature reserves:

Eardley Road Sidings (Bates Crescent, SW16 5AP, off Abercairn Road and Greyhound Lane)

Unigate Wood (Namba Roy Close, SW16 2QD, off Valley Road)

Norwood Grove (Covington Way, SW16 3BY) A large park adjacent to Streatham Common, with formal gardens and wooded areas. Norwood Grove Mansion is in the park and is set in its own ornamental gardens.

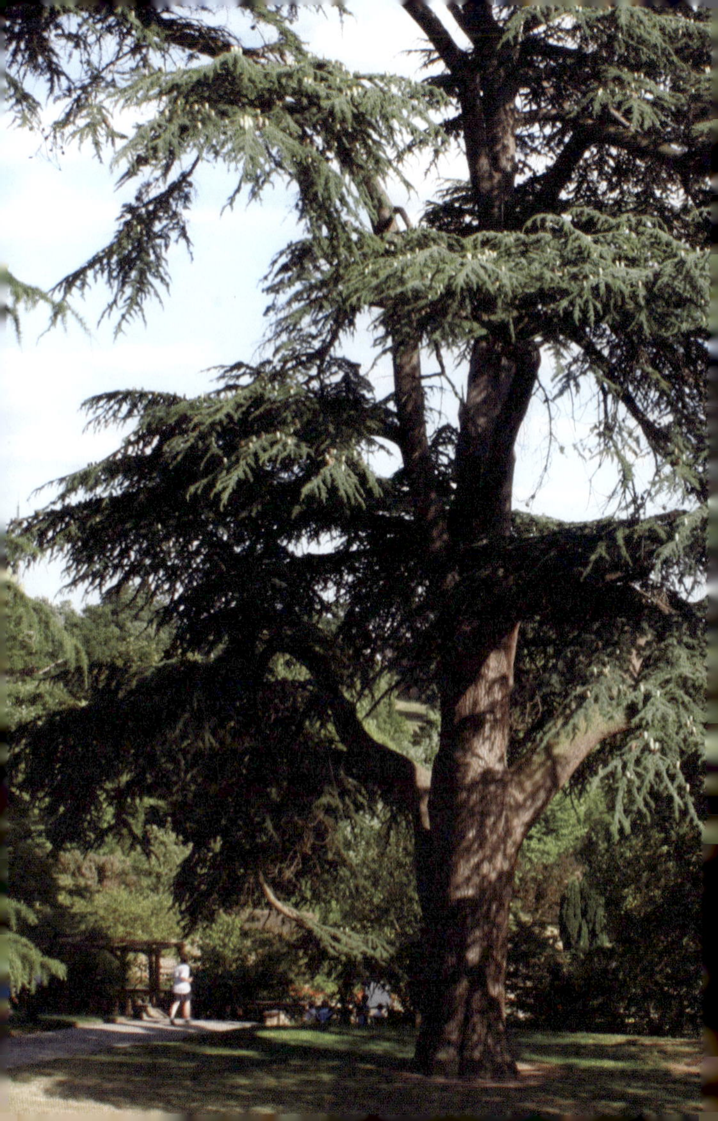

Streatham Rookery

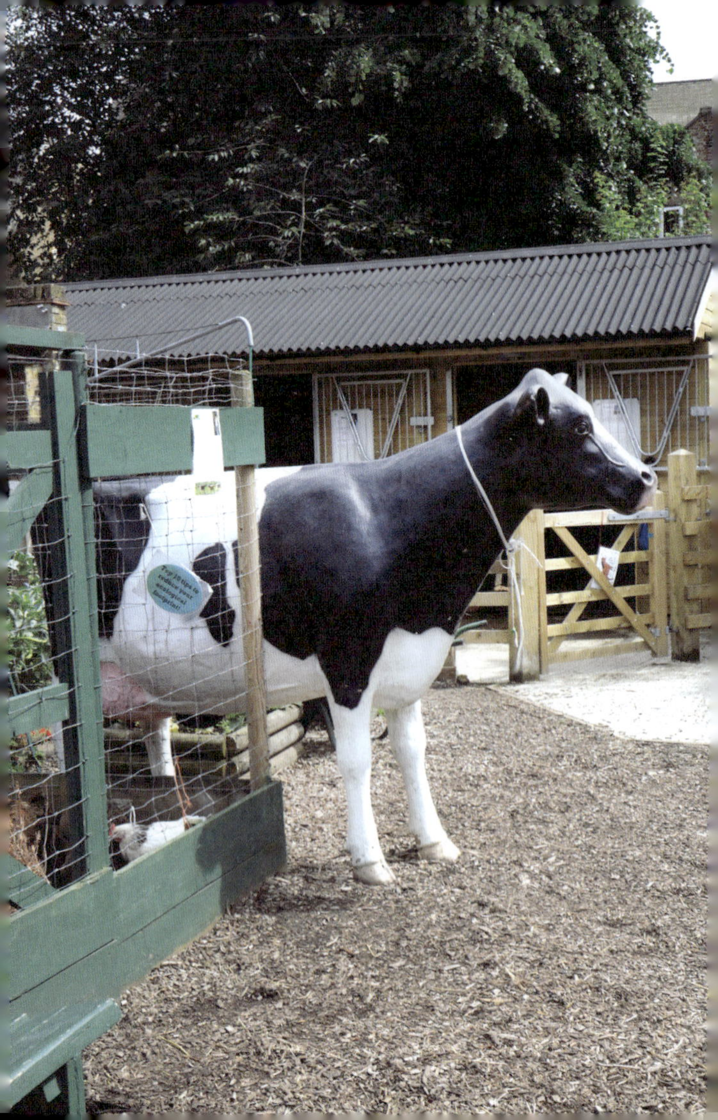

South-west

Vauxhall City Farm

165 Tyers Street, SE11 5HS
Wed-Sun 10:30-16:00
www.vauxhallcityfarm.org
020 7582 4204
Transport: Vauxhall LU & Rail
Area: 1.2 acres
Facilities: Riding centre, workshops, animal meet & greet, therapeutic and educational services, café
Admission: Free

Birthday parties, riding lessons and a young farmers' club are just some of the activities that take place in this urban farm that justifiably touts itself as 'a little piece of the countryside in Central London'. It's actually somewhat southeast of the centre but there's no arguing with the fact that Vauxhall City Farm is a wonderful respite from the apartments and office blocks that dominate the area.

A charity run by volunteers, it sits at the edge of the restored Vauxhall Pleasure Gardens (see page 114). Modestly-sized, it has plenty of goats, sheep, pigs, ducks, chickens and rabbits who you can feed and you can even buy fresh eggs from the chicken coops to take home. An adopt-a-pony scheme runs at the riding centre, and the farm's horses and ponies (around 10 of them in total) are regularly booked for lessons, riding therapy and riding for the disabled. A group of local textile artists run wool activity days at the farm and cultivate dye plants in the farm's community garden.

South-west

Vauxhall Park

Lawn Lane, SW8 2EJ
7:30 until dusk
020 7926 9000
www.vauxhallpark.org.uk
Travel: Vauxhall LU
Area: 8.5 acres
Facilities: Children's playground, tennis courts, basketball court, café

Vauxhall Park was opened in 1890 by Albert Prince of Wales. It's a modestly-sized area bordering South Lambeth Road and Fentiman Road. By the late 1990s, it was looking a bit scruffy, but improvements over the next few years included spruced-up lawns and a lush lavender garden, which replaced a dilapidated bowling green. The two tennis courts are well used in the summer, and there's a popular Parco Café, which offers a good children's menu and delicious hot and cold snacks and cooked breakfasts that draw in Vauxhall residents, builders and even tourists.

A mix and match of themes within the park include a Victorian fountain with cascading water, a rose garden and a 1940s model village nestling among fir trees and flowerbeds. Donated to the park in 1947 by a retired engineer, Edgar Wilson, the doors and windows of the tiny cottages are made of lead, while the concrete was painted by hand.

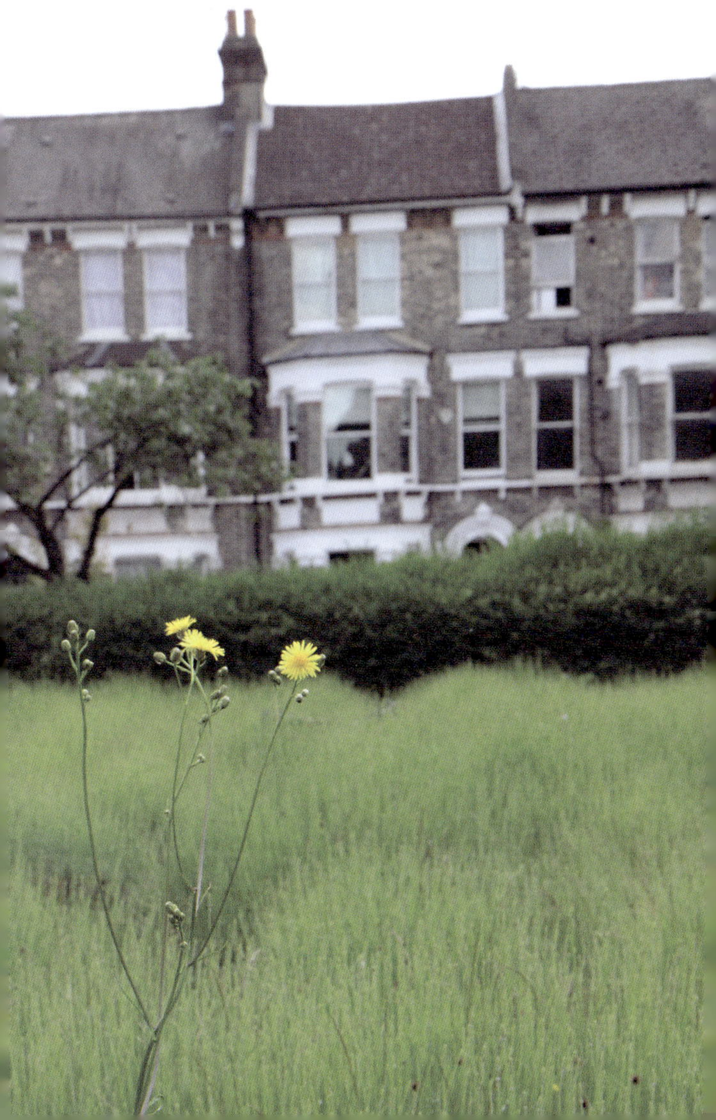

South-west

Vauxhall Pleasure Gardens

New Springs Gardens Walk, SE11 5HL
Daily 24 hours
020 7926 9000
www.lambeth.gov.uk
Travel: Vauxhall LU
Area: 8 acres
Facilities: Multi-use games area, café

2012 saw the opening of the newly refurbished Vauxhall Pleasure Gardens. With a history that goes back to the 17th century, in its heyday it was the venue for orchestras, promenades, circuses, and lion tamers and was regularly patronised by the likes of Shelley, Casanova and Charles Dickens (who was rather scathing about what he saw as the park's 'faded splendour' in the 1830s). The gardens were so popular that Vauxhall station was built in 1848 to cater for the visitors. Other competitors were the pleasure gardens at Marylebone and the Ranelagh gardens in Chelsea (which can be seen as part of a visit to the Chelsea Flower Show).

Vauxhall's original pleasure garden became a model for Copenhagen's Tivoli Garden amusement park, which opened in 1843 and is now the oldest of its kind in the world. By the early 1840s the public's craze for pleasure gardens was on the wain and Vauxhall gradually declined before its final closure in 1859. This history adds to the importance of the current park, whose new features include landscaped hills and mounds on the west side of the park, recently planted trees and a free all-weather sports pitch. The most eye-catching additions are the two 18-metre high concrete pillars at the Kennington Lane entrance.

During the summer there are outdoor film screenings (weather permitting) and fireworks in the winter. There are horse-riding paddocks within the park that are run in association with the adjoining Vauxhall City Farm (see p.111).

The Tea House Theatre (139 Vauxhall Walk, SE11 5HL) looks out over Vauxhall Pleasure Gardens and serves delicious cake and hot food in a charming converted Victorian public house.

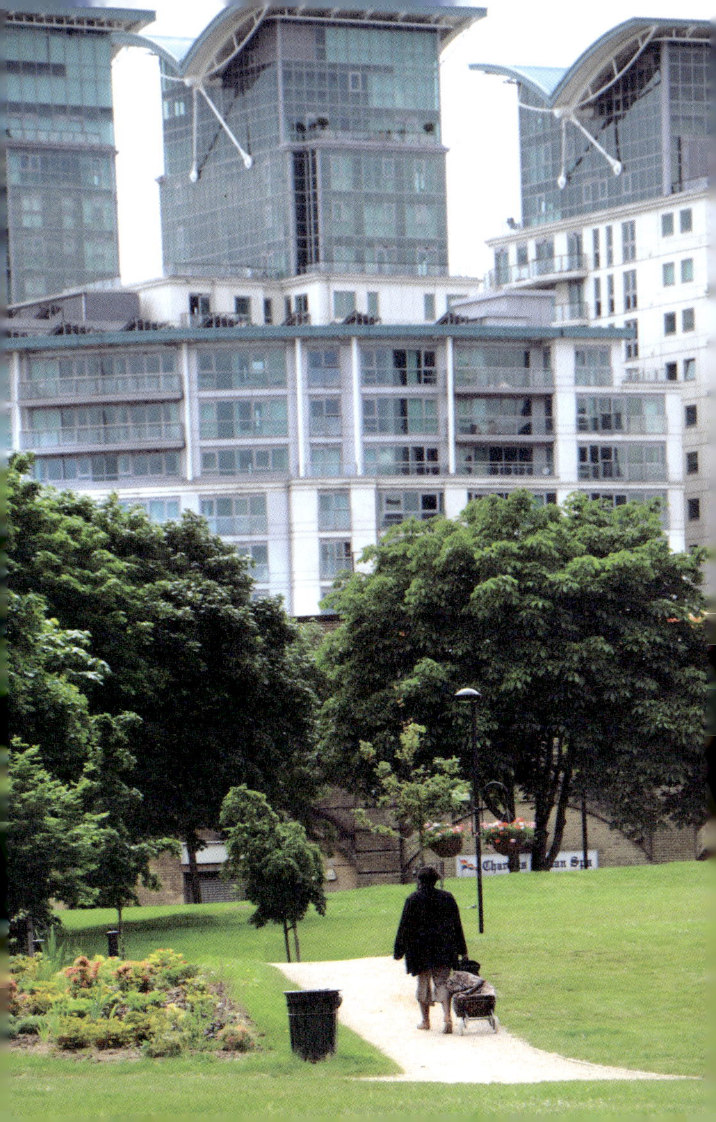

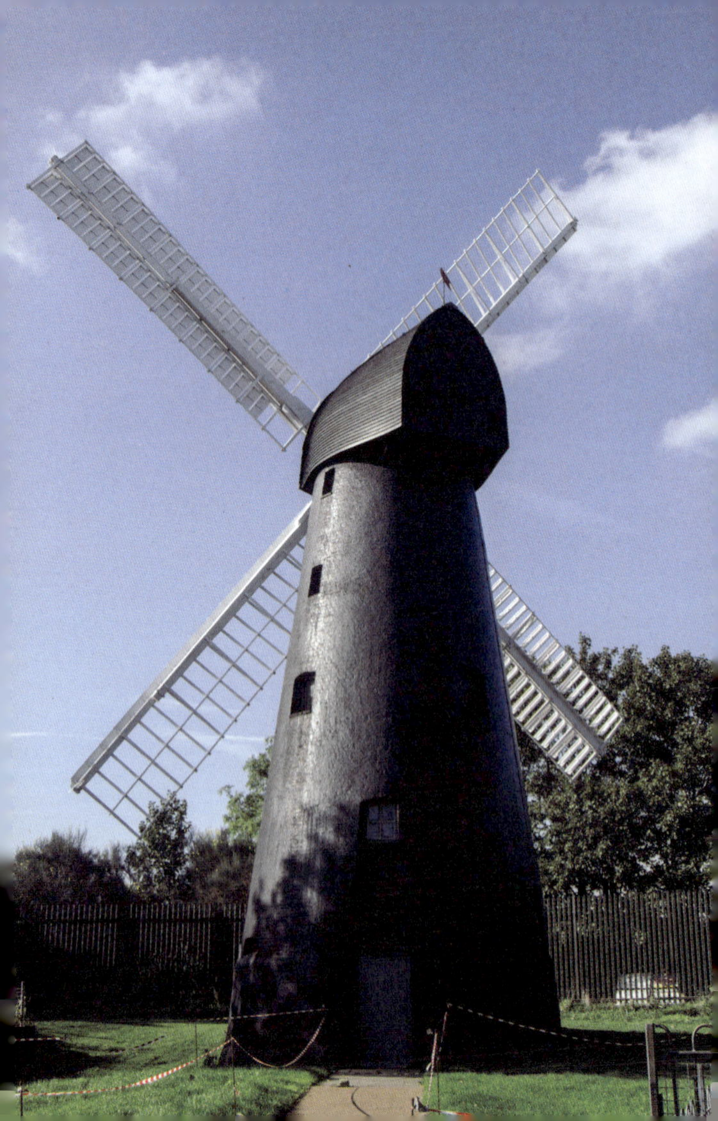

Windmill Gardens

Blenheim Gardens, Brixton, SW2 5EU
Daily 24 hours
020 7926 9000
www.brixtonwindmill.org
Travel: Brixton LU & LO
Area: 1.3 acres
Facilities: Children's playground, table tennis tables, medicinal herb garden

Tucked away behind the Blenheim Gardens Studios and estates of Brixton Hill is this park and archaeological site. A compact green space with a stay and play facility and a medicinal herb bed, this little garden is best known for the old Brixton Windmill. The structure stands 12 metres tall and was built in 1816 when SW2 was nothing but open fields. Formerly known as Ashby Mill, it was a working mill right up to the early 20th century and is the only one to have survived of 12 other sites that have been identified in Lambeth. Even as far back as 1917, it was considered something of a fascination, with a piece in the Daily Chronicle newspaper poetically stating that the windmill was 'a relic of an age which is fast becoming a memory approached by a small roadway hedged with privet over which nods acacia' limes and filberts and lots of fowl.' Now a Grade II listed building, the windmill with its eighteen-inch thick brickwork seems destined to remain here for many more centuries. It pretty much dominates the landscape, particularly with its black colouring, which replicates the original tar that protected it from the elements.

Other than Saturday morning Tai Chi classes, they host a busy programme of community events throughout the year which include a Beer and Bread festival, Art in the Park in August and a Harvest Festival in September. They even have a Santa in the Windmill every Christmas for the little ones.

Peckham Rye Park

SOUTH-EAST

SOUTH-EAST

Bermondsey Spa Gardens **123**
Brockwell Park 125
Burgess Park **131**
Crystal Palace Park 134
Dulwich Park **140**
Geraldine Mary Harmsworth Park 144
Greenwich Park **147**
Greenwich Peninsular Ecology Park 153
Horniman Gardens **154**
Kennington Park 156
Leathermarket Gardens **157**
Myatt's Fields 158
Oxleas Woods **160**
Peckham Rye Park 161
Ruskin Park **164**
Slade Gardens 165
Southwark Park **166**
Sunray Gardens 167
Sydenham Wells Park **168**
Tabard Gardens 169
Walworth Garden Farm **171**
West Square Gardens 172

Southwark Park

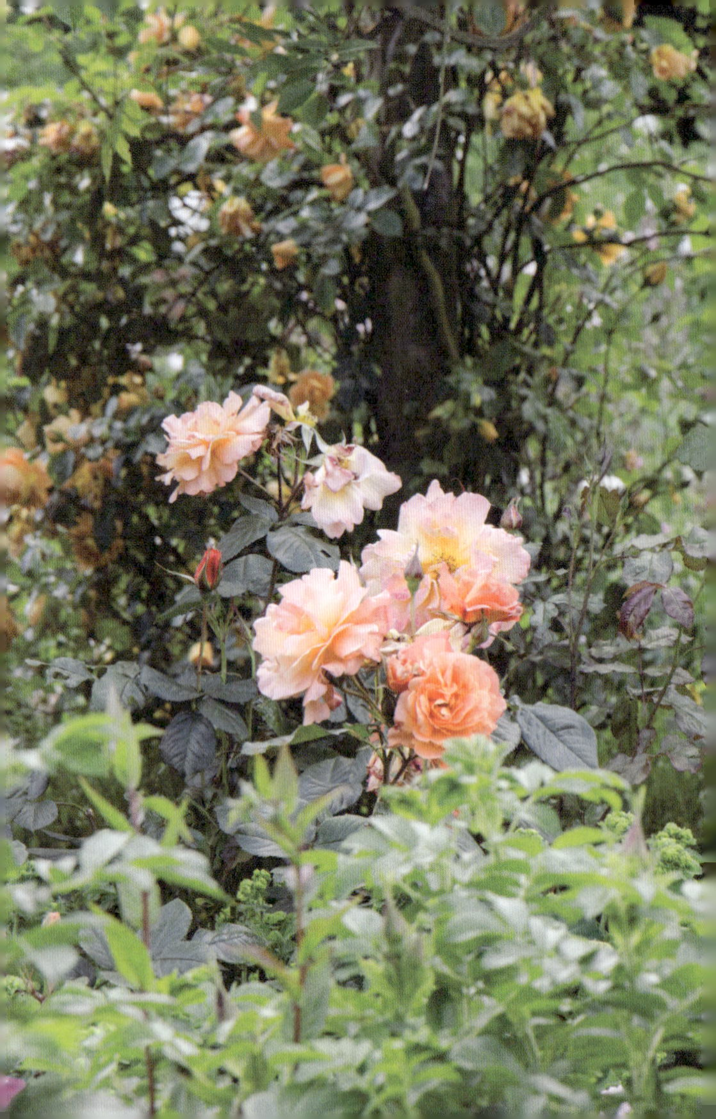

Bermondsey Spa Gardens

Spa Road, Bermondsey, SE16
Daily 7:30 until dusk
020 7525 2000
www.southwark.gov.uk
Travel: Bus 1 & 78
Area: 4.5 acres
Facilities: Picnic areas, children's playground, multi-use games area, play centre, running track, café

Officially re-opened in 2006 after a refurbishment programme, Bermondsey Spa Gardens is a modestly sized green gem in a built-up area of Bermondsey. The park's history dates back to the mid-1700s when the landowner, Thomas Keyse, opened a tea garden in the area, offering attractions such as a concert hall, picture gallery and firework displays. The 'spa' part of the equation came with the discovery of a supposedly health-giving chalybeate spring, which sprang from the River Neckinger, one of London's lost rivers. Bermondsey Spa closed sometime after Keyse's death in 1800 and the modern park that bears its name was opened in 1954, on the ground formerly occupied by terraced houses. Today you can stand at the central point of this flat green space and see pretty much all the facilities on offer. These include new seating benches lining the sandy walkways, swings and slides in the playground, a dog walking area, a running track and the Ellen Brown Children Centre, a building which caters for children and their families. There's also a good café – Bell's Café – for fresh coffee, homemade cake, food and ice-creams.

South-east

Brockwell Park

SE24 9BJ
Daily 7:30 until dusk
020 7926 9000
www.brockwellpark.com
Travel: Herne Hill Rail
Area: 128 acres
Facilities: Lido, children's playground, wet play area, tennis courts, football pitch, basketball court, bowling green and badminton court, paddling pool, BMX track, community greenhouses, miniature railway, cafés

The sloping grounds of Brockwell Park first opened to the public in 1892. Formerly a private estate, it is bordered by Tulse Hill, Norwood and Brixton. An expansive arena, its dimensions are big enough for the park to feel perennially underpopulated, even in the summer when its grassy slopes are pleasantly dotted with dedicated sunseekers. It's only when the annual festivals roll into town that any real crowds start to gather, the park has become the mainstay of many musical events including the Mighty Hoopla, Cross the Tracks, City Splash and a succession of funfairs and circuses throughout the year. Over the last year or so, the park has introduced occasional outdoor theatre and concerts throughout the summer, with plays such as Shakespeare's Midsummer Nights Dream going down well with ticket holders as well as the slightly bemused early evening joggers or dog walkers who stop at the edge of the seating area to take a look at the action.

One of Brockwell's hidden gems is the beautiful walled rose garden. Its gate is located just beyond a small white porticoed shelter that was once a private chapel but is now an additional and much-welcome public loo. Inside the garden, wooden benches are placed among the shrubs and seasonally changing flowers, and an overriding sense of serenity makes this an excellent spot for quiet contemplation. Permanent features include an old mulberry tree and an array of well-coiffed box and yew hedges. There's also an old well that's covered by grating, and a sundial suspended from

Brockwell Park

the wall in the far corner – though it's often swamped by a mass of wisteria. For a less manicured dip into nature, the nearby community greenhouses offer a full range of art and nature-related workshops that can be booked for children and families.

Visitors are welcome on open days when plants such as organic kitchen herbs are on sale in the greenhouses. Other pleasures within the main park are the willow and oak-lined duck ponds. These miniature lakes are separated by a small humpbacked bridge and have been tidied up and reshaped in recent years. This has resulted in even more Canada geese, mallards and mute swans, and fewer of the water rats that used to take some of the joy out of a stroll by the water.

For leisure pursuits, there are tennis courts, a football pitch, a bowling green and a basketball court that is popular with the locals, but the real sports draw is the Brockwell Lido, which has a pool-side sauna, is open all year round, and has been here since 1937. The Grade II listed building that surrounds it has been extended and is now a health and fitness centre. Along the grassy edges of the park, wooden keep-fit apparatus are dotted around to look like art installations. Situp benches, log stacks, stride jumps and horizontal ladders have all been provided by Fenland Leisure Services, although their sculptural appearance has baffled a few park visitors.

Snacks and occasional themed barbecues can be found at the poolside Lido Café. Closeby is the Brockwell Park miniature railway, which opens on Sundays from March to October. There's even a shop for railway souvenirs. However, if you and yours are set on walking, all upward leading paths take you to the brow of the steepest hill. It is here that the Grade II listed Brockwell Hall – now the family-run Brockwell Park Café – stands. Originally built between 1811 and 1813, it was at one time a late Georgian centrepiece of the Brockwell estate of John Blades – a well-off City glass maker. It survived fires in 1990 and 2001 and after reconstruction now presents a combination of 'free Grecian' and Victorian splendour. To the left of the main stone-pillared entrance, fronted by cedars and oak trees on the south side, is a veranda with seating for alfresco dining. At the weekend just follow the appetising smell of early morning fry-ups and you are sure to find the busy café. On the north side of the hall, the black Tritton clocktower now ticks again thanks to a restoration programme in early 2014. The tower straddles a series of paths that offer terrific vistas of the south London skyline. From here you can see Battersea Power Station to the north, the London Eye and Houses of Parliament to the west, while to the east the BT Tower, Norman Foster's 'gherkin', the 306m tall Shard and the winking tip of Canary Wharf are laid out in the distance. Not bad for a vantage point that's just a ten-minute walk from Brixton.

Did you know?

- In 1992, the Effra Redevelopment Agency launched a campaign to bring back the part of the Effra River that once flowed along the edge of Brockwell Park.

- Brockwell Park was the setting for the music video 'Do Your Thing' by Basement Jaxx, who started as a local band in Brixton.

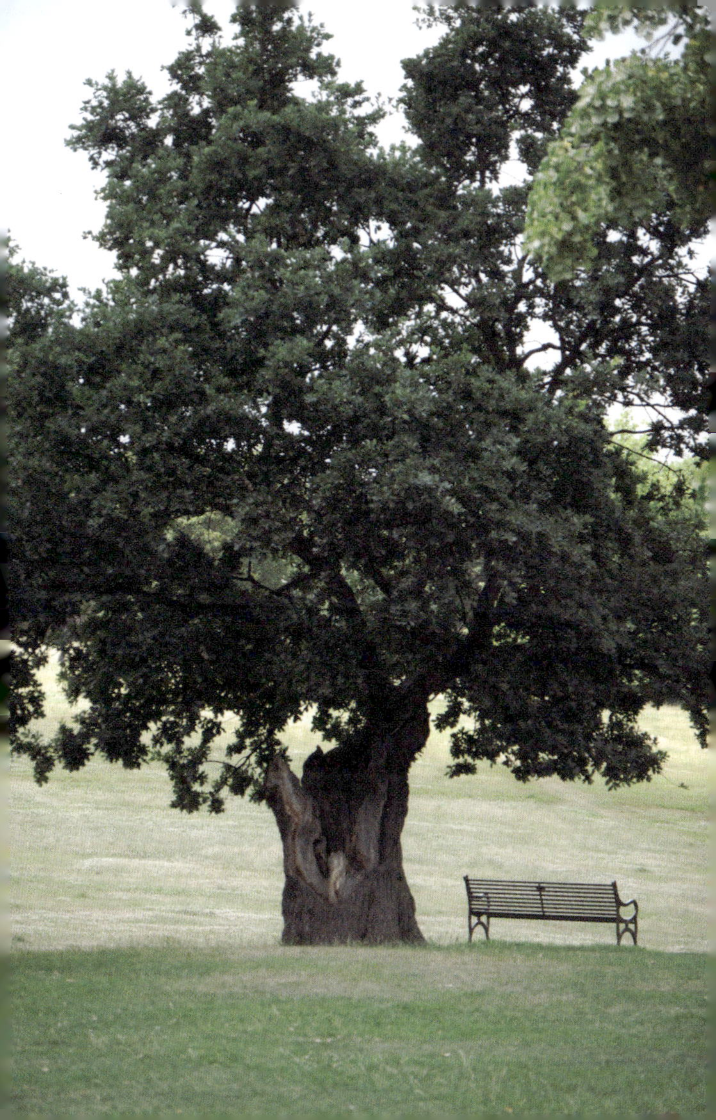

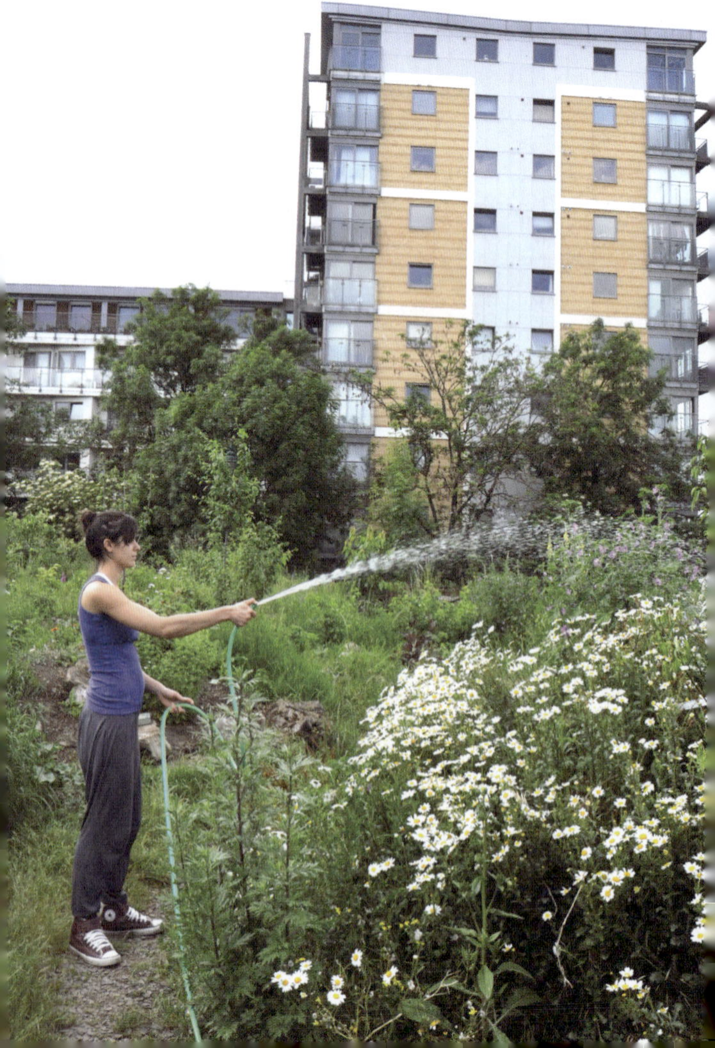

Burgess Park

Albany Road, SE5 7QH
Daily 24 hours
020 7525 2000
www.southwark.gov.uk
Travel: Elephant & Castle LU & Rail
Area: 138 acres
Facilities: Play areas, fishing lake, community garden projects, sports centre, BMX track

Burgess Park sprang up in 1943 and involved levelling streets and rows of houses, with the understandably disgruntled residents being packed off to occupy the nearby Aylesbury Estate. The park runs from Camberwell to the Old Kent Road, and in the 19th century, much of the land was industrial. Remnants of those commercial days are discernable in landmarks like the old lime kiln.

The Camberwell end of Burgess Park is edged with high slopes of wildflower meadows and includes the Burgess Park Community Food Project. A large team of volunteers garden this enclosed area and produce food which is shared among them.

Beyond this entrance, the park is a vast expanse of land with long avenues ideal for rollerblading and a large hill providing shelter for picnickers and great views across London. This is a park that really serves its diverse population well with a popular Latin festival in the summer and local youth carnivals or football games that reflect the Caribbean, African, British and Latin communities of the SE5 area.

On the northern edge, Chumleigh Gardens is a throwback to the 19th century, with its neatly-kept almshouses near Albany Road and cottage-style garden plots. The planting here reflects the traditional English, Caribbean, Islamic, Mediterranean and Oriental styles, and just outside this garden area is the Park Life café. Further on, at Old Kent Road end, there's a huge duck pond with plenty of wildfowl. Part of the lake is stocked for anglers who can buy Thames Water day or annual fishing licences. Hilly mounds, tree-lined paths, picnic areas and woodlands make this the far more serene end of the park. Burgess Hill is a surprising treat and is well worth exploring.

Burgess Park

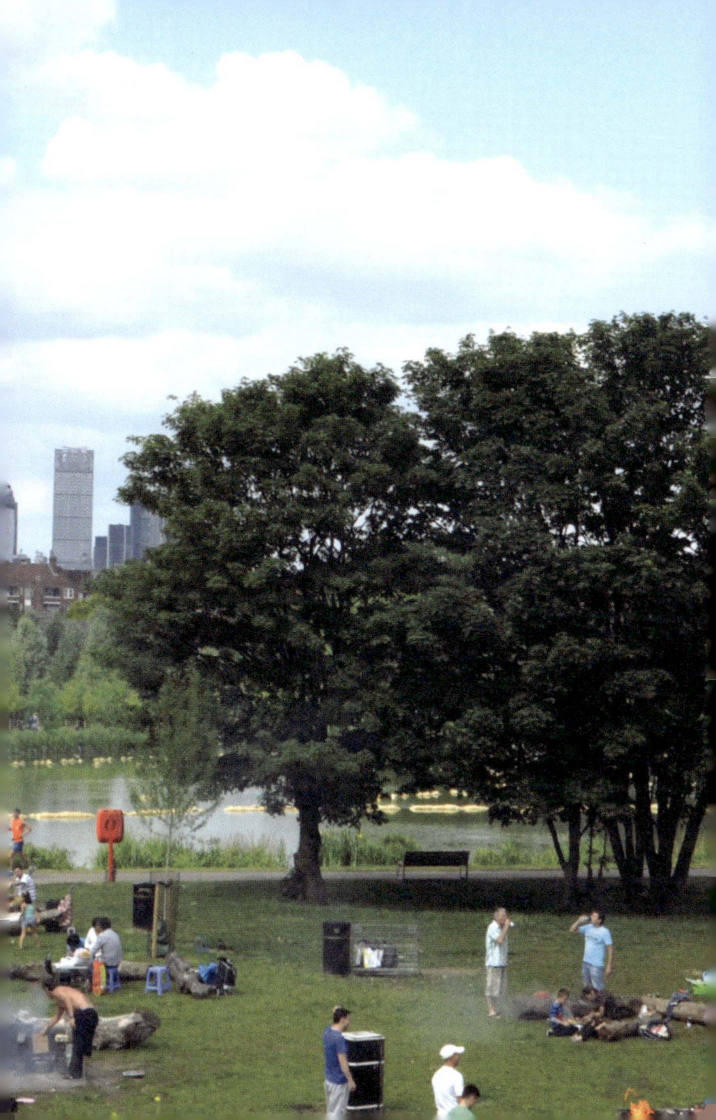

South-east

Crystal Palace Park

Thicket Road, SE19 2GA
Daily 7:30 until dusk
020 3236 0078
www.crystalpalaceparktrust.org
Travel: Crystal Palace Rail
Area: 200 acres
Facilities: Cricket pitch, athletic stadium, National Sports Centre, fishing lake, children's farm, museum, concert bowl, children's play area, café

The 200 acres of Crystal Palace Park are steeped in 19th and early 20th-century history. It's no surprise that there's constant disagreement as to how to recapture its former glory, and the unveiling of a £500 million redevelopment plan to build a 'new' Crystal Palace in the form of a cultural attraction on the site of the park's original Victorian building has swelled the numbers of residential and other interest groups. Regardless of how things shape up, there's no altering the park's history. The area began with the world-famous Crystal Palace glass hall. Designed by Joseph Paxton, it was originally constructed for the 1851 Great Exhibition in Hyde Park. Three years later it was moved to Sydenham Hill and opened by Queen Victoria. Three times the length of St Paul's Cathedral, it housed everything connected with British industry, empire and culture, from kitchen utensils and machinery to ancient Egyptian and Renaissance art and architecture. A fire devastated the venue in 1936, but remnants of its Victorian splendour are marked by the bust of Joseph Paxton at the entrance to the National Sports Centre, and the ruins of the grand Italian terraces that run along the main avenue from the Anerley Hill entrance. Back in the Palace's heyday, the terraces' steps and plinths had statues representing the national dress of each country of the British Empire.

Now only one fenced-off figure survives on a level just below the two Egyptian sphinxes in the upper north-west corner. These two enigmas provide the highest viewing point in south-east London, where an awesome panorama reveals hills, meadows and industry. On a good day, the view includes the white towers of the Queen Elizabeth II Bridge over at Dartford.

The Crystal Palace grounds are actually split between the 1970s-style concrete areas around the sports centre and car parks, and the parkland which takes up the southern half of the complex. Some recent restructuring within the green areas means that the famous dinosaur lake – with its anatomically incorrect models – has been fenced off and landscaped to include better rock formations, tidier islands and a better flow to the tidal lake that sits beside it. While this is an improvement, regular users

Crystal Palace Park

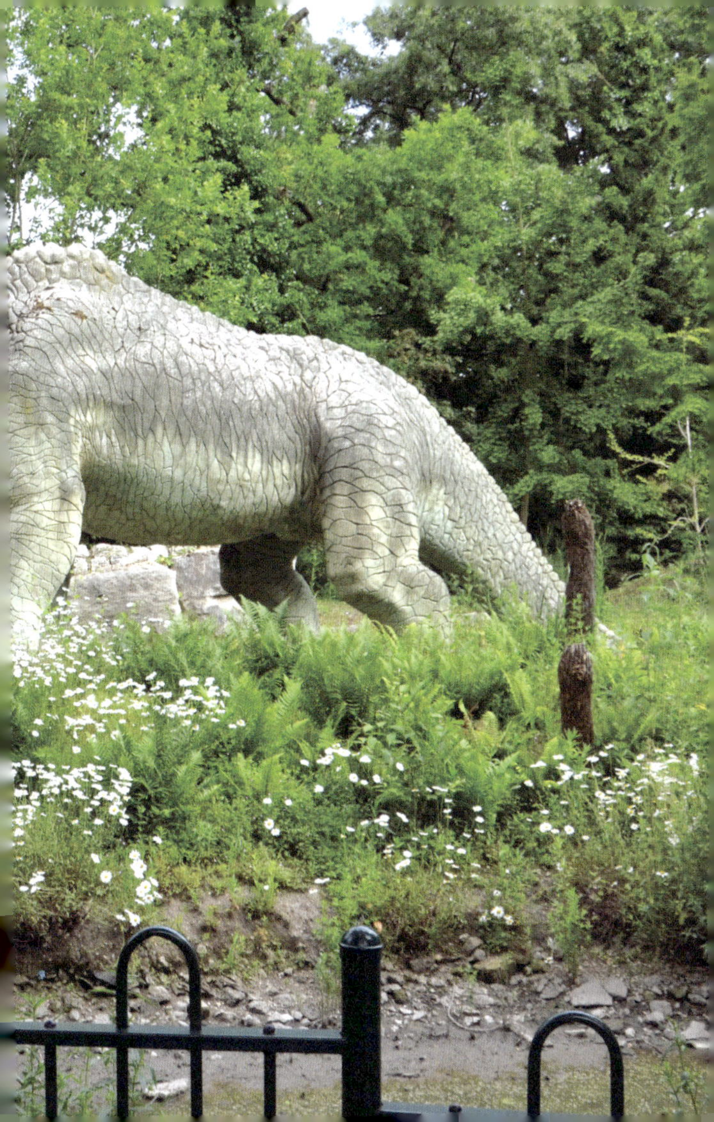

complain that children can no longer sit in the mouths of the gigantic beasts. The restrictions are, however, inevitable given that these original figures have been granted listed building status. Children can still get a kick out of the park's farm, close to the rail station entrance, where llamas and huge black pigs have entertained many school groups. There's also a museum – a volunteer labour of love close to the car park – where the history of Crystal Palace and the Great Exhibition are laid out in a small building that looks like a school hall.

Another park landmark is the concert bowl, a concrete structure surrounded by a lily pond which is best seen at night when the floodlights are on. It's the site of summer music festivals with local musicians, and children's events on the surrounding lawns, but has in the past hosted big-name visitors such as The Cure, Bob Marley and John Lee Hooker. Just behind the moated bowl, a gravel path is the last remnant of a former motor racing track that was originally built in 1928. It is now surrounded by the flower beds of an English landscaped garden that leads to the entrance of a circular maze reconstructed in its original Victorian style and planted with rhododendron bushes, hornbeams and poplars. Beyond this, the members-only fishing lake sits at the edge of a hilly woodland area that slopes down along a path leading to the wide and open cricket field. At the far end of the lawn, the children's play area and information centre building sit just beside a glorious path of elegantly arching London planes.

Did you know?

- 20 FA Cup Finals took place at Crystal Palace between 1895 and 1924.

- The Crystal Palace fire happened on the night of 30 November 1936. It took 90 fire engines to put out the flames, which could be seen from as far away as Brighton.

- When the Crystal Palace glass structure was built it was the largest of its kind in the world.

- Crystal Palace was the venue for The Sex Pistols final 'Jubilee' gig in July 2002.

- The huge metal structure of Crystal Palace transmitting station within the park was constructed in the 1950s among the ruins of Crystal Palace. In 2007 Ofcom confirmed that it would remain an A group transmitter after the digital switchover from analogue TV.

- The sports centre now has an outdoor beach volleyball area thanks to the popularity of the game, and inspired by the Brazilian team who used the site to practice during their stay for London's 2012 Olympics.

Beach Volleyball at Crystal Palace Park

South-east

Dulwich Park
College Road, SE21 7BQ
Daily 7:30 until dusk
020 8693 8635
www.southwark.gov.uk
Travel: North Dulwich and West Dulwich Rail
Area: 72 acres
Facilities: Children's playground, Francis Peek Centre, cricket pitch, tennis court, bowling green, boating lake, outdoor gym, café

The seventy-two acres of Dulwich Park were once used as farmland (known as Five Fields) before being landscaped for the public in 1890. Oaks were used as the farm's boundary markers, and many of the ancient trees still stand within the park today. Sandy paths beyond the sports pitches are used by horse riders from the Dulwich Riding School, and for the non-horsey, there are bikes for hire from London Recumbents with lessons on tandems, trikes and horizontal bikes all bookable from the Ranger's Yard. The park is situated near three schools, making its open lawns a popular place for organised sports sessions on the football and cricket pitches.

Of the four entrances, the main College Road gate faces the John Soane-designed Dulwich Picture Gallery - the oldest purpose-built gallery in the world. Central to the park is the lake, where boats can be hired all year round (weekends only during the winter). The lake's south side is where a 1970s Barbara Hepworth 'Two Forms' sculpture once stood on a grassy knoll – until it was stolen by suspected scrap metal thieves in 2011. Two years later, a competition to replace the artwork was won by Conrad Shawcross, a rising star of the British art scene. His work, 'Three Perpetual Chords', is a series of cast iron sculptures, each created in relation to the mathematical patterns found in music. Over towards the north side of the lake, the white wood and glass-fronted Dulwich Clock café serves full meals and is especially busy on weekend mornings. At the back of the building is the pretty dry garden, where aromatic plants including lavender and other herbs offer up their scent. This isn't the only garden within the park. A few others are scattered throughout, but the American Garden, with a healthy selection of rhododendrons and azaleas, stands out. Best appreciated in late spring for its colourful blooms, it also has a number of large silver birches that shade the flowers when the sun is out. The paths away from the lake lead towards the playground – through the trees you can spot the top of the Crystal Palace transmitting station identifying Dulwich Park's much larger neighbour. There are a few other smaller parks that are also worth exploring...

Dulwich Park

Nearby green spaces:

Sydenham Hill Woods
Sydenham Hill and Crescent Wood Road, SE26 6LT
020 7261 0447
Travel: Forest Hill Rail

Sydenham Hill Woods lies closer to Crystal Palace Park. Owned by the London Wildlife Trust, it has a ruined monastery and is one of the largest remnants of the Great North Wood.

Belair Park
Gallery Road, SE21 7AB
020 7525 2000
Travel: West Dulwich Rail

Closer to Dulwich Park is the beautifully refurbished Belair Park. The only Grade II listed landscape in the borough, it features the upmarket Beauberry House restaurant, a central lake, a park lodge, a stable building, a skate park and pitches for cricket and football.

South-east

Geraldine Mary Harmsworth Park

(next to Imperial War Museum), St George's Road, SE1 6ER
Tel: 020 7525 0874
Transport: Elephant and Castle LU/Rail, Lambeth North LU;
bus 171, 176, 188, 344, C10
Open: Daily 8am-9pm (summer) and 8am-4.30pm (winter)
Facilities: basketball court

The Geraldine Mary Harmsworth Park opened in 1934 and is named after Viscount Rothermere's mother (the viscount having donated the land to the 'spendid struggling mothers of Southwark'). At the centre of the park lies The Imperial War Museum, which tells the story of people's experience of modern warfare. If you don't have time to visit the museum, the Soviet War Memorial by Sergey Shcherbakov to the west of the museum, commemorates the 27 million Soviet citizens who perished in WWII.

Just next to the museum and by the two imposing ship guns that dominate the entrance is a fragment of the Berlin Wall that originally stood in the Kreuzberg district and was acquired by the Imperial War Museum in 1991.

Fittingly, the park also contains a Peace Garden which was opened in 1999 as a place of peace and harmony. The entrance has a stone Language Pillar, each side carved with a message of peace. Three carved steps at the top of the pillar represent peace, understanding and love. The garden's central focus is a bronze mandala, with eight meditation seats. More westernised sculptures are laid out to the north, south, east and west corners of the garden, with these areas representing the four elements of air, fire, earth and water. Scattered throughout are herbs and plants with climbing plants like honeysuckle and scented roses all adding to the sense of tranquillity.

One of the best things about the park is the charming Songbird Café which has extensive outdoor seating and serves great food and coffee.

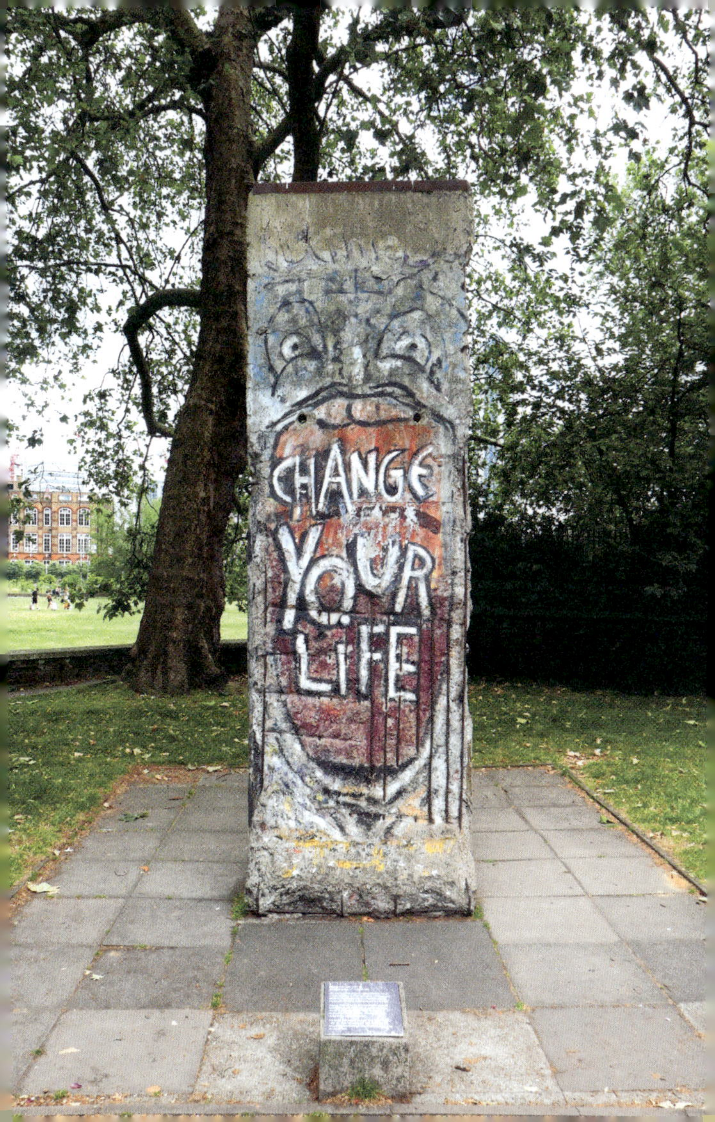
CHANGE
YOUR
LIFE

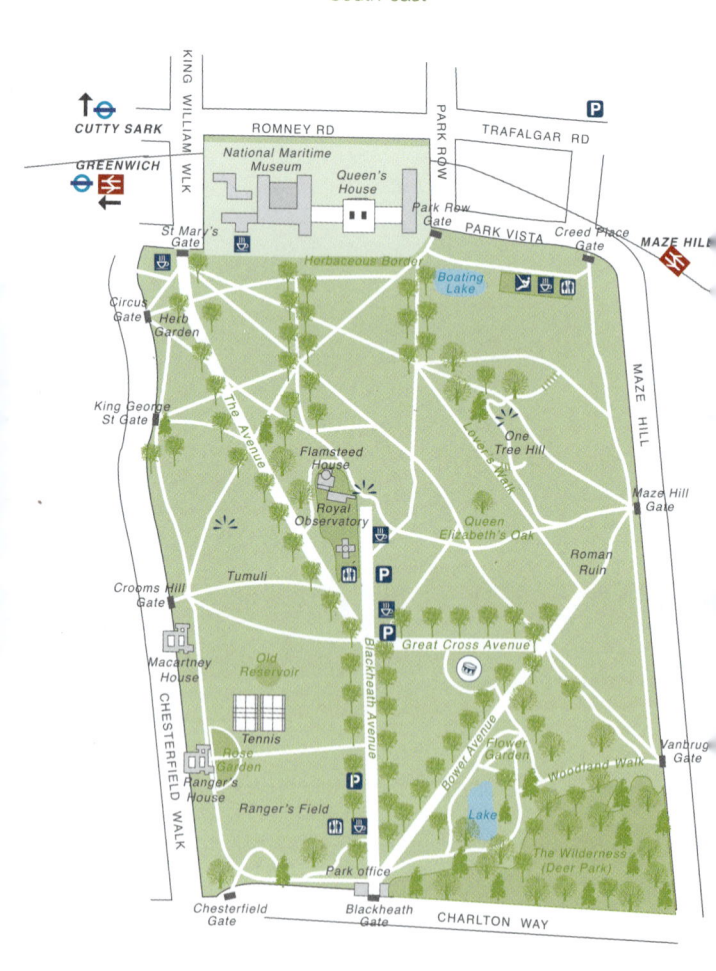

South-east

Greenwich Park

Blackheath Gate, Charlton Way, SE19 8QY
Daily 6:00 until dusk
0300 061 2380
www.royalparks.org.uk
Travel: Cutty Sark DLR
Area: 183 acres
Facilities: Children's playground and boating pond, tennis courts, cricket pitch, rugby pitch, bandstand, cafés, museum

The site of the start of the annual London Marathon, Greenwich Park is the only royal park east of Central London. Lying between Blackheath and the Thames, it is just a few miles to the south of the Olympic Park in the Lower Lea Valley.

Having stood in its 183 acres of grounds since 1427, the park has been lavished with care and attention due to its royal connections and maritime history. This riverside location was once the site of the Palace of Placentia, the birthplace of Henry VIII and his daughters Mary and Elizabeth. It was a favourite royal residence with 200 acres of enclosed pasture, wood and heath in an area that now makes up the current royal park.

Undeniably magnificent, Greenwich Park offers huge expanses of flat and spectacularly hilly green areas, that are cut through with grand avenues and smaller paths. There are many noteworthy historic buildings in the area including the former Royal Naval College (now the University of Greenwich), The Old Royal Observatory and Planetarium, The Queen's House (see page 310) and Ranger's House.

If you enter the park from the Maritime Museum entrance, you might want to fuel up at the white-washed St Mary's Lodge Café. Doubling up as a snack spot and information centre, it offers cakes, hot drinks and sandwiches, as well as leaflets and a potted history of the park from the adjacent information centre. The Maritime Museum is also the chosen venue for the permanent display of artist Yinka Shonibare's 'Nelson's Ship in a Bottle'. The scaled down replica of HMS Victory formerly occupied Trafalgar Square's Fourth Plinth and now sits outside the museum's new Sammy Ofer wing.

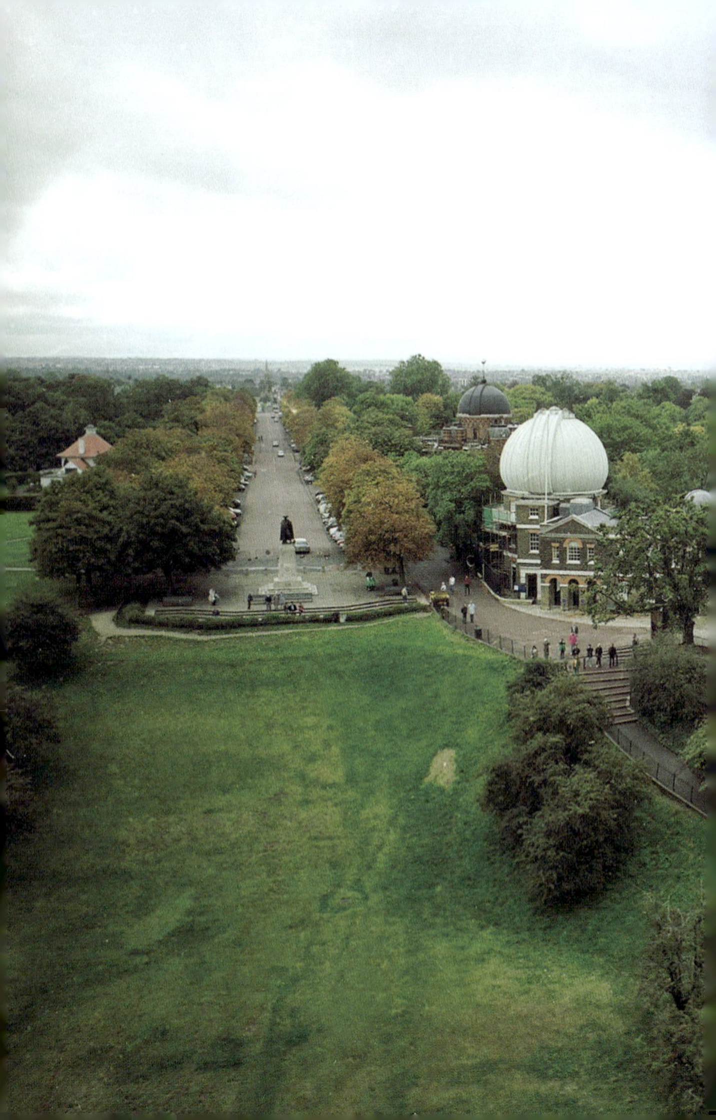

Greenwich Park

Within the park, a huge 'tidying up' programme takes place during autumn and winter, when thousands of daffodil and crocus bulbs are planted, alongside equally large numbers of plants like pansies and wallflowers. The borders and seasonal planting schemes are planned with a great deal of care and recently award winning garden designer Chris Beardshaw has helped create the spectacular herbaceous border outside Queen's House.

For the best views, the park's highest point is at the Royal Observatory where the imposing monument of General James Wolfe stands. It is here that the tree-lined Blackheath Avenue meets Great Cross Avenue. At around fifty metres above sea level, you can look down onto the Thames, and take in the panoramic view of St Paul's Cathedral, Tower Bridge (on a good day) and Canary Wharf. The main art deco Pavilion Café is also found at the park's summit, while a short walk from here is the Queen Elizabeth Oak. A natural monument to bygone times, it is said to have been planted in the 12th century. Storms tipped over the long dead husk in 1991, and it's now preserved within a metal-gated enclosure. Linked with Queen Elizabeth I, who used its six foot hollow trunk as a resting spot, and Henry VIII and Anne Boleyn, who danced round it – at one time it also had a door added as a lock up for criminals.

The areas towards Blackheath are the lushest parts of the park. The flower garden beside the enclosed deer park offers some glorious bursts of colour during the summer, while the cedars have branches low enough to provide some privacy for those wanting to relax in the shade. Sturdy clusters of thick oaks and birches make this area seem like a park within a park, especially with the central lake, fountain and wildfowl. There's a stunted look to some of the trees here, a consequence of their branches having been cut during the Second World War to widen the firing range for anti-aircraft guns. Greenwich has a smattering of signs saying where you can't cycle, play sports or unleash your dogs but seems a lot more relaxed than other royal parks like Hyde Park or St James's Park. There are more than enough sports areas to compensate for the restrictions. Close to Blackheath Gate on the park's south side, the Rangers' Field is marked out for cricket, where teams can hire the pitch and pavilion. At the edge of the field, the Dell is a lovely enclosed rhododendron and azalea garden, surrounded by a path that leads on to the lively rose garden not far from the putting green. Rangers House (020 8853 0035) is located here and is one of the park's gems, containing a fine art collection which is well worth a visit. Nearby, the Greenwich Park Tennis Centre has six hard courts, which open from April to September (phone 020 8293 0276 for times), and an adjacent putting green with equipment for hire. Summer and school holidays bring puppet shows and workshops for children, with Sunday concerts in the bandstand.

Did you know?

• Members of the public have been enjoying the park since the early 1700s when passes were issued to local people. In 1830 the park was opened to all.

• The tumuli are a series of saucer-shaped mounds inside Greenwich Park. Many were destroyed by planting, but in 1784, when several of them were opened, human hair, scraps of woollen cloth and glass beads were discovered.

• The second wedding in *Four Weddings and A Funeral* was filmed in the chapel in the Old Royal Naval College. On the opposite side of the park, Vanbrugh Castle at 121 Maze Hill was used in the 1986 film *Mona Lisa*, and close to the entrance of Greenwich Park, the Gloucester Pub was featured in the 1996 film *Beautiful Thing*. Greenwich Park was one of the locations used for the 1995 film *Sense and Sensibility* starring Emma Thompson.

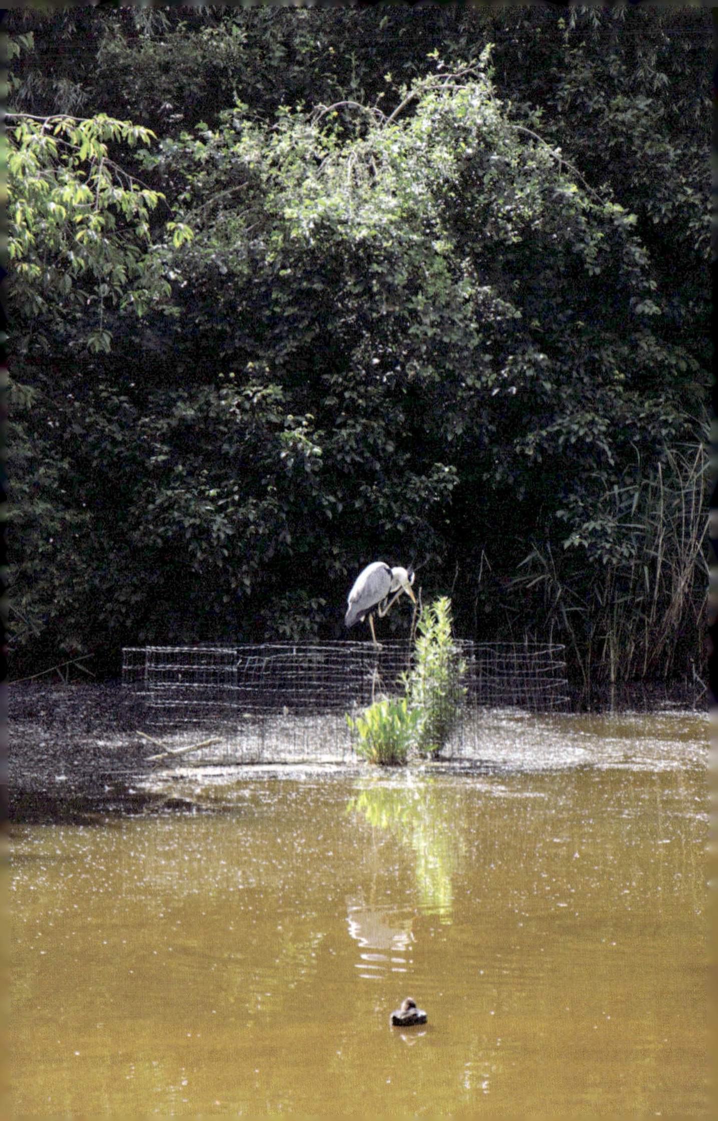

Greenwich Peninsular Ecology Park

Thames Path, John Harrison Way, SE10 0QZ
Wed-Sun 10:00-17:00
020 8293 1904
www.tcv.org.uk
Travel: North Greenwich LU
Area: 4 acres

Along the Thames Path, and behind the contemporary Millennium Village housing complex, with its apartments and shops, is this wonderful ecology park. A marshy oasis for visiting and resident wildfowl, it's an area made up of two lakes surrounded by woodland. There's free public access to the outer lake at any time, but the inner lake can only be reached through the gatehouse and information centre during opening hours. Mondays and Tuesdays are reserved for school visits during term time, when children can take part in quizzes, nature trails, pond dipping and bird spotting.

At one time this was agricultural land, which was industrialised from the late 1880s. With the closure of the gasworks in the 1970s, the land slowly fell into dereliction. The four-acre park was finally created by English Partnerships in 1997, and is now run by the Trust for Urban Ecology.

There are in fact eight main habitats in the park – lakes, marsh, shingle, beach, shallow pools, wildflower meadow, willow beds and woodland. Together they form a thriving home for wildlife. During a walk around both lakes visitors can see butterflies, dragon and damselflies, stag beetles as well as newts, frogs and voles in their favoured habitats. The riverbank is an ideal spot for watching the varied birds that visit the park throughout the year. The specially designed hides allow keen spotters to observe the seasonal changes in feathered traffic, from gulls, geese and moorhens to ducks, reed warblers and kingfishers. Like Thames Barrier Park, this green space is often quiet, offering visitors the chance to bond with nature or simply escape from the bustle of the city.

Horniman Gardens

100 London Road, Forest Hill, London, SE23 3PQ
Mon-Sat 7:15 until dusk
020 8699 1872
www.horniman.ac.uk
Travel: Forest Hill Rail
Area: 16 acres
Facilities: Sunken garden, sound garden, bee garden, nature trail, bandstand, café

Forest Hill's best known landmark has to be the Horniman Museum with its collections of natural history, artefacts from different cultures around the world and musical instruments. The museum is well worth a visit, but so are its surrounding acres of gorgeous gardens. Beautifully maintained since the building opened in 1901, there are formal and natural landscapes and expansive views which look across the valley to Kent and the South Downs. Within the grounds, the fine rose garden and sunken Italian gardens are ideal for a peaceful stroll. The central bandstand that dates back to 1903 is also worth a visit, and now that it's available for hire, big public events like Brazilian capoeira have taken place here in the summer. Other features include a Grade II listed conservatory by the museum's café, a five acre nature trail and an animal enclosure with goats, rabbits and turkeys. The conservatory is occasionally used for functions and concerts, but during the summer, the gardens' lawns are also a venue for music festivals, visiting bands or children's days.

On Sundays the gardens play host to the fabulous Horniman Market which combines locally produced groceries, delicious street food and a few designer makers offering quality gifts from vegan cosmetics to organic kid's wear. Having bought food from the market the gardens provide a perfect place for an impromptu picnic.

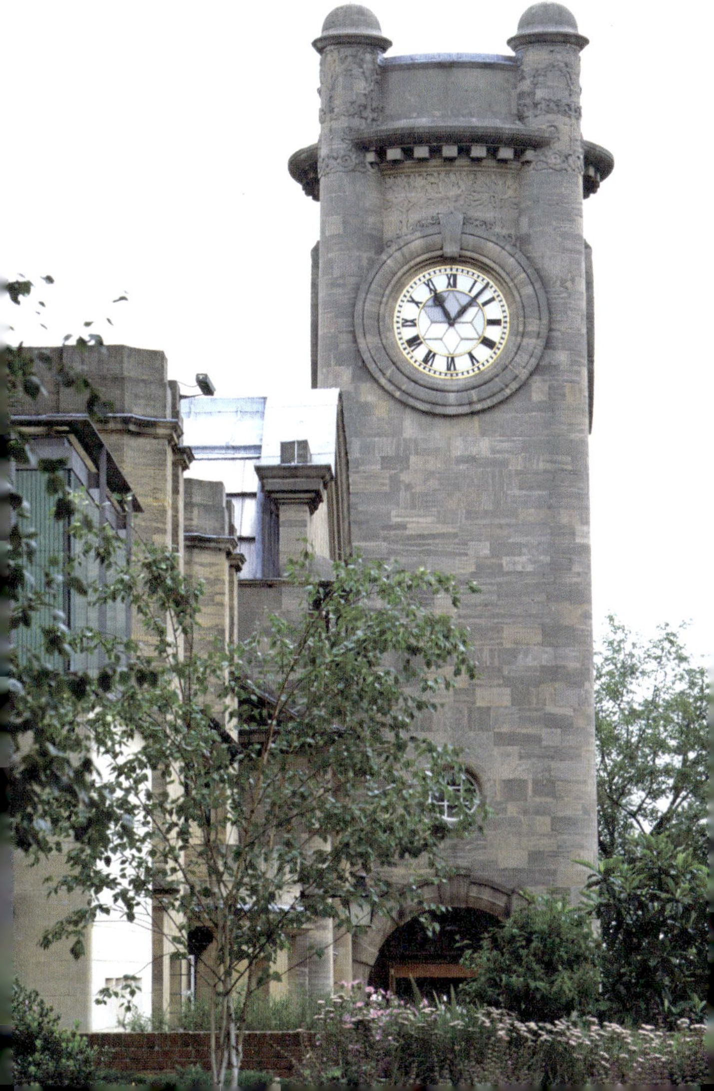

South-east

Kennington Park

Kennington Park Road, SE11 4BE
020 7926 9000
Daily 7:30 until dusk
www.kenningtonpark.org/
Travel: Oval & Kennington LU
Area: 36 acres
Facilities: Children's playground, outdoor gym, café, toilets, astroturf sports pitches for football and netball, tennis courts, cricket court, bee keeping centre

A perfect respite from the busy Kennington Park Road thoroughfare, this is a park with a history dating back to 1854. The first open space in Lambeth to be dedicated for public use and pleasure, it was previously a common and the site of cricket matches and open air sermons by the likes of John Wesley. Back then, it was most famous for being the site of the 1848 'monster rally' of 25,000 Chartists, who were demanding voting rights for the working classes. In 2023 the park celebrated the 175th aniversary of the rally with a dedicated trail and podcast.

Inside the park, a central, white-fronted café seems to be a big focus. Outdoor benches and a picnic area are popular in the summer, while to the east of this there's an historic flower garden and a designated area for organised ball games. Over at the Kennington Park Road entrance to the park, there is the area's best-known landmark – the Kennington Park skate bowl. First built in 1978 it was condemned as unsafe and closed not long afterwards. It took until 2011 for the US Converse shoe company's 'Fix to Ride' programme to shake things up, with Kennington's skate bowl being the first of its international roster of concrete sport areas to receive help. £50,000 later the park opened in May 2012 and is now one of the few original 1970s skate bowls remaining in London. Bijou in size and less competitive than the larger skate park over in Stockwell (SW9) or the iconic and much-treasured one at London's South Bank (SE1), it's a valued site within London's skateboard community.

South-east

Leathermarket Gardens

Weston Street, SE1 3HS
Daily 24 hours
020 7525 2000
www.southwark.gov.uk
Travel: London Bridge LU & Rail
Area: 3 acres
Facilities: Basketball court, children's play area, café

A gem of a green space in Bermondsey, Leathermarket Gardens is built in clear sight of London's Shard, with the upper stories of the glass construction providing a dramatic addition to skyline. The park is just a few steps from the Leathermarket business complex, an historical spot that was once home to a nineteenth century leather market and tanneries before becoming a housing estate in the 1950s. By the 1970s, the gardens (which actually date back to the 1930s) were fully established and in 1999, the eastern section was restored to the point that the western area seemed neglected and was poorly connected to the main gardens. What exists today is an elongated strip of green space that is well maintained and carefully designed with sculpted flowerbeds, rose bushes and in the spring and summer, trees full of blossom and daisy-covered hills. In the summer months the gardens are a popular retreat for local office workers and the doctors and nurses from the nearby Guy's Hospital. The place is also well used by locals with basketball courts and a children's play area featuring small swings and mini slides. The gardens are just a few minutes walk from Bermondsey Street where you can find lots of cafés and pubs as well as The Fashion & Textile Museum and White Cube gallery.

Myatt's Fields Park

Cormont Road, SE5 9RA
Daily 7:00 until dusk
020 7926 6200
www.myattsfieldspark.info
Travel: Loughborough Rail; Bus P5
Area: 10.4 acres
Facilities: Playgrounds, water play area, bee house, gardening club, café

A modestly-sized Victorian space in a quiet corner of Camberwell, Myatt's Fields is a well maintained and much loved park that has been recognised with a Green Flag award and is run as a charity by local enthusiasts. Surrounded by neat residential red-brick houses, it's a park that is popular with the locals. The name derives from Joseph Myatt, an early Victorian farmer, respected for his skills in growing strawberries, but who made his fortune by growing rhubarb, which was then a luxury food in the UK.

The park's features include a bandstand, an ornamental garden, a cluster of well-tended flowerbeds and lawns as well as a small picnic area. The children's playground includes a play area, a sensory trail, plants, seating areas and lawns. Beside the playground, the Mulbery Centre has a One O'clock Club during the week, which can also be privately hired. Within the rest of the park, dog areas are conscientiously used by owners anxious to avoid the punishing £1,000 fine for any canine misdeeds.

Dusk is a lovely time to visit, particularly during the spring and summer months, when early evening joggers lap the park's oval edges. The couples hanging out in the garden seem content to soak up the relative quiet only sporadically broken by cheers from the football pitch.

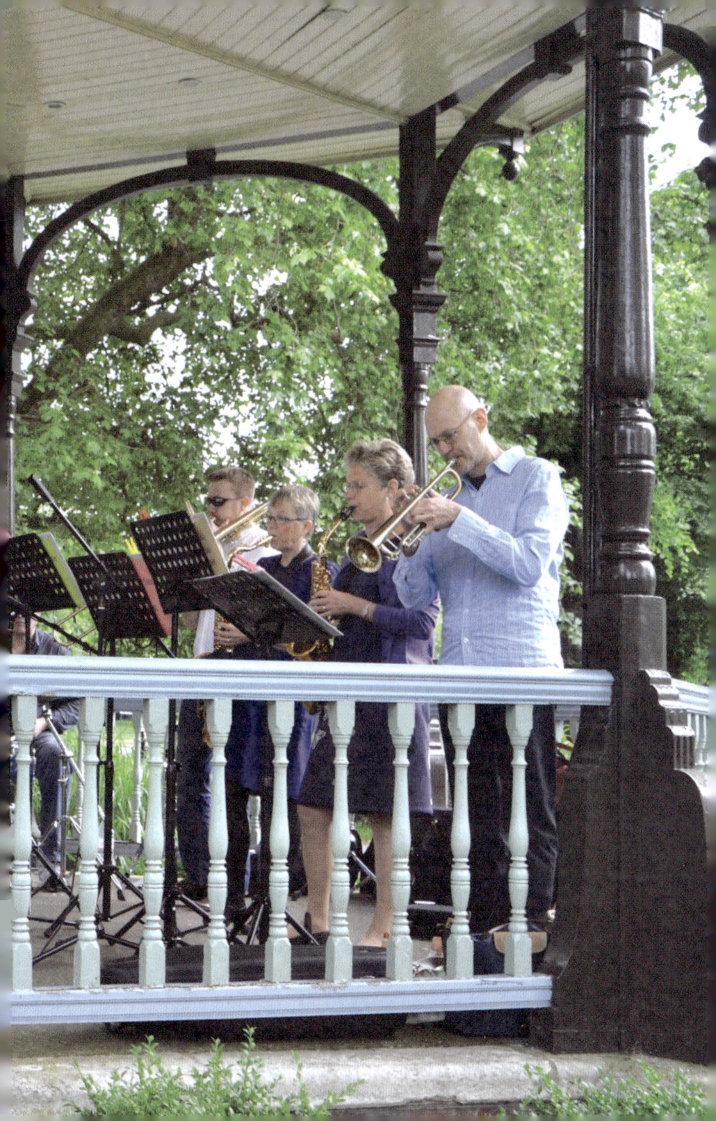

Oxleas Woods

Shooters Hill, Eltham, London, SE18 3JA
Daily 24 hours
020 8856 0100
www.oxleaswoodlands.uk
Travel: Falconwood rail
Area: 190 acres
Facilities: Outdoor gym, café

There's so much history packed into the ancient site of Oxleas Woods – all 190 acres of it. A large continuous area of woodland and parkland, it lies on the south side of Shooters Hill. Some parts of the wood date back 8,000 years to the last Ice Age. The woodland areas contain oak, hornbeam, silver birch and coppice hazel and there are various landmarks dotted throughout. One of these is Severndroog Castle, a 60-foot high, eighteenth century triangular brick-built tower designed in the gothic style by architect Richard Jupp. Built in 1784 as a memorial to William James of the East India Company, it stands in its namesake Castle Wood. Next to this area is Jack Wood, which has a terrace garden offering wide-reaching views across London, as well as a pretty rose garden. Since the wood and parkland are huge expanses to walk around, it's worth noting that the Oxleas Woods Café sits at the top of Shooters Hill, with panoramic views extending as far as the Kent border.

South-east

Peckham Rye Park & Common

SE15 3HU
Daily 7:30 until dusk
020 8299 0861
www.southwark.gov.uk
Travel: Peckham Rye Rail
Area: 49 acres
Facilities: Bowling green and pavilion, football pitches and cricket pitches, skate park, adventure playground, outdoor gym, café

Peckham Rye Park was once the site of the late 19th-century Homestall Farm. It lies on the northern boundary of the larger Peckham Rye Common (see page 286) towards Forest Hill and leafy Honour Oak. Although the park's flat outer edges are mainly open fields split by paths and interspersed with a few old wooden climbing frames, it does have the added appeal of the Peck River. The river runs along the east side of the park and flows underground into the park's pond. It also feeds the stream which is a central feature of the beautiful Japanese Garden, that sits within the park's woodland-surrounded middle section. Here can also be found the American Garden, the Sexby English Garden, flowered arbours and Visitor Centre all restored to their original 19th-century glory. Contemporary additions to the park are the wildlife and conservation area.

The busy café is located at the entrance to the park at the boundary with the larger common. It is one of London's best caffs, serving delicious hot and cold food and locally produced ice cream in the summer months.

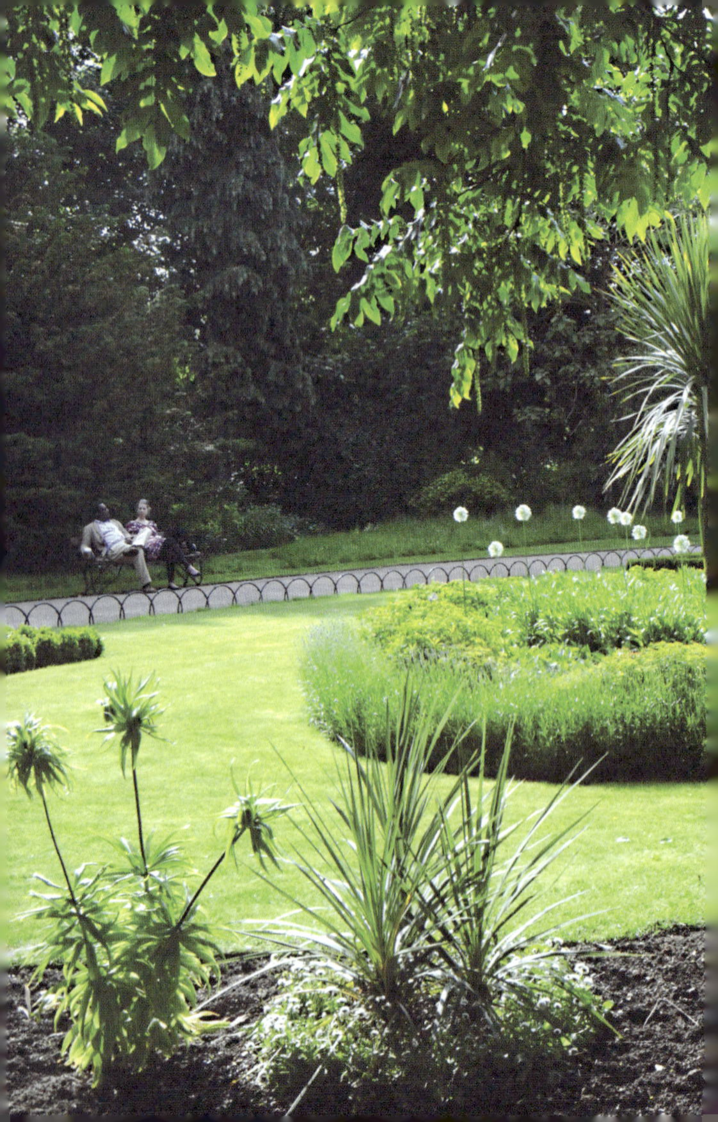

Peckham Rye Park

Ruskin Park

Denmark Hill, SE5 8EL
Daily 7:00 until dusk
020 7926 9000
www.lambeth.gov.uk
Travel: Denmark Hill Rail
Area: 37 acres
Facilities: Children's playground, paddling pool, sports pitches, kiosk, outdoor gym, bandstand, community garden, tree walk

This park is named after the Victorian artist and critic, John Ruskin, who lived nearby. In the heat of the summer, the large shallow paddling pool at the north-west corner of the park is alive with the yelps of delight from hordes of children splashing around to their hearts' content. A small picnic area and adjacent playground make this the most happening spot during summer holidays.

The rest of the park also has some fine features. A wide meadow area is circled by a path that's a jogger's delight, while the northern end has a large duck pond and a flower garden with a bricked and arboured walkway with overhanging plants, dramatically tangled branches and rhododendron bushes. The enclosed area next door with its raised lawn, hedges and shaded benches for summer readers can get spectacularly overgrown during autumn and winter, but the outer surrounding lawns and bright pockets of flowerbeds are always immaculately kept, and serve as a favoured spot for sunbathers. They have also become a regular location for many a wedding photocall over the years. One particular focal point is the wooden bandstand towards the Denmark Hill entrance to the park. Fully restored in 2006 it occasionally offers live music events.

Never overcrowded, Ruskin Park is perfect for sitting and doing absolutely nothing, and watching the huge population of squirrels who are so laid back they'll practically eat out of your hand.

Slade Gardens

Stockwell Park Road, SW9 0DD
Daily 8:00 until dusk
020 7926 9000
www.lambeth.gov.uk
Travel: Stockwell LU
Area: 1 acre
Facilities: Children's playground, outdoor gym, dog exercise area

'The little park with big plans' is how Stockwell's Slade Gardens touts itself. From the blink-and-you'll-miss-it gate between tall terraced houses at the residential Lorn Road entrance, the park opens out into a wide and flat open space with a central circular herb garden, and to the right of this an enclosed children's play area. The rest of the grassy areas are fairly nondescript, but changes have started, which includes more protection for trees to encourage more growth and guard against vandalism. An adjoining Slade Garden Adventure Playground has been in the community for years and is run by a separate charity. It offers huge wooden climbing frames and traditional rope and tyre swings for children. For Slade Gardens itself, the Friends organisation is campaigning to bring the maintenance of the park up to scratch and to preserve this historic green space. The park was once owned by the Slade family, which included William Slade (1790-1868), who established the Slade Chair of Fine Art at Oxford University.

Southwark Park

SE16 2TX
Daily 7:30 until dusk
07882 641 923
www.southwark.gov.uk
Travel: Bermondsey LU
Area: 64 acres
Facilities: Bandstand, wildlife garden, children's playground, bandstand, boating lake, bowling green, football, tennis courts, gallery, café

A ten-minute walk from Bermondsey tube station, this large, flat park is perfect for joggers. The park's long history dates back to 1869. Changes along the way have include the building of the dome-topped bandstand, which can be seen if you enter by the Jamaica Road entrance closest to Bermondsey tube station. Acquired for the park after the 1884 Great Exhibition in South Kensington, it's one of London's better kept public platforms, and hosts regular live performances during the summer.

The busiest area is around the lake and café at the centre of the park, where visitors converge on the aptly named Park Café, wildlife garden and play area. Here can also be found the Café Gallery London (www.cgplondon.org, tel: 020 7237 1230) – a bright white building with an equally pristine interior, it offers free exhibitions. It is a 'sister' gallery to the newly renovated Dilston Grove Gallery, a larger artists' space a few minutes walk away, towards the east of the park. A Grade II listed former church, its high ceilings make it a perfect spot for showing large-scale installations and performances.

The park also boasts free tennis courts, an annual Bermondsey carnival, and for those more interested in flora and fauna, a lake with wildfowl and an ornamental garden with well-tended plants and benches. If traveling to the park by car, it's worth noting that there is easy parking in the central avenue of the park.

Sunray Gardens

Sunray Avenue, SE22 9PL
Daily 7:30 until dusk
020 7525 0874
www.friendsofsunray.com
Travel: North Dulwich Rail
Area: 4 acres
Facilities: Playground, recreation area

This Grade II listed neighbourhood park at the bottom of a hill, was once the water garden of 'Casina', the villa which was built for lawyer Richard Shaw in 1796. The grounds originally covered 15 acres, with the estates and houses that now surround the present day park replacing a series of gardens and small fields leading down a slope to the current park and pond.

The park got its current name in 1923, and its boundaries follow that of the original Casina villa. The gardens now include a colourful children's playground with a wooden ship being the most popular piece of climbing equipment. There's also a picnic area with rock features that work well as extra seating, small flowerbeds, paved walkways, and at the far southern end, a large duck pond with a feeding platform. At different seasons you can look out for Canada geese, mallards, rock or wood pigeons and carrion crows. Labelled trees circle the pond, with a weeping ash, a ginkgo biloba and a dramatically leaning horse chestnut taking pride of place.

South-east

Sydenham Wells Park

Wells Park Road, Sydenham SE26 6LA
Daily 8:00 until dusk
www.lewisham.gov.uk
Travel: Sydenham Wells Park
Area: 19 acres
Facilities: Playground, tennis courts, outdoor gym, multi-sports ball courts, a water-play system, a sensory garden

Close to Crystal Palace, the smaller but well-loved Sydenham Wells Park sits in an area that was once part of a landscape of sweeping hills, streams and valleys that occupied over 500 acres of what is now urban south east London. Today, the relatively compact park has a series of contemporary features including two tennis courts, a multi-sports ball court, a summer putting green, ponds and a large children's playground. The park achieved Green Flag status in 2004, no doubt for its beautifully landscaped gardens boasting a banquet of shrubs, trees and seasonal bedding. The state-of-the-art water-play fun facility has also gone some way in helping take Sydenham Wells Park out of the shadow of the better-known Crystal Palace Park and is packed with scores of children and families during the hot summer months.

Water has always featured in Sydenham Wells Park, with its name deriving from the medicinal springs that were discovered in Sydenham in the mid-17th century. For a while, these were a popular attraction for the village, turning it into a spa resort, until the novelty of drinking the bitter-tasting valley water wore off in the early 19th century. A number of the 12 original wells still lie within the park's grounds and the water-play area is sourced by the springs. Officially opened to the public in 1901, this park continues to be one of the gems of south-east London.

South-east

Tabard Gardens

Tabard Street, SE1 4JU
7:30 until dusk
03330 050 403
www.southwark.gov.uk/
Travel: Borough LU
Area: 4 acres
Facilities: Children's play area, outdoor gym, table tennis tables, multi-use sports pitches

About a ten-minute walk from Borough tube station, this elongated strip of green land is divided up into sports, play, nature and meadow areas, all nestling between low and high rise office and apartment blocks, with the Shard and the Gherkin visible in the distance. A big attraction is the free outdoor gym that's overlooked by the park's basketball court. During quiet times you can take your pick from the seven machines – shoulder press, cross trainer, hand bike, recumbent bikes, ski machine, fitness bike and bench press. The public workouts can get pretty competitive, but it's all good fun and draws different strands of the community together.

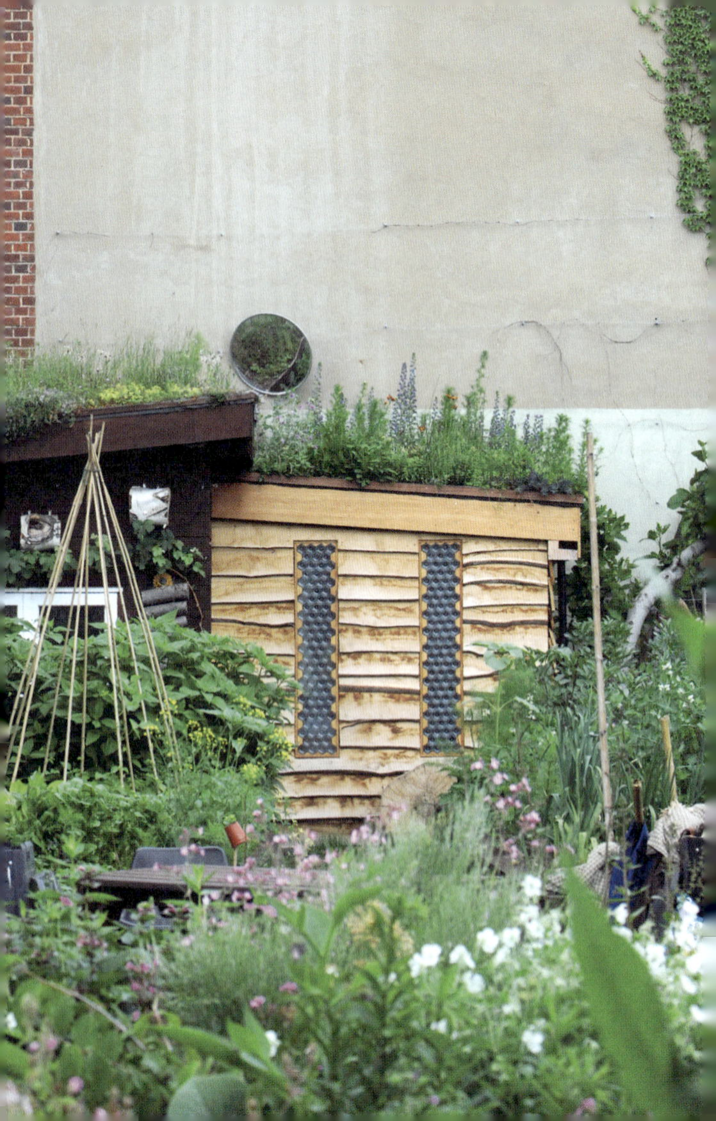

South-east

Walworth Garden

206 Manor Place, SE17 3BN
Mon-Fri 8:00-17:00, Sat & Sun 10:00-17:00
www.walworthgarden.org.uk
020 7582 2652
Travel: Kennington LU

Push open the huge cast iron gate that's studded with insect sculptures and step into this gorgeous little enclave, just a short walk from Kennington tube station. Compact, but wonderfully lush, the garden stretches out from a central staff hut, and is carefully divided into areas for planting, sitting or general meandering. Wooden benches with backs intricately carved into butterfly shapes add character to this unique green space. Run by a local charity established in 1987, the farm sits on what was once a derelict site. It offers a wide range of courses including bee keeping, professional and amateur gardening (including free courses for beginners), decorative metalwork, horticultural therapy and herbal medicine. There's a gate to a small wildlife area where visitors can see frogs, newts and insects, while over at the back of the garden there are glasshouses, a polytunnel and raised herb and vegetable beds.

For more boisterous running around, Pasley Park sits directly opposite Walworth Garden Farm. Save for a small children's playground the park is a fairly sparse stretch of green but it does have an interesting history. Once the site of the Royal Surrey Zoological Gardens, it was a go-to attraction from 1831, when a man named Edward Cross moved his collection of rhinos, leopards, snakes, elephants and giraffes there. The park was also home to a 12,000 capacity music hall and lavishly themed outdoor spectaculars that featured erupting volcanoes and even the city of Rome. The theme park was a favourite of Queen Victoria and the Royal children. The zoo and the theme park are long forgotten, with Edward Cross's animals being sold off by 1855, and the music hall destroyed by a fire in 1862. The park closed in 1877, and it wasn't until 1950 that it was relandscaped and renamed as today's much more humble Pasley Park.

South-east

West Square Gardens

West Square, Elephant & Castle, SE11 4SP
Daily 7:30 until dusk
Travel: Elephant and Castle LU

A compact, circular (despite its name) delight, West Square is open to the public during the day but locked every night. Surrounded by much sought-after Georgian terraced houses, it was built during the nineteenth century on land owned by the West family. It lies east of the site of the Bethlem Hostpital, which is now the Imperial War Museum. Back in the 1800s, many of the Bethlem staff were housed in the square, but since the park area was developed, it's become a peaceful retreat from the traffic-laden St George's Road. These days, because of the square's proximity to the London College of Communication, you might find a few students or office workers hanging out on the benches at lunchtimes, but the space never seems to get overrun and always retains its sense of peaceful tranquillity. There's usually a dedicated park gardener keeping things neat and tidy, and if you walk round the square itself, you'll spot a plaque on the house where chemist J.A.R. Newlands (developer of the periodic table) was born.

Did you know?

- As a young child, Charlie Chaplin (1889–1977) lived at 39 West Square for a short time.

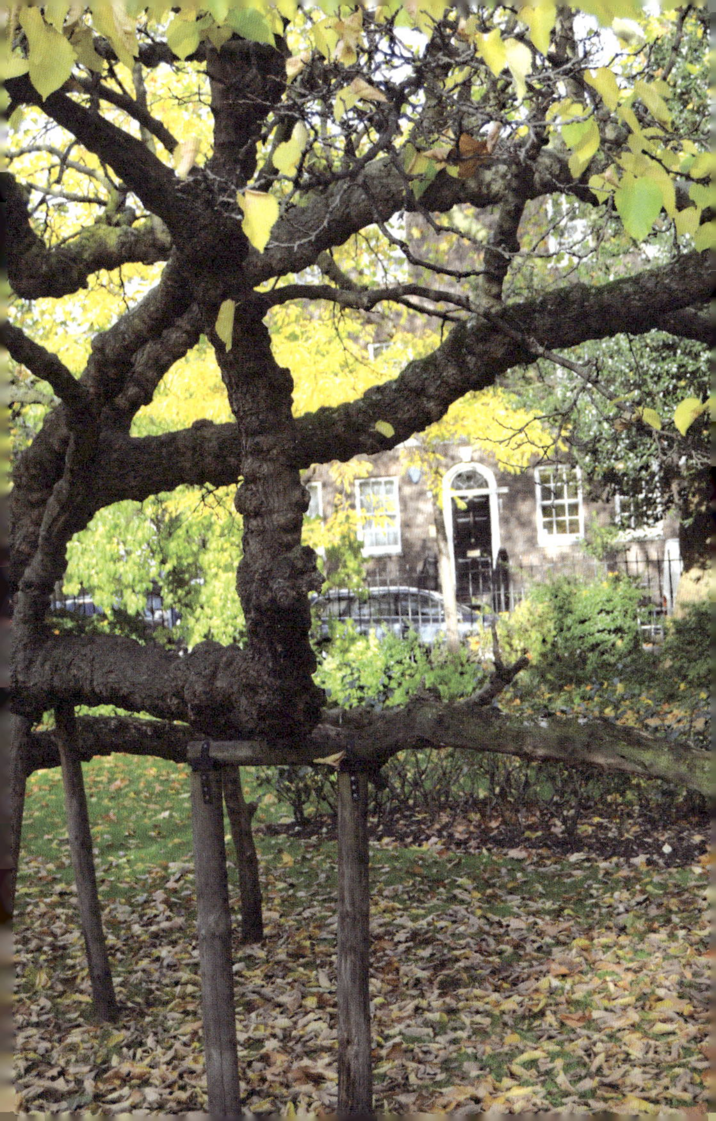

Queen Elizabeth Olympic Park

EAST

EAST

Island Gardens Park 178
Hackney Marshes 179
Haggerston Park 182
London Fields 185
Mile End Park.......................................186
Queen Elizabeth Olympic Park......189
Springfield Park 194
Thames Barrier Park..........................198
Valentine's Park..................................201
Victoria Park 202
Wanstead Flats...................................206
West Ham Park 207

Queen Elizabeth Olympic Park

Island Gardens Park

Saunders Ness Road, E14 3EA
Daily 24 hours
www.towerhamlets.gov.uk
020 7364 5227
Travel: Island Gardens DLR
Area: 3 acres
Facilities: Kiosk

The namesake of the Island Gardens DLR stop opened as a public park in 1895, nearly a century before the automated metro system got underway in 1987. With a backdrop of the rolling hills of Greenwich Park, Island Gardens is a bijou park with a wonderful view over The Thames of the Cutty Sark and the National Maritime Museum. This is in fact the modern-day version of the view of Greenwich which was captured in the 18th century painting *A View of Greenwich from the River* by Canaletto – although apparently the Italian painter never stepped foot in this part of town. The entrance to the Greenwich foot tunnel sits within the park and from here visitors can walk to Greenwich under the Thames. The foot tunnel has recently been refitted and is a popular attraction, being used by some 1.2 million pedestrians each year.

Hackney Marshes

Homerton Road, London E9 5PF
Daily 24 hours
www.hackney.gov.uk
020 8986 7955
Travel: Lea Bridge Rail, Homerton LO
Facilities: Football pitches, rugby and cricket pitches, café bar and roof terrace, cricket pitches

The Hackney Marshes area has long been considered a footballer's paradise –even Lionel Messi got helicoptered in for an appearance on the green in 2010. The Hackney and Leyton Sunday Football League has been running here since 1946 and the marshes are home to some 82 marked-out football, rugby and cricket pitches. Parts of the marshes were used for training during the 2012 Olympics, and after the event, the south eastern section of the arena fields became what is now the Queen Elizabeth Olympic Park (see page 189). Aside from sport, the marshes are good for spotting wildlife. Mature trees including black poplar, plane, willow, ash and lime were planted here over 100 years ago, while the River Lea on the east side of the marshes is where you'll find mallard, tufted ducks, cormorants and gulls, although a few species seem to find that the nearby car park is just as good for a gathering spot.

Did you know?

- In 1981 a reported sighting of the so-called 'Hackney bear' resulted in 50 police officers and helicopters searching the area.

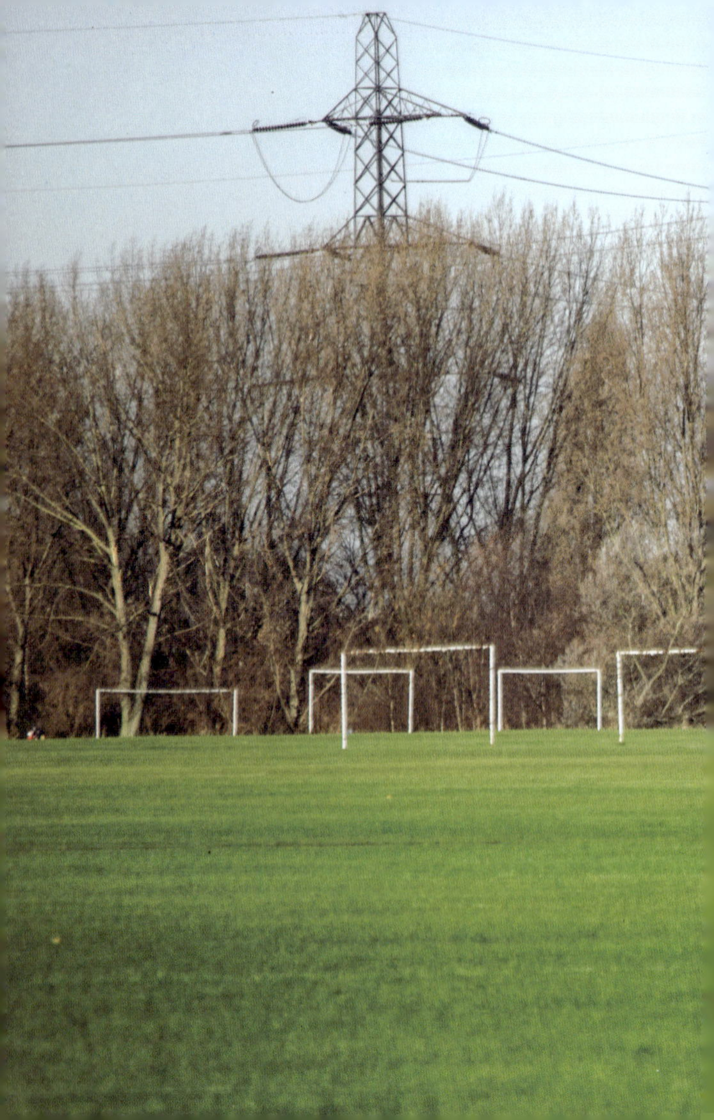

Hackney Marshes

East

Haggerston Park

Yorkton Street, E2 8QH
Daily dawn until dusk
020 8356 3000
www.hackney.gov.uk
Travel: Haggerston LO
Area: 15 acres
Facilities: Football pitch, BMX cycle track, children's play area, athletics track, table tennis tables, community orchard, city farm, kiosk, multi-use game centre, trim trail

Home to the wonderful Hackney City Farm, Haggerston Park emerged as a peaceful public open space in the late 1950s from the rubble of Shoreditch gasworks, which was hit by a V-2 rocket in 1944. Today's park has a nature reserve, which consists of a section of meadowland, with banks of shrubs and tall grasses in view of a fenced and turfed football pitch and children's play area. The biggest draw of the park is the BMX track which is busy at the weekends with kid's practicing their tricks. Hackney City Farm (see page 312) is also a very popular destination with farm animals to feed and stroke and a range of courses on offer. A visit to the farm and park would be incomplete without trying the delicious food on offer at the Frizzante Café, which has earned itself a great reputation since it opened in 1992.

At the weekend, nearby Broadway Market (E9) is open, while on Sundays many people can be seen walking home laden with plants from Columbia Road Flower Market which is just 5 minutes walk away.

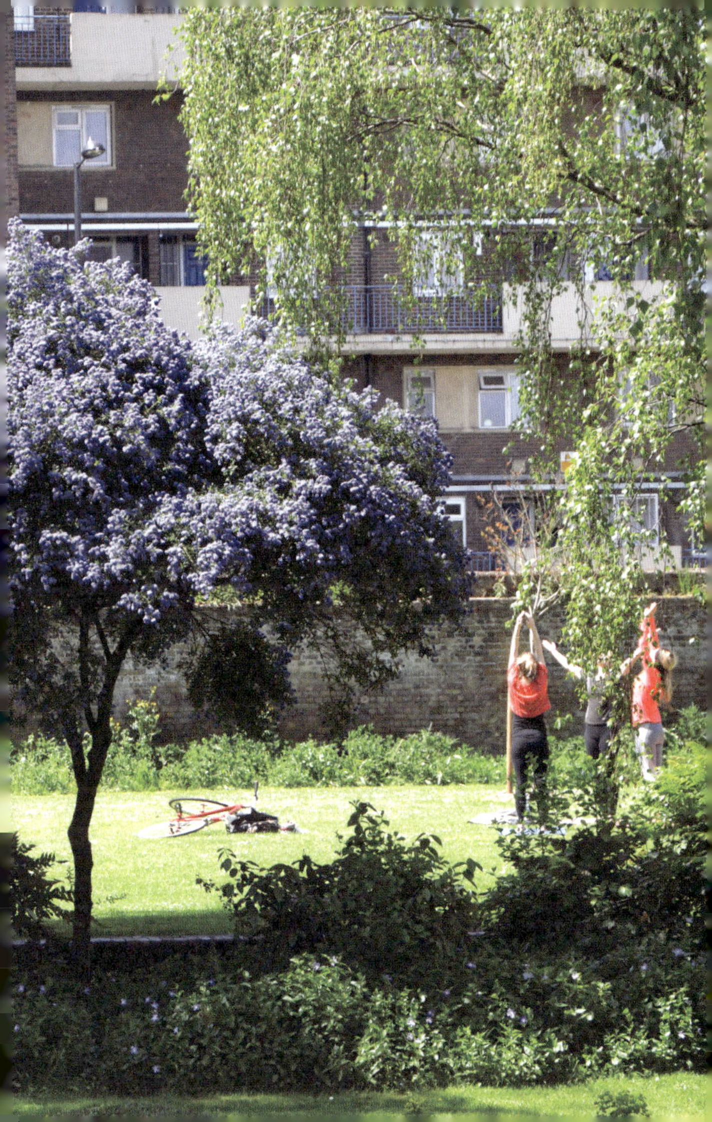

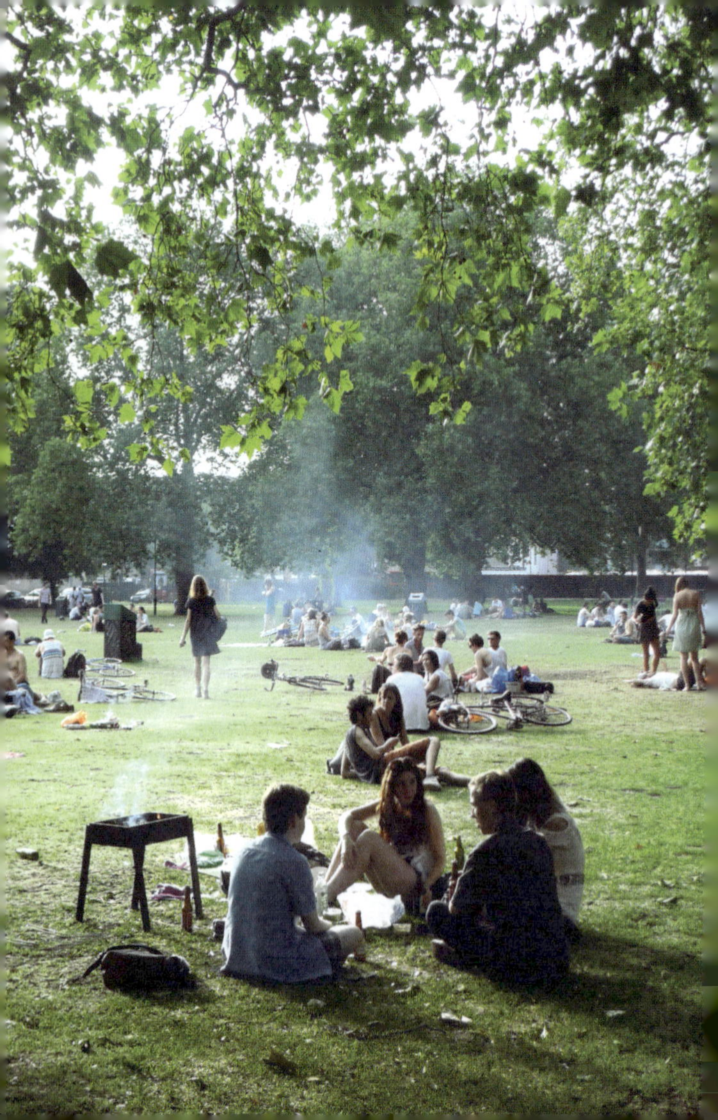

London Fields

Lansdowne Drive, Hackney, E8 3EU
Daily 24 hours
020 8356 3000
www.hackney.gov.uk
Transport: London Fields LO
Area: 30 acres
Facilities: Children's play areas, cricket pitch, lido, outdoor gym, table tennis table, tennis courts, wildflower meadow, café

London Fields is first mentioned in 1540 as common land used by farmers to graze cattle before sending them to market. In the last two hundred years Hackney has been swallowed up in London's expansion and London Fields has become an oasis of green amid the urban sprawl. The late Martin Amis used the area as the title for his 1989 novel, but the book's dystopia of cheap lager, dodgy geezers and semi-pro darts is a long way from the gentrified area of today. The nearby Broadway Market is now a very popular food market at the weekend which attracts an increasingly wealthy local population.

The park itself is a pleasant, if rather flat, 30 acre green space complete with tennis courts, several playgrounds and an outdoor table tennis table. A wildflower meadow now flourishes in an area that was once gritty and underused, the honey scent attracting butterflies and bees in the summer months.

The cricket strip hosts competitive matches throughout the summer and is the home of London Fields CC. In 2006 the 50 metre lido was reopened, having been closed for 15 years. The lido is open throughout the year and is popular with the local sporting fraternity – London Fields even has its own triathlon club!

Visitors looking for relaxation will find plenty of shade from the many mature trees in London Fields. There's a café adjacent to the lido and also The Pub on the Park to the eastern side, which has a balcony overlooking London Fields and there are plenty of eateries on nearby Broadway Market.

Mile End Park

Mile End Road, E3 4HL
Daily 24 hours
www.towerhamlets.gov.uk
020 7364 5227
Travel: Mile End LU
Facilities: Ecology Park, Arts Park, the play pavilion, children's park, leisure centre, stadium, climbing wall, outdoor gym, go kart track

An East End treasure, Mile End Park is an elongated strip of green land that stretches from Limehouse along the Regent's Canal towards its larger sibling Victoria Park. The unenclosed acres were made available to the public in 1945 and underwent extensive refurbishment in 2002 with the help of £25 million of funding. The development involved the creation of distinct areas within the park including the Arts Park, Ecology Park and Terrace Garden all near Mile End Road, which cuts through the middle of the park.

The Mile End Arts Pavilion is an earth-covered building that once inside, reveals itself to be a well-lit gallery space that overlooks a small lake. From the arts pavilion you can see an unusual hill which was created from the rubble of the Blitz and offers spectacular views along the Regent's Canal and of the spectacular skyline of Canary Wharf. From here you can also see the ascending path of the Green Bridge which provides a grassy, tree-lined walkway and cycle path that crosses over Mile End Road and gives the park some continuity and more great views of the city.

Down at the southern end of the park, there's a change of focus in the facilities, with an open space for ball games, circus events, funfairs and festivals. Further along there's a sports stadium, featuring an eight-lane athletics track, grass and artificial football pitches, a weight training room, changing facilities and swimming pool. An established attraction is the Mile End Climbing Wall (020 8980 0289), a few minutes from Mile End tube station at Haverfield Road. Classes are available for children and adults of all standards.

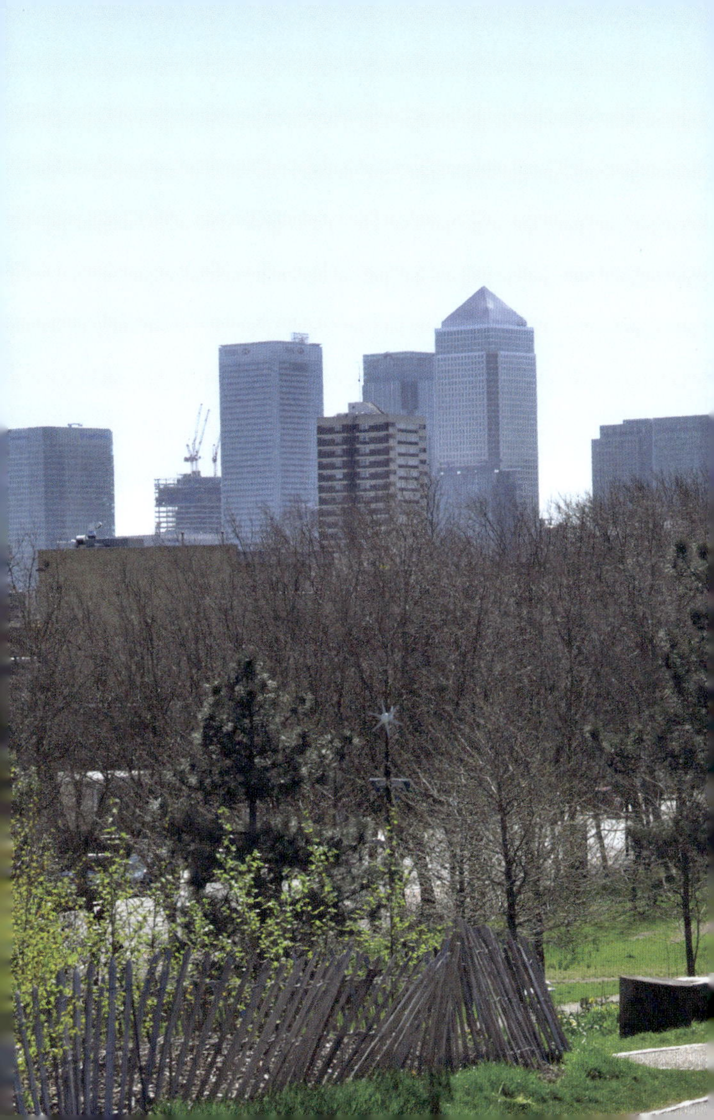

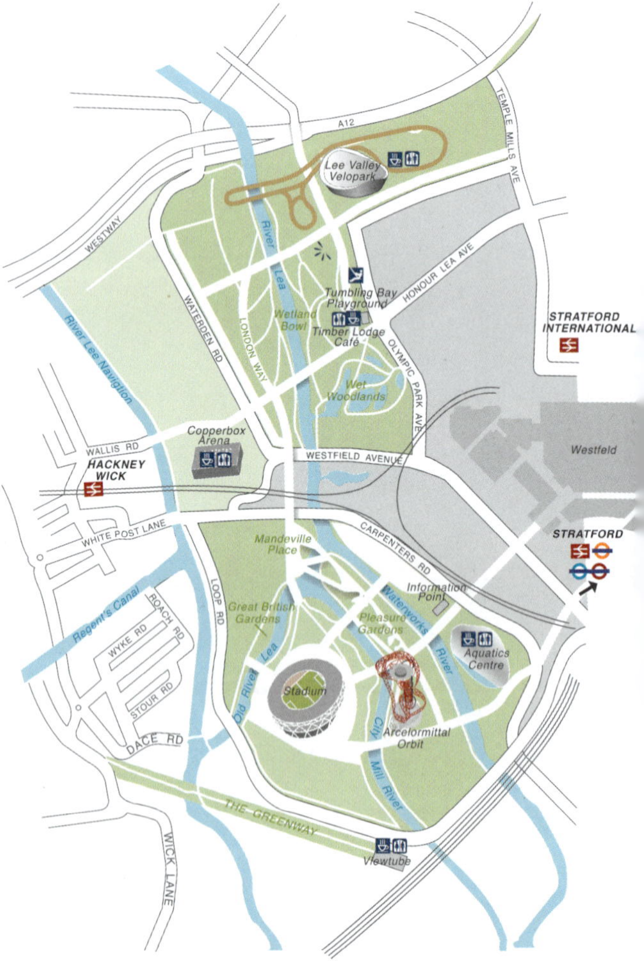
A12
TEMPLE MILLS AVE
Lee Valley Velopark
WESTWAY
River Lea
Tumbling Bay Playground
HONOUR LEA AVE
Wetland Bowl
Timber Lodge Café
STRATFORD INTERNATIONAL
WATERDEN RD
LONDON WAY
OLYMPIC PARK AVE
River Lee Navigation
Wet Woodlands
Copperbox Arena
WALLIS RD
WESTFIELD AVENUE
Westfeld
HACKNEY WICK
WHITE POST LANE
Mandeville Place
CARPENTERS RD
STRATFORD
Information Point
LOOP RD
Regent's Canal
ROACH RD
Great British Gardens
Pleasure Gardens
Waterworks River
WYKE RD
Aquatics Centre
Old River Lea
Stadium
STOUR RD
City Mill River
Arcelormittal Orbit
DACE RD
THE GREENWAY
Viewtube
WICK LANE

East

Queen Elizabeth Olympic Park

E20 2ST
Daily 24 hours
0800 072 2110
www.queenelizabethpark.co.uk
Travel: Hackney Wick LO
Area: 560 acres
Facilities: Stadium, Copper Box sports arena, Aquatics Centre, playground, Velopark, tennis centre, cafés, slide

Step out of Stratford tube station and follow the signs through the sprawling Westfield shopping centre to get to Queen Elizabeth Olympic Park. Originally given the simpler Olympic Park title, it adopted the regal name after the 2012 Olympic games. A huge talking point during the international sports event, the park is one of the largest urban green spaces to be built in Europe for more than 50 years. Officially opened in early 2014, the area is still being developed with the arrival of UCL East Campus in recent years and the imminent opening of V&A East and Saddlers Wells East, just beyond the park.

The park combines areas for gentle relaxation with family and friends, and areas for wildlife to flourish alongside some of the world's best sporting facilities. The greener spots sit within the borders of the sporting complexes and feature a wetland area, meadow, lawns and areas for kite-flying, as well as a playground, water fountain, café and planted borders that, once mature, will provide a lush environment for wildlife. A standout landmark is the ArcelorMittal – better known as the Orbit. A 376 feet high bright red steel sculpture and observation tower, designed by the Turner Prize winning artist Anish Kapoor. Located between the Olympic Stadium and the park's Aquatic Centre, it's a structure that's impossible to miss. There are two observation towers, offering spectacular views of the whole park and its surrounding areas, although these views are not free and a family ticket will set you back £64 at peak times.

However the main legacy of the Queen Elizabeth Olympic Park will always be its sporting venues. When millions of eyes were on this part of east London for the 2012 Olympics and Paralympics, venues such as the Olympic Stadium and the Velodrome became recognised across the world. The Olympic Stadium held the opening and closing ceremonies and has now been converted into a 54,000-capacity venue and the permanent home of West Ham United Football Club and British Athletics. The Velopark, which sits at the northern end of the Olympic Park, is home to the spectacular Velodrome, a BMX racing track, a mile-long road course and a mountain bike track.

The park's London Aquatics Centre was another of the main Olympic venues. It opened to the public in early 2014 and with two 50-metre swimming pools and a 24 metre diving pool, it caters both for serious swimmers and divers, as well as those just wanting to enjoy splashing about or learning to swim.

At the Hackney Wick station entrance to the park, the Copper Box Arena is an indoor multi-use venue for sports competitions including basketball and handball. It's also the home of the London Lions basketball club.

The Queen Elizabeth Olympic Park has been designed to reference the 2012 games in various other ways such as featuring number-crunching facts about the event. These are documented in green squares painted onto various pathways within the park. Facts include the 'roar of Super Saturday' when team GB took three golds including Mo Farah for the 10,000 metres, and Jessica Ennis for the heptathlon.

This is a park for everyone, from serious and amateur sports fanatics to families out for a stroll. A further legacy of the Olympics is the vast Westfield shopping complex which can be seen in the distance and has well-signed routes through to the main entrance into the park for those seeking some relaxation after their retail therapy.

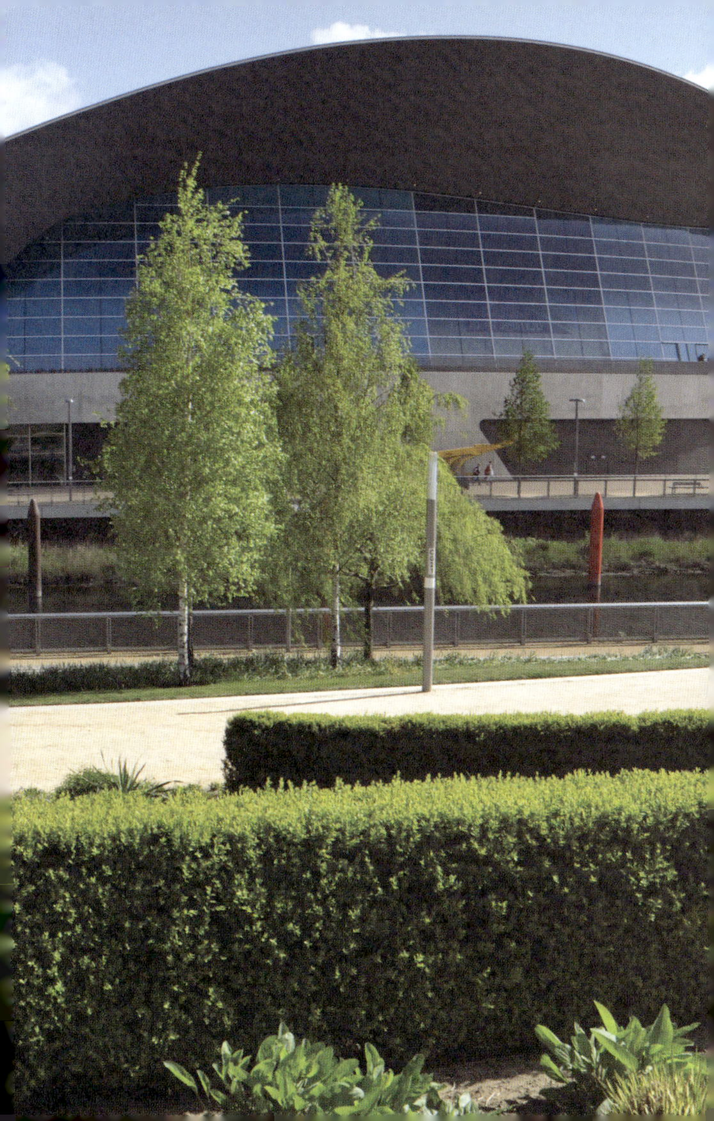

Velodrome at the Queen Elizabeth Olympic Park

Did you know?

• The Queen Elizabeth Olympic Park has been allocated its own E20 postcode from the Royal Mail. The postcode had previously only appeared in the TV series East Enders, which takes place in the fictional suburb of Walford.

Springfield Park

Springfield Lane, E5 9EF
Daily 24 hours
020 8356 3000
www.hackney.gov.uk/springfield-park
Travel: Stoke Newington & Clapton LO
Area: 36 acres
Facilities: Athletics track, bandstand, children's playground, conservation area, cricket pitch, fountains, organic food growing, outdoor chessboards, café, table tennis table, tennis courts

Opened in 1905, Springfield Park overlooks the River Lea and the expanse of the Walthamstow Marshes. Spanning the steep grounds of what used to be three private houses, only the park's Springfield House (known as the White Lodge Mansion) survives. Inside the Grade II building, Springfield Park Café is open every day of the year, except Christmas Eve and Christmas Day, and has long been known as a venue where local artists can show their work. There's a seasonally changing menu and the owners are happy to take suggestions from customers. From the east side of the lodge, the duck pond widens out from the bottom of a sloping path. You can step right down to the edge, where the wildfowl pick at reeds in water that also holds koi carp.

The old glasshouses on the other side of the café have now become a tropical conservatory, with green-fingered activity by the volunteer group, Growing Communities, who host Open Sunday sessions every third weekend. Salad crops such as basil and oakleaf lettuce are some of the spoils, as well as oyster mushrooms in a composting area. Figs, olives and grapes are work in progress in one of the greenhouses. Elsewhere, pockets of dense (but safe) woodland make excellent hide and seek areas for energetic children, while mature trees (including copper beech, plane, sweet chestnut, silver birch, lime and mulberry) stake out their territory on the lawns. Down the park's slope lie the tennis courts, children's playground and allotment area and beyond this is the Springfield Marina where

East

a colourful hotchpotch of boats are moored. Cross over the white bridge to the Lee Valley which contains the ditches, ponds and shrublands of the Walthamstow Nature Reserve. The park's connection to the Lee Valley's network of canals and waterways is one of its great features. From here you can walk or cycle south to Hackney Marshes or further on to Victoria Park (see page 202), alternatively head north to Walthamstow Marshes or even further on to Waltham Abbey. If you're feeling particularly energised, the nearby Lea Valley Walk is a 50-mile long-distance path between Limehouse in east London and Leagrave, the source of the River Lea near Luton.

Thames Barrier Park

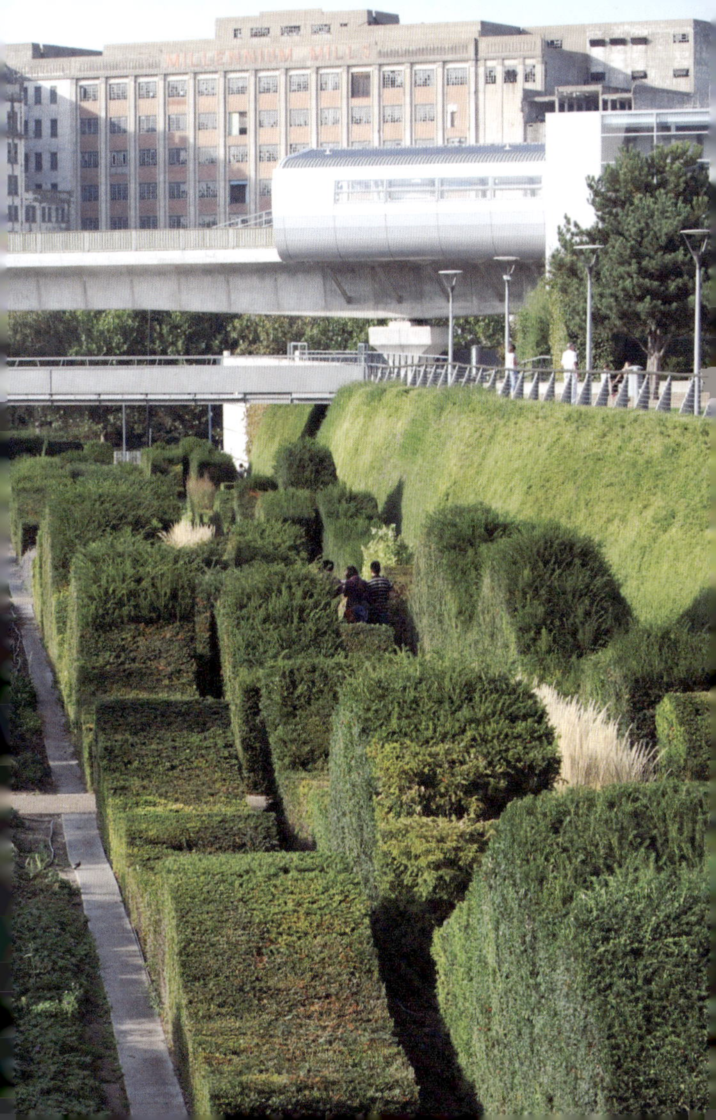

Thames Barrier Park

E16 2HP
Daily 7:00 until dusk
020 7476 3741
www.london.gov.uk
Travel: Pontoon Dock DLR
Area: 22 acres
Facilities: Children's playground, 5-a-side football, basketball court, café

Completed in 2000 on undeveloped river bank, the park's biggest claim to fame is that it overlooks the huge metal fins of the Thames Barrier floodworks.

The park is a perfect haven for high and low tide wildlife that is attracted to the shore. From the Pavilion of Remembrance (which honours the victims of the Blitz) visitors can see herons, teal, shelduck and mallards. In the wildflower meadow a population of crickets creates a cacophony during the summer and fountain plaza – with blasts of rising water jets – is also a treat for excitable children (and adults) on hot days. There's a children's play area and small unfenced basketball court, which looks like a bit of an afterthought, with a rickety ballpost at one end and a miniature football net at the other.

The Green Dock is a sunken rectangular garden of hedges, flowerbeds and paths, which is cut into a scooped landscape between the riverfront and the fountain area. Viewed from the overhead walkways, this strip of greenery looks like it's been set within the remnants of a concrete strip of motorway, although it is actually a very lush area with hedges and neatly cut flower beds.

The Visitor Pavilion is the central glass-fronted building with oakwood frame and iroko decking containing a café for drinks and snacks. Despite the fact that you could probably get round the whole park in 20 minutes, it's worth taking your time and enjoying this unique part of London.

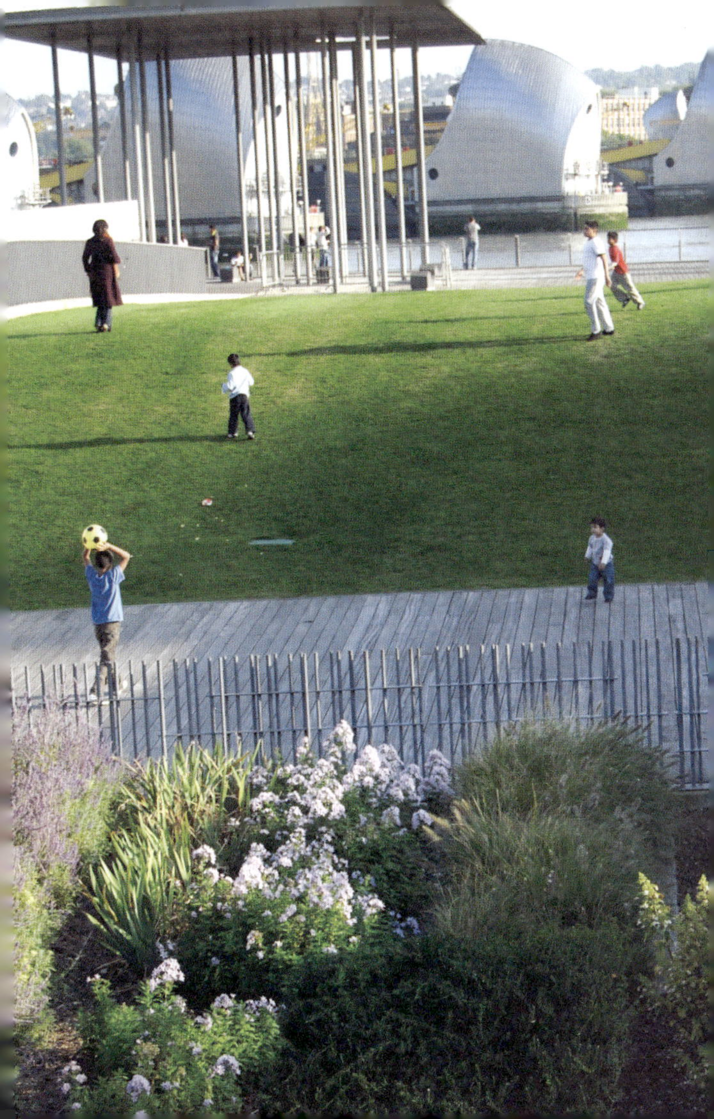

Grotto seat in Valentine's Park

East

Valentine's Park

Cranbrook Road, Ilford, IG1 4TG
Daily 8:00 until dusk
020 8708 5437
visionsrcl.org.uk/centre/valentines-park/
Travel: Gants Hill LU
Area: 128 acres
Facilities: Children's playground, multi-use games area, lake with rowing boats for hire, café, tennis court, cricket ground, mansion, outdoor gym, café

If you enter Valentine's Park at the pond side Cranbrook Road entrance you might attract loud noises from the hungry ducks and there's also duck food on sale for the unprepared. Opposite the pond, the walled rose and Old English gardens have bricked archway entrances where the scent of fresh herbs lead you to the Gardener's Cottage café and terrace area. If your seeking sporty recreation the park has one of London's largest outdoor gyms.

A focal point of the park is Valentines Mansion. Free entry reveals the life style of its past owners and their servants, and the house itself has a history that goes back to 1696, when it was built for Lady Tillotson, the widow of the Archbishop of Canterbury. Visitors can now snoop around the servant's domain including the kitchen, scullery and dairy as well as exploring the grander upstairs drawing room, parlour room, bedchambers. while in the rest of the park on any given day you can check out features such as the long water canal, the glade, the south lawn, the grotto and horse pond. The park also hosts open air theatre events during the summer.

Did you know?

- A great Black Hamburg Vine was planted at Valentine's mansion in 1758. In 1769 a cutting was taken to produce the still-existing vine at Hampton Court.

Victoria Park

Grove Road, E3 5TB
Daily 7:00 until dusk
020 8985 5699
www.towerhamlets.gov.uk
Travel: Mile End LU, Bethnal Green LU, Hackney Wick LO
Area: 213 acres
Facilities: Model boating lake, fishing lake, playgrounds, tennis courts, sports pavilion, water park, cafés, bandstand, community room

Victoria Park's opening followed a petition from over 30,000 local residents, presented to Queen Victoria in 1840, for some decent outdoor space. An Act of Parliament was duly passed in 1841 and Victoria Park became the first park in London to be designed for the public. It was an immediate success but also the site of political controversy serving as the venue for the Chartist protest of 1848.

The fact that there are 19 separate entrances to the park gives an indication of its sprawling size. The 213 acres – which cover parts of Bethnal Green, Hackney and Bow – is big enough to host regular festivals including the annual All Points East music festival, fêtes and running events and fun runs for children. Bounded by the Regent's Canal to the west, Victoria Park is joined by the Hertford Canal along its southern edge, and boasts a staggering number of trees (over 4,500 throughout), many of which are as old as the park itself. Three special walks designed by Tower Hamlets (www.towerhamlets.gov.uk) allow full appreciation of these fine specimens, with the areas to the east, west and along the park's outer avenues planted with sycamores, maples, false acacias, Kentucky coffee trees, London planes and limes.

Often considered as three parks in one, due to divisions made by major avenues, Victoria Park is transected by Grove Road on the west side between the Royal Gates and Crown Gates and by a grand pedestrian avenue that connects Gore and Approach Road even further to the west. The larger end of the park to the east is more open, with tennis courts, a cricket pitch, the old lake and duck pond, running track and bandstand being some of the features surrounded by open areas of mainly flat lawns and grassland. The popular Old English Garden in the eastern side of the park is edged by neatly cut, staggered hedging to give different sight lines through the oblong-shaped garden and there's plenty of benched seating throughout. A more recent addition to this part of the park is the outdoor gym that is found just next to the tennis courts and is very popular with local fitness enthusiasts. This part of the park also has the great Hub Café and there are public table tennis tables, although you'll need to bring your own bats.

On a historical note, the entrance to the west side of the park has the famous statues of the crazy-looking Dogs of Alcibiades. Donated to Victoria Park in 1912, over the years they've gone through cycles of cleaning, restoration and vandalism. They are in good shape these days and now observe Victoria Park Market on Sundays that offers delicious street food and quality groceries and even a flower and plant stall. Just a minute's walk from the dogs is the huge lake within the park's grounds with its powerful fountain and a good number of ducks, geese and other wild fowl. This is also the site of the Pavilion Café which serves delicious but expensive food using local and organic produce (www.the-pavilion-cafe.com).

Victoria Park is a stone's throw from the Olympic Park (see page 189), you could – if you felt up to it – take a full six-mile tour of east London's green spaces by starting off from Mile End Park (see page 186), continuing along the Union and Hertford Canals, through Victoria Park and on to the Olympic complex.

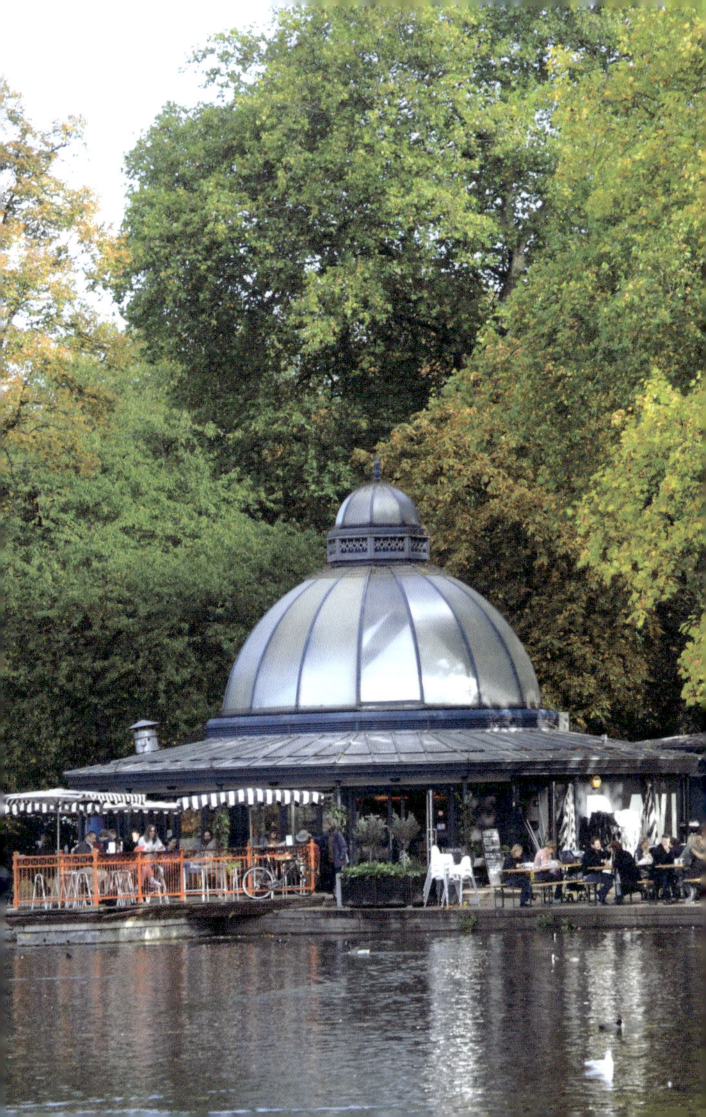

Wanstead Flats

Epping Forest, London E11 2LT
Daily 24 hours
020 8532 1010
www.cityoflondon.gov.uk
Travel: Manor Park Rail LO
Area: 113 acres
Facilities: Playing fields, pond dipping platform

Wanstead Flats sits at the southern tip of Epping Forest, with most of the area surrounded by a ditch and a bank to keep out all vehicles aside from bikes or work trucks. Its expanse of open grassland contains bridlepaths for horses, a number of small woods and copses, and in the north west corner of the Flats, an avenue of sweet chestnut trees – known as Evelyn's Avenue after the 17th century writer and gardener John Evelyn, who planted it. Other features including three ponds, the largest of which is Alexandra Lake, also known as the Sandhills because of its dry banks.

A site of special scientific interest, Wanstead Flats is a haven for wildlife and a popular spot for birders on the lookout for meadow pipits and migrating birds.

Did you know?

- In WWII Wanstead Flats was home to the P.O.W camps, as well as temporary housing and defensive artillery.

West Ham Park

Upton Lane, London E7 9PU
Daily 7:30 until dusk
020 8472 3584
www.cityoflondon.gov.uk
Travel: Stratford LU & LO, West Ham LU
Area: 77 acres
Facilities: Children's playground, tennis courts, football pitches, cricket pitches, all weather pitch, summer running track, rounders area, bandstand

A Corporation of London treasure, West Ham Park has excellent public sporting facilities with nine tennis courts, two cricket squares, two football pitches, a large rounders area and running track. It is well used by local schools and athletics clubs.

Opened to the public in 1874, the park is thought to date from the 16th century. Naturally flat, there are a few man-made hills giving the vast green areas surrounding the sports facilities a tad more character, as well as providing ideal areas for a picnic. Up to a million visitors a year pass through the park, many heading straight for the exquisite enclosed ornamental garden at the far south-eastern edge. An alpine rockery forms the centre of this area, with paths separating the surrounding sections of rhododendron and heather beds, the terrace and footbridge, as well as the three separate walled, iris and rose gardens.

Behind the first cricket pitch towards the south-east of the main park, the nursery, with its huge computer-controlled greenhouses, provides thousands of seasonal bedding plants for the City of London. In terms of the park's trees, the sweet gum is one of the newer additions, joining cedars, weeping ash, hornbeam and oak. Summer activities for children include puppet shows, live music and wildlife activities such as spider surveys and bat walks.

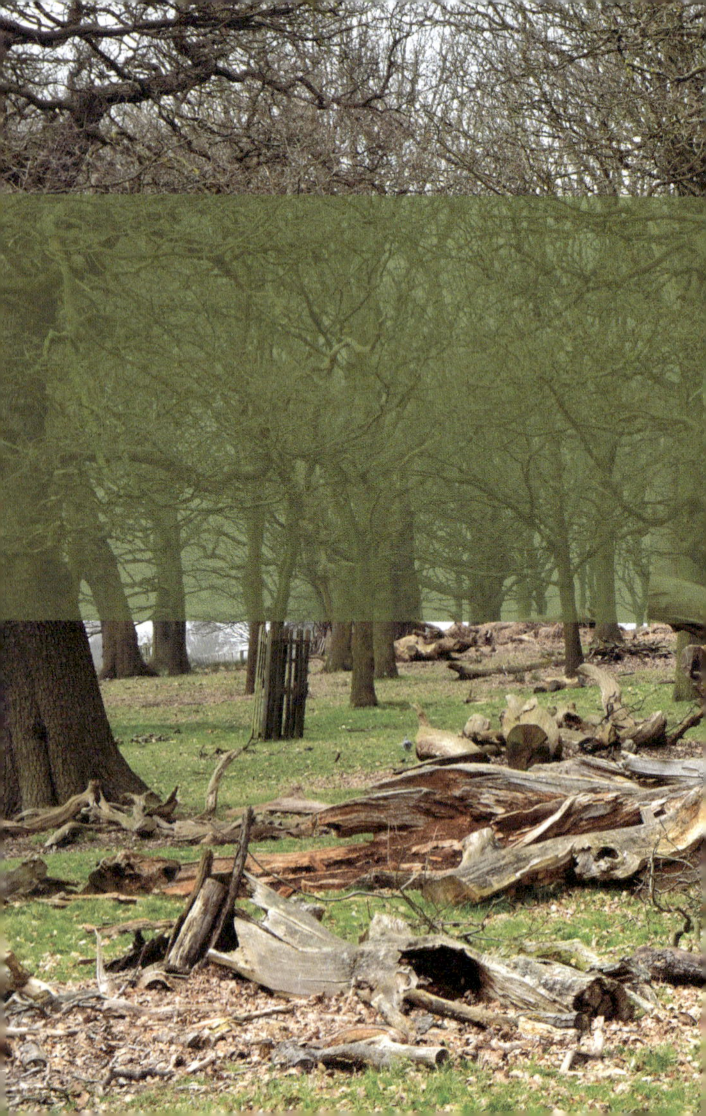

OUTER LONDON

OUTER LONDON

Bushy Park.. 212
Epping Forest..................................... 215
Morden Hall Park 217
Osterley Park..................................... 219
Richmond Park 222

Osterley Park

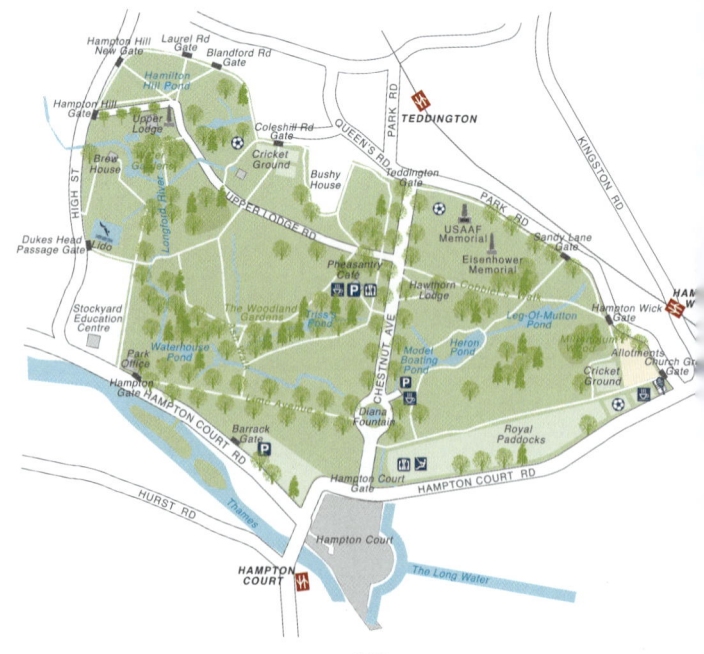

Outer London

Bushy Park

Hampton Court Road, Hampton Hill, TW12 2EJ
Daily 24 hours
0300 061 2250
www.royalparks.org.uk
Travel: Hampton Court, Kingston or Teddington Rail
Area: 1100 acres
Facilities: Adventure playground, football pitches, cricket and rugby pitches, hockey pitches, tennis courts, heated open air pool, fishing ponds, café

Outer London

This is the second largest of London's eight Royal Parks, and its expansive and flat landscape is well worth a trip out of London to visit. Lying to the north of Hampton Court Palace, it has some historical links with the regal building, which in the 17th century suffered from a chronic lack of water. It was Charles I who came up with the idea of creating an artificial river in Bushy Park as a much needed reservoir to supply the parched royal household. It took nine months to build the Longford 'River', which still runs through the park today. At thirteen miles long, its source is at Longford Point on the River Colne, beyond Heathrow Airport. A linear nature reserve stretches for around nine miles outside the park's boundaries, with grass banks, shrubs and trees along the length of the river.

There's plenty of water within the park itself with streams and ponds attracting swans, coots and other wildfowl. There are also lakes for fishing and facilities for horse riding. The Upper Lodge Water Gardens are where you'll find a stunning collection of pools, fountains and a canal. It's an area that served as a hospital for Canadian troops during WW1. After that it was used as a swimming pool as part of a school for East End boys with respiratory diseases. In WW2 it was turned into a barracks and then faded into disrepair for decades. It wasn't until 2010 that the area was refurbished with new cascade walls and a finely tuned pumping system to create what's essentially a throwback to the Baroque splendour of this section of the park.

Elsewhere in the grounds there are two woodland gardens, one of which has a café. A wildlife treat are the red and fallow deer that graze in the park – around 320 in number – which means that spotting clusters of them from time to time is pretty likely.

The park's most formal area is the central Chestnut Walk, a beautiful mile-long avenue of huge chestnut trees, which runs between Hampton Court Road in Hampton and Sandy Lane in Teddington. Seasonal walks take place to celebrate when the chestnut blossoms appear in the park. Other events include activities like fairs, live bands and classic car and bike runs.

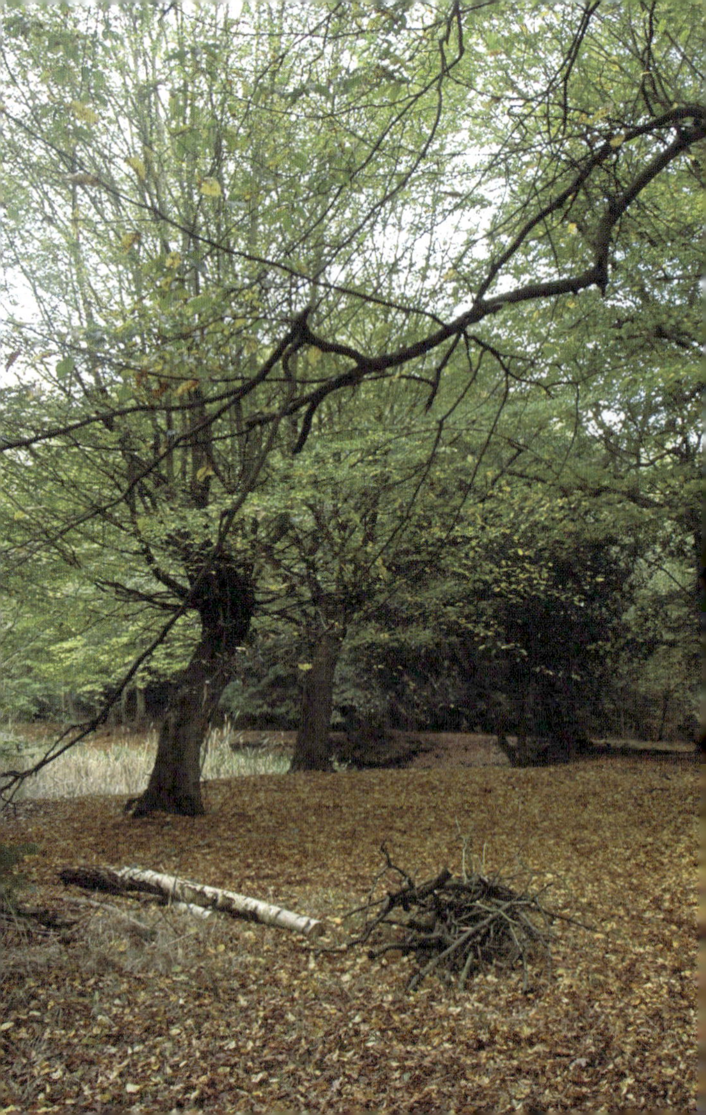

Outer London

Epping Forest

High Beech Forest Centre, High Beech, Loughton, Essex, IG10 4AE
Daily 24 hours
020 8508 0028
www.cityoflondon.gov.uk
Travel: Loughton, LU
Area: 6118 acres
Facilities: Football and cricket pitches, campsites, golf, cycle tracks, horse riding, visitor centre, café

Delightful, awesome and overwhelming are some of the adjectives that could be used to describe this ancient forest which extends over 6,000 acres on the western and northern edges of Loughton, Essex. The area near to Chingford station is where you'll find the Visitor Centre, better known as The View (020 7332 1911), which opens seven days a week. From here you can check out interactive displays as well as changing art and history exhibitions, and go on a forest trail, which starts at the back door of the centre.

A Forest site worth exploring is Queen Elizabeth's Hunting Lodge, which was built under the orders of Henry VIII in 1543 and offers visitors a glimpse into the forest's Tudor past. The High Beach Forest centre is another area where information and maps about the forest are available. It also has a bird observation window and gift shop. Within the High Beach area can also be found Holy Innocents Church with its 128 ft tower and spire. The area was once the home of a 19th-century private asylum, where poet John Clare was a one-time resident. Another resident (of the area, not of the asylum) was Alfred Lord Tennyson, who lived in Beech Hill House from 1837 to 1840.

The Temple is another listed site in Wanstead Park, which lies within the forest. Dating from the late 18th century, the Temple is believed to have been built for Lord Tylney, owner of the now-demolished Wanstead House. Displays here tell the story of Wanstead Park from the Romans to the modern era. This park also has ornamental ponds, a ruined grotto and carpets of bluebells in early spring.

There are a whole range of features and services within Epping Forest, including 60 football pitches, an eighteen-hole golf course, three cricket pitches and horses for hire if you want to take advantage of the numerous riding tracks throughout.

As one of the last surviving areas of the great oak forests that framed London until medieval times, Epping Forest is London's largest open space and a dedicated conservation area as well as a Site of Special Scientific Interest. Whether you're a wildlife aficionado or a complete novice, expect to see hundreds of rare plants, animals and insect species with anything from dragonflies to grass snakes crossing your path.

Before a visit, it's worth downloading the maps from the City of London website (www.cityoflondon.gov.uk). These will help you navigate to the View, as well as give you an idea of the size of this vast and beautiful forest.

Did you know?

- In the 18th century, the monarchy lost interest in hunting, which affected areas like Epping Forest. It became a shelter for thieves and outlaws who would frequently attack nearby villages at night.

Outer London

Morden Hall Park

Morden Hall Road, Morden, SM4 5JD
Daily 24 hours
020 8545 6850
www.nationaltrust.org.uk
Travel: Morden LU, Phipps Bridge Tramlink
Area: 125 acres
Facilities: Garden centre, bookshop, café

This beautiful National Trust green space is cut through by the River Wandle, which flows from Croydon, Sutton and Wandsworth on its way to join the River Thames. Features within the park include the Riverside Café, garden centre and the 18th-century Morden Hall House that's a popular restaurant and wedding venue.

One of the Park's prettiest spots is the large open rose garden, with scattered rectangular flowerbeds that display a collection of over 2,000 roses in the summer. The building beside this is the Old Snuff Mill – now an environmental study and workshop centre for everything from stained glass to wood turning. The original water wheel on the outside wall was used to grind snuff until 1922. Beneath its black iron spokes a gushing section of the River Wandle travels under a sturdy concrete bridge, its downstream journey leading on to a decorative white cast-iron footbridge in the distance. Next to the mill is an excellent second-hand bookshop offering paperbacks for just 50p.

It's possible to cross the river many times from within the park and in doing so you'll see lush wetland areas, riverbanks and islands where a diversity of plants, insects and birds flourish.

Oak, beech, ash and birch trees are planted throughout the woodlands, with their ages spanning the 18th to the mid 20th centuries. To the north of the park, the marshland areas are popular havens for herons and kingfishers. A stable block, garden centre and riverside café are all on site.

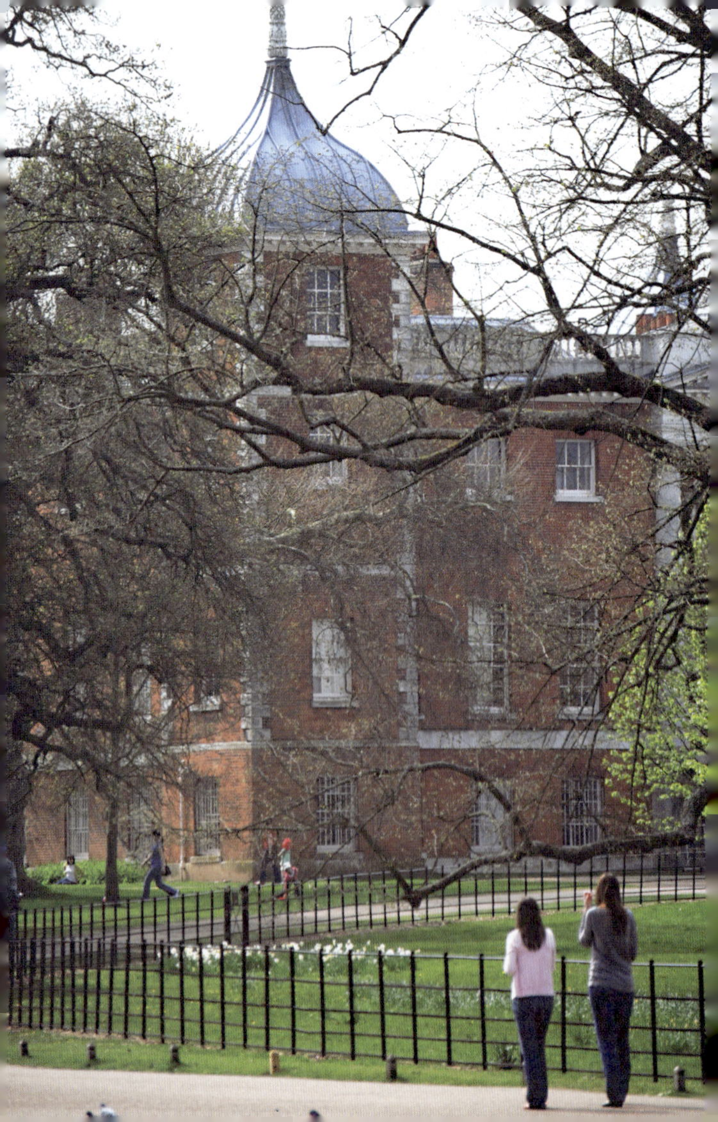

Osterley Park

Isleworth, Middlesex, TW7 4RB
Daily 10:00-17:00
020 8232 5050
www.nationaltrust.org.uk
Travel: Osterley LU
Price: £4-£8
Area: 350 acres
Facilities: Osterley House, Jerwood Art Gallery, cycle hire, bookshop, kiosk, café

For many, the main reason for visiting Osterley Park is to snoop inside the red-bricked and white-pillared Osterley House. In 1761, the building was a crumbling Tudor pile before fashionable Scottish architect Robert Adam transformed it into a lavish country villa, set in a suburban landscape. Today, the house is presented in much the way it would have looked in the 1780s, and that includes displays of some of the house's original gilt-framed family portraits and items of furniture that were brought back to the property in 2014 on a ten year loan. This now allows visitors to glimpse some of the faces behind Osterley's history. Stories about the house will no doubt have an added resonance when you can gaze at works such as an 18th century pastel of Osterley's owners Robert, Sarah and their daughter Sarah-Anne Child, who managed to get herself disinherited for eloping to Gretna Green to marry the Earl of Westmorland.

Within the house there's said to be a 'secret room' that can be accessed from the library, but is unavailable for visitors – which gives the building a sense of mystery. The National Trust took over the grounds in 1949 and acquired the farmland in the late 1990s. A room within the house is devoted to books – many of them second-hand and donated by generous booklovers. There is incidentally another second-hand shop (the non-affiliated Osterley Books) that sits at the entrance to Osterley Park, which also has a good selection.

With the support of the Friends of Osterley Park, the Trust has funded the growing of flowers for displays in the house, created picnic areas and provided bench seating throughout the grounds, including a circular seat around the willow tree by the main lake.

From the main Jersey Road entrance into the park, a long driveway cuts through two huge fields occupied by horses and cows. This gives a rural feel to the place, despite the fact that it's located in a residential part of west London.

The farm shop at the end of the cowfield offers seasonal vegetables, all grown in the grounds. Wherever you find yourself within the park – the picnic area, pleasure grounds or the lakes – the four pineapple-shaped turrets of the main house can always be seen and make navigating the outdoor spaces a great deal easier. There's a huge uncultivated meadow that can be freely walked through, navigated via mown paths. It's a rough and ready haven for butterflies, beetles and grasshoppers.

A walled area at the far end of the pleasure grounds reveals a series of well-tended vegetable gardens. Back in front of the main house, the picnic area beside the lake has bright flowers in the summer and deckchairs provided on good days. It's an undeniably tranquil spot – even with the nearby Heathrow flight path making its presence known with its regular inbound arrivals.

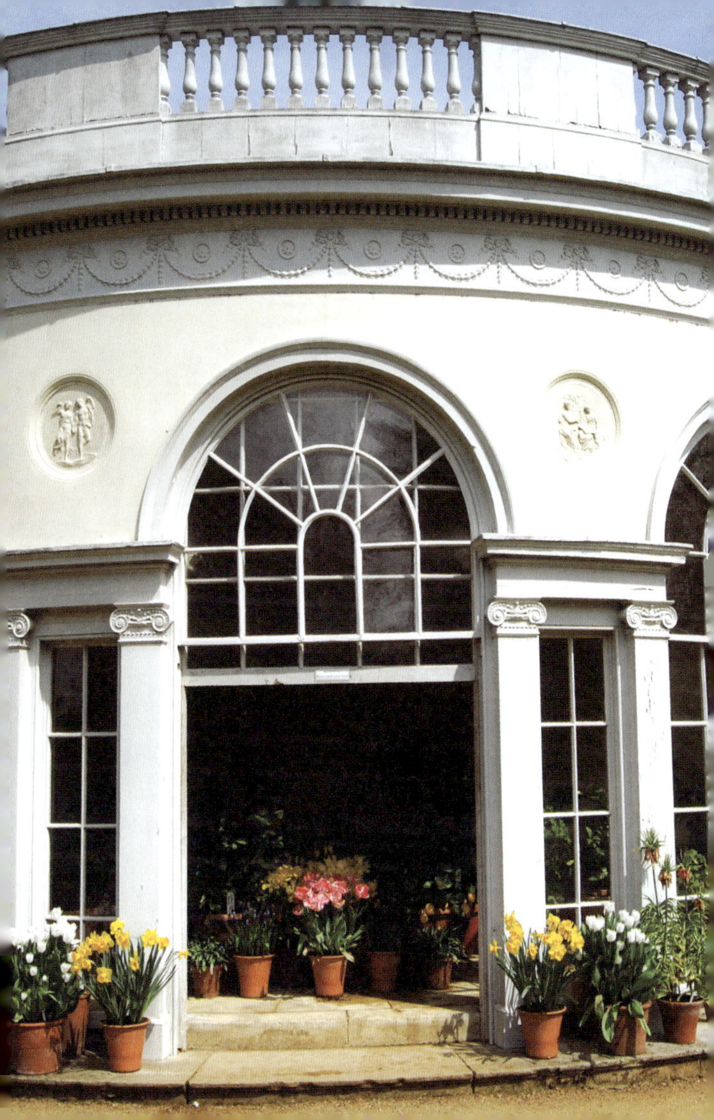

Outer London

Richmond Park

Richmond, Surrey, TW10 5HS
Daily 24 hours (except during deer cull season)
0300 061 2200
www.royalparks.org.uk
Travel: Richmond LU & LO
Area: 2,500 acres
Facilities: Golf courses, playgrounds, cafés, kiosk, viewpoint

Like a beautiful open gym and recreation centre, Richmond Park is an ideal place for cross-country running, hill walking, cycling, horse-riding and picnicking; all of which take place within the expanse of this Royal Park on the edge of south-west London. However, it's the deer that are the biggest draw for the legions of visitors. Red and fallow deer have grazed this land for centuries, and now have signs allowing them right of way across the roads that cut through the park. Some may be skittish but the majority are so used to humans that you'll often find them hanging around close to the edges of the running, cycling or strolling paths on any given visit. They've obviously come a long way since they were quarry for the royal court, Charles I having set the area aside for hunting in 1637. The monarch first came to the area in 1625, and holed up in Richmond Palace to escape the plague of that year which killed 35,000 people in London.

Richmond Park Cycle Hire (www.parkcycle.co.uk, tel: 07050 209249) rents out two-wheelers for anyone wishing to take to the paths that surround the park. For sporty types, there is an area of grassland to the north of Roehampton Gate, with three winter rugby pitches, although at weekends it's hired out exclusively to Rosslyn Park Rugby Football Club. The park has fishing ponds and two 18-hole golf courses, as well as riding stables. Richmond Park is also popular with lycra clad cyclists seeking a place to exert themselves away from London's busy roads.

A designated Site of Special Scientific Interest and a Natural Nature Reserve, the park consists of meadows, open lawns, lush tree-lined paths and woodland. The park's central Isabella Plantation is a gorgeous organically run woodland garden with rich plant life. Here you will find an enclosed playground, wooden bridges, streams, benches and shaded grassy areas that are perfect in the height of the summer and make for a relaxing haven in an already tranquil part of outer London.

Sustenance can be found at the Pembroke Lodge Café. This is a Georgian mansion, set within landscaped grounds, that was once the home of Bertrand Russell.

Horse carriage rides take place in the winter (advance booking required), and in the area near Richmond station you can walk along the Thames or stop off in any of the pubs or restaurants close by. If you want more order to your visit there are free walks organised by the Friends of Richmond Park (www.frp.org.uk).

Although well preserved, there's a nice rugged feel to the park that's missing from more pristine royal spaces like Regent's Park. Other nearby alternatives to Richmond are Kew Botanical Gardens (see page 275), Hampton Court Palace and Gardens (see page 269), Bushy Park (see page 212) and Syon Park and Gardens (see page 280).

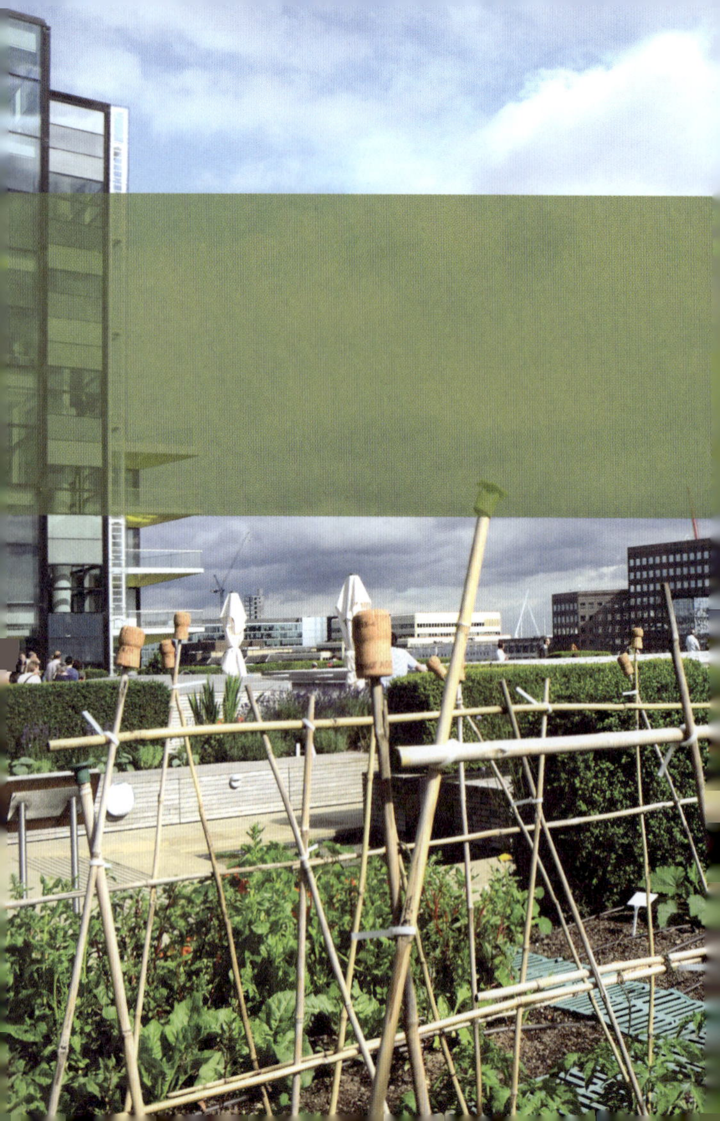

GARDENS & SQUARES

Open Gardens Weekend

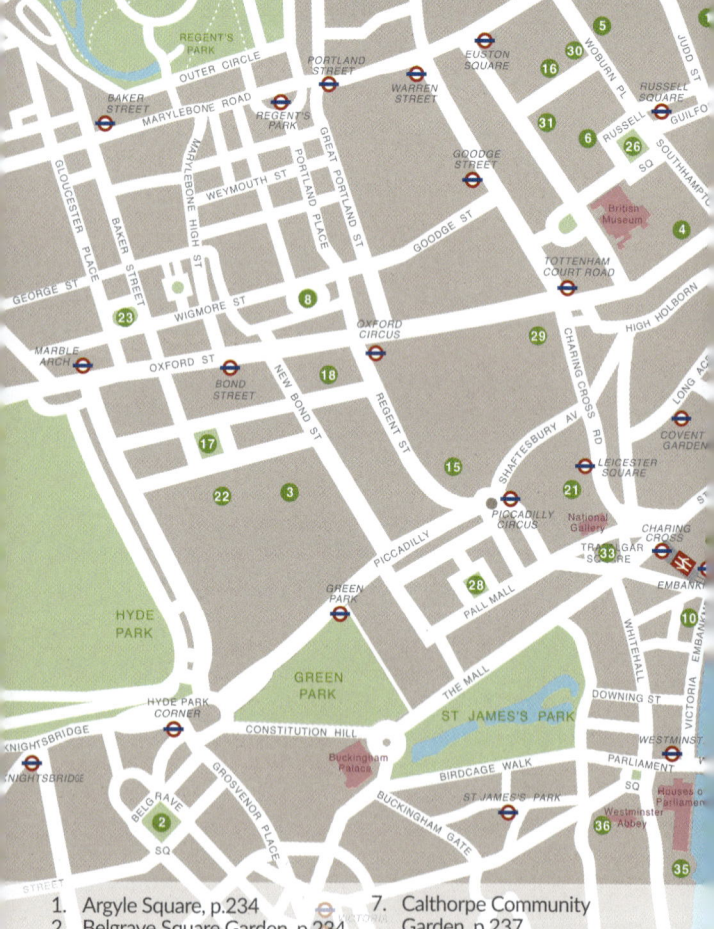

1. Argyle Square, p.234
2. Belgrave Square Garden, p.234
3. Berkeley Square, p.234
4. Bloomsbury Square, p.235
5. British Medical Association Garden, p.235
6. Brunei Gallery SOAS Roof Garden, p.237
7. Calthorpe Community Garden, p.237
8. Cavendish Square, p.237
9. Charterhouse Square, p.238
10. Devonshire Square, p.238
11. Draper's Hall Garden, p.238
12. Embankment Gardens, p.239
13. Finsbury Circus Garden, p.239

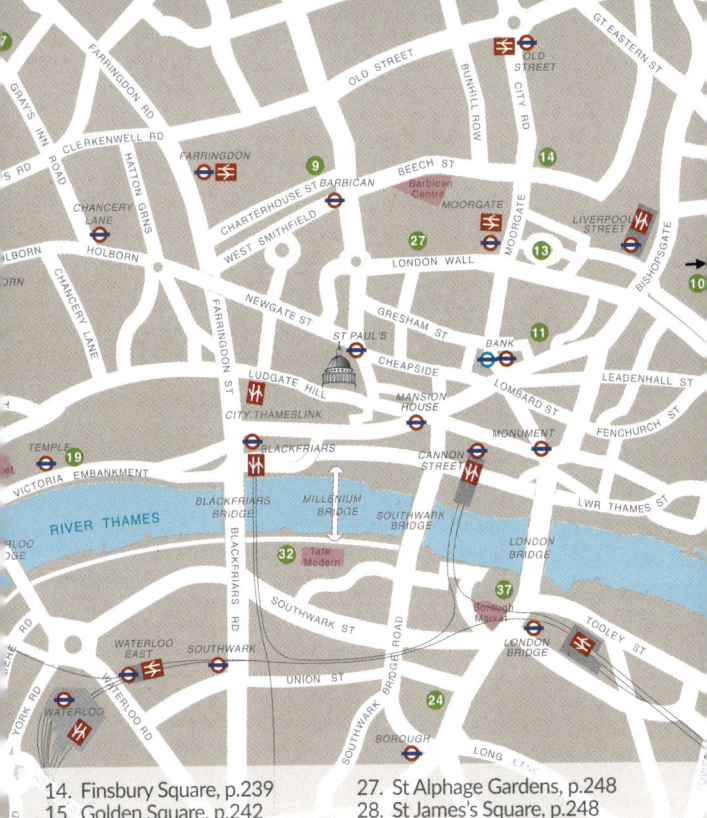

14. Finsbury Square, p.239
15. Golden Square, p.242
16. Gordon Square, p.242
17. Grosvenor Square, p.243
18. Hanover Square, p.243
19. Inner Temple Garden, p.243
20. Jubilee Gardens, p.244
21. Leicester Square, p.244
22. Mount Street Gardens, p.244
23. Portman Square, p.245
24. Red Cross Garden, .p.245
25. Red Lion Square, p.247
26. Russell Square, p.247
27. St Alphage Gardens, p.248
28. St James's Square, p.248
29. Soho Square, p.248
30. Tavistock Square, p.249
31. Torrington Square, p.249
31. Tate Modern Garden, p.249
32. Torrington Square, p.249
33. Trafalgar Square, p.250
34. Tradescant Garden, p.250
35. Victoria Tower Gardens, p.251
36. Westminster Abbey College Gardens, p.251
37. Southwark Cathedral Churchyard, p.258

GARDENS & SQUARES

This book would not be complete without some attention being paid to London's many squares and gardens. These small areas are not as dramatic or grand as the Royal Parks, but they are perhaps more useful, offering little oases of calm amid the capital's noise and chaos. Cavendish Square is a great example of how beneficial such a green space can be – just a few minutes from Oxford Circus and yet offering grass lawns, trees and benches to the weary shoppers and office workers of the area.

Although gardens and squares provide the same vital service they vary greatly in their origins. The public gardens of London are the product of historical accident and differ as much in shape as they do in age. In contrast the squares of London are a creation of Georgian and Regency architecture and planning. The late 18th century was the time of London's expansion under the management of the landed gentry who developed vast areas of land in the Georgian style complete with elegant squares. John Nash continued this process with the patronage of the Crown. Most of London's squares either date from this period or are built with reference to it.

London's gardens and squares are among its greatest assets and are a vital part of what makes London unique as a world city. Some of London's 600 gardens and squares are reviewed in the following pages, but we cannot hope to be comprehensive. The annual Open Gardens Weekend draws attention to the contribution that London's garden squares make to the capital's culture and environment and is a great opportunity to explore some of the squares that are not usually open to the public.

London Open Gardens

Mid-June annually
londongardenstrust.org

Run by the London Parks and Gardens Trust, this is the one weekend when many of London's private garden squares and other gardens open their gates to the public. A number of special activities take place in over 200 gardens which range from traditional or historical to experimental spaces, with around 25 of London's boroughs taking part.

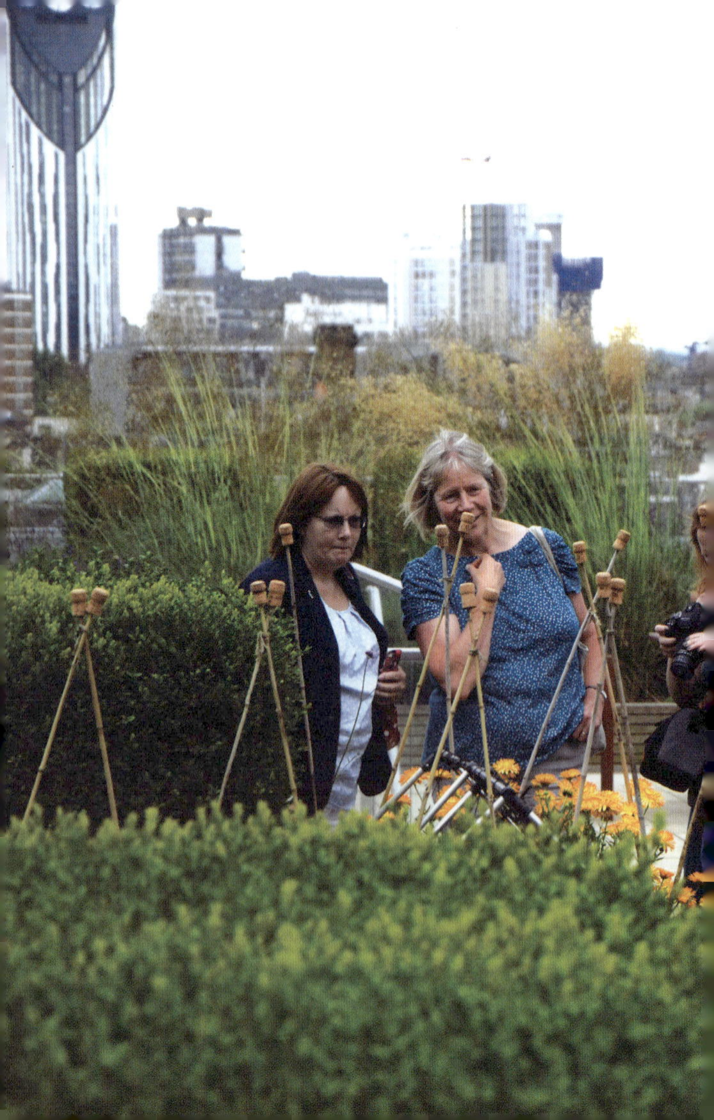

Open Gardens Weekend

CENTRAL

Argyle Square, WC1H 8AL
Travel: King's Cross St Pancreas LU & Rail
Way back in the late 18th-century, this area was simply a field which had become a repository for the rubbish of the nearby city and so a mountainous dust heap accumulated which became a famous landmark. In the 19th-century the pattern of roads that exists today was built, but the area never escaped its seedy reputation and was for many years renowned for prostitution. It was in the late 20th-century that the area was finally redeveloped and this pleasant square created, complete with a basketball court and enough trees and benches to make it a great place of escape from the traffic of nearby King's Cross.

Belgrave Square Garden, SW1X 8PA
Travel: Hyde Park LU
This circular garden in the middle of Belgrave Square has been restored to its original 19th-century layout with wisteria, roses and passion flowers. The garden is private and can only be accessed with a key, but it does participate in the London Open Gardens Weekend (see page 231) as well as hosting occasional events such as cinema nights which allow access to the general public.

Berkeley Square, W1J 5AD
Travel: Green Park LU
Named after Lord Berkeley of Stratton, a Civil War commander, this Mayfair enclave was built on the gardens of Devonshire House. It has a central garden of maple trees planted in the late 18th century. Famous residents of the area have included Winston Churchill, Horace Walpole and PG Wodehouse's comic creation, Bertie Wooster.

Bloomsbury Square, WC1A 2NS
Travel: Holborn or Russell Square LU

A green flag award winner, this is London's oldest square. It has kept some of its Georgian charm, with many fine surrounding buildings – although none of them are original. The square itself is large with a broad paved area, lawns, a good selection of trees and plenty of benches. It's a great place to relax on a fine day when you've been shopping in Holborn. The most prominent feature of the square is the monument to Whig politician Charles James Fox which was erected in 1816. There is also a blue plaque to Sir Hans Sloane, the benefactor of the British Museum, in the north-east corner of the square.

British Medical Association Council Garden, WC1 9HP
Travel: Russell Square LU

This garden is tucked away behind the south wing of BMA House and medicinal plants are a feature of the planting. One of the walls has a plaque surrounded by stones from the foundation of the house that Dickens lived in from 1851-1860, and where he wrote *Bleak House*, *Hard Times* and *Great Expectations*. Call to find out the times for tours of the garden and talks on its plants and history.

Brunei Gallery / SOAS Roof Garden

Brunei Gallery
SOAS Roof Gardens, WC1B 5DQ
Travel: Russell Square LU
Opposite the main entrance to the School of Oriental and African Studies, the Brunei Gallery has a Japanese-style roof garden that was developed in 2001. Open in conjunction with the gallery, the garden is dedicated to Forgiveness.

Calthorpe Community Garden, WC1X 8LH
Travel: King's Cross St Pancreas LU
A community gardening resource set around a purpose-built day centre and meeting venue. The central building's large verandas lead to the landscaped community gardens where activities such as planting, weeding and composting take place. The organisation involves local schools in the maintenance of the garden as part of a series of ongoing community projects. There's also a 5-a-side football pitch on the site.

Cavendish Square, W1G 0LA
Travel: Oxford Circus LU
This square was laid out for the 2nd Earl of Oxford in 1717 and is a small circular patch of green just to the north of Oxford Circus. On fine days the square is packed with people catching some sun. Past residents of the square include Lord Nelson. Below the square is a large underground car park.

Gardens & Squares

Charterhouse Square, EC1M 6AN
Travel: Barbican LU

The former site of Charterhouse School, the square was built between 1700-1775. It still contains a few Georgian brick houses, some with their original ironwork and doorways. In 2014 workers on the Cross Rail transport project discovered evidence here of a large burial plot for plague victims dating from the mid 14th century. Just next to the square is the Charterhouse Museum which is one of the most interesting museums in the capital and well worth a visit.

Devonshire Square, EC2M 4WQ
Travel: Liverpool Street LU & Rail

This square still has a few of its original Georgian houses. It is one of the few quiet spaces around Liverpool Street and Aldgate and a great haven if you want to escape the crowds, although those in search of vegetation will be disappointed as the square is paved. Events like the World Food Festival take place here during the summer along with performances by live bands.

Drapers' Hall Garden, EC2N 2DQ
Travel: Bank LU

These gardens are behind Drapers' Hall in Throgmorton Street, and represent only a small area of what once stretched all the way to London Wall. Although diminished in size the present gardens are still home to long established mulberry trees, one of which was planted by the late Queen in 1955 and another by that royal lover of shrubbery, Prince Charles, in 1971. The garden is not open to the public but does participate in the Open House and Open Gardens Weekend (see page 231).

Gardens & Squares

Embankment Gardens, WC2N 6PB
Including Victoria Embankment Gardens, Middle Temple Gardens and Whitehall Gardens
Travel: Temple, Embankment LU

The Embankment Gardens are little known treasures extending along the north bank of the Thames and serving as an archipelago of calm amid the noise of central London. Middle Temple Gardens are just behind the Strand and directly outside Temple underground station. It is a relatively small space, but has lots of flower beds and mature trees as well as some fine monuments. Victoria Embankment Gardens is just in front of Embankment station and is a grand affair with many monuments and a very good café. Whitehall Gardens lies beyond Northumberland Avenue and is perhaps the most beautiful of the gardens with three striking monuments and a great deal of lush plants and trees. In the summer there are deckchairs and a bandstand with live events.

Finsbury Circus Garden, EC2M 1NB
Travel: Moorgate LU/Rail

One of the largest open spaces in the City, this circular garden is surrounded by modern, high-tech architecture. Although the garden is rather sparse it does have a central bowling green, live bands in the summer and the City's only Japanese Pagoda tree.

Finsbury Square, EC2A 1AE
Travel: Moorgate LU/Rail

This large square is located just off City Road and close to the busy Old Street roundabout. The area is now largely composed of modern office blocks but there are a few original Georgian buildings on the square. There's also the famous Bunhill Fields Burial Grounds just opposite, where many famous non-conformists are buried including Daniel Defoe, John Bunyan and William Blake.

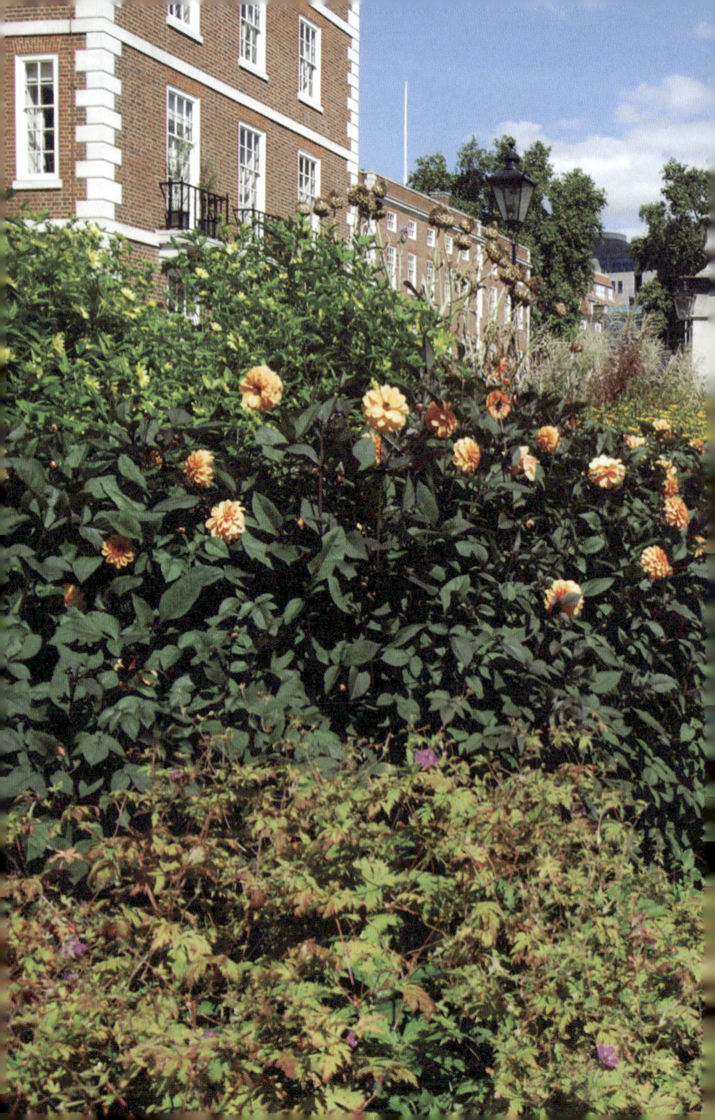

Inner Temple Garden

Golden Square, W1F 9AA

Travel: Piccadilly Circus LU

Once known as Gelding's Close, this square was built between 1670 and 1700. It lies just north of Piccadilly, and is a great place to escape from the crowds of Regent Street. The square itself is small and attractive with a few modest flower beds, a considerable expanse of paving, and a good number of benches. There is a monument to George II which was erected during his reign. Charles Dickens refers to Golden Square in *Nicholas Nickleby*.

Gordon Square, WC1H 0AG

Travel: Russell Square, Goodge Street LU

This was originally a private square for residents, with a number of the surrounding houses once occupied by the Bloomsbury Group of British intellectuals, philosophers and artists. Since 2006 the square has been owned by the University of London whose offices now occupy the surrounding grand buildings. Gordon Square is open to the public with a large expanse of lawn and plenty of mature trees surrounding its borders. Another important feature of the square is the wonderful Momo's Garden Café that offers delicious vegetarian fare and great coffee from a tiny kiosk at the entrance.

Gray's Inn Gardens, WC1R 5ET

Travel: Holborn & Chancery Lane LU

Known as 'The Walks', the pretty Gray's Inn gardens were laid out by Sir Francis Bacon in 1606. Todays sloping banks are where a high wall and privet hedges once stood. Red oaks and London planes are the dominant trees lining the paths today.

Gardens & Squares

Grosvenor Square, W1K 2HD
Travel: Bond Street LU

The second largest square in London (after Russell Square), this area was designed and constructed between 1725-1731 by the Grosvenor Estate. The square is close to Oxford Street, but the lawns are dotted by tall trees with benches along the paths, making this a peaceful retreat from the bustle of central London. The square's most famous feature was the United States Embassy that dominated the western end for many years until it moved to Nine Elms in 2017, but the monuments dedicated to the Eagle Squadron and three American presidents still remain as a reminder of the square's special relationship with America. The site is currently under development as a smart hotel that will not require the high security barriers and security that once dominated the square.

Hanover Square, W1S 1HA
Travel: Oxford Circus LU

The first of the Mayfair squares, Hanover Square is modest in size but lush and well maintained. It has Oxford Street to the north and Regent's Street to the east and is a great place to escape both busy thoroughfares. The square is home to the statue of the British Prime Minister, William Pitt the Younger.

Inner Temple Garden, EC4Y 7HL
Travel: Temple LU

This fine garden dates from the 12th century and derives its name from the Knights Templar residence that stood here. The gated garden offers well-maintained herbaceous borders, roses, a fountain and fine trees surrounded by grand gothic buildings that serve as lawyers' chambers and apartments. The garden can only be entered from the main gate opposite Crown Row Office. There are several other gardens along the Embankment (see page 239).

Gardens & Squares

Jubilee Gardens, SE1 8XX
Travel: Waterloo LU

This garden was established in 1977 to commemorate the late Queen's Silver Jubilee. It is next to the London Eye and during the summer serves as a music venue. The garden has undergone a huge refurbishment since 2012 and features a modern under-11's children's playground, new paths, flowerbeds and seating.

Leicester Square, WC2H 7DE
Travel: Leicester Square LU

Famous for its cinema complexes and movie premières, Leicester Square got its name from the second Earl of Leicester, who bought the land in 1630. It is one of the best known of London's squares and a popular rendezvous point. For this reason it is not a quiet place but a hive of activity with crowds, buskers and just a few token trees overshadowed by the cinema hoardings. Artist William Hogarth lived on the square and there's a bust of him as well as statues of Sir Isaac Newton, William Shakespeare and Charlie Chaplin.

Mount Street Gardens, W1K 3AH
Travel: Green Park LU

Song thrushes, crows, goldcrests, blackbirds and magpies are some of the birds that nest at Mount Street Gardens, which is a peaceful retreat from the busy Mayfair surroundings. The gardens are well kept, and you're likely to see staff cutting and trimming the grass on any daytime visit here. Visitors are also kept in order with signs warning against loud music, alcohol, cycling, squirrel feeding and ball games. All the benches in the garden have been donated, mostly by Americans associated with the US Embassy that stood on Grosvenor Square until 2017. A nice feature is the palm trees that are dotted around the area.

Gardens & Squares

Myddelton Square, EC1R 1XX
Travel: Angel LU
The square is in the grounds of St Mark's Church, but is open to the public. It contains a playground for children, shrubs, mature trees and plenty of benches. A great refuge from Islington's crowds.

Pimlico Gardens, SW1V 3LA
Travel: Pimlico LU
This lush little space on the banks of the Thames is close to Vauxhall Bridge. It contains seating, a drinking fountain and a monument to William Huskisson – the Victorian politician who was killed by a train (George Stephenson's *Rocket*) having just opened the Liverpool to Manchester railway line.

Portman Square, W1H 7BG
Travel: Marble Arch LU
This square was developed in the late 18th century. The two and a half acre site includes well maintained hedges, shrubs and trees as well as a children's play area. It has long been associated with the homes of dukes, earls and viscounts and was once the site of the Courtauld Institute. The square is private and only accessible for residents of the area.

Red Cross Garden, SE1 1HA
Travel: Borough LU
This small community garden and the charming cottages that stand beside it are the work of Victorian philanthropist Octavia Hill. The cottages and garden are now run by a trust and have been restored to their original splendour with serpentine paths, benches, carefully planted borders and a pond. Even in the middle of winter this is a peaceful place to stop and relax, just a stones throw from Borough High Street and the busy market.

Russell Square

Gardens & Squares

Red Lion Square, W1R 4HQ
Travel: Holborn LU
Named after a Holborn inn, this square was laid out in 1684. Although much has changed in the area, the square remains a pleasant green space with lots of trees and shrubs and plenty of benches. Located just north of High Holborn and within walking distance of Oxford Street, it's a great place to evade the crowds. There are several monuments within the square including one to the philosopher Bertrand Russell, who was once a local resident.

Riverside Walk Gardens, SW1P 4RP
Travel: Pimlico LU
This garden was redesigned in 2004 with meandering paths, fibre-optic lighting and a Henry Moore sculpture entitled *Locking Piece*. The resulting garden is minimalist in style and offers great views of the Thames.

Russell Square, WC1B 5BA
Travel: Russell Square LU
The largest of London's Georgian squares was built on the grounds of Bedford House in 1800. Its landmark building is the huge terracotta-bricked and elaborately styled Russell Hotel. The square's café is popular with local office workers who flock here for alfresco lunches. The square's other attractions include a central water fountain and a rather grand statue of the Duke of Bedford. In 2003 Russell Square was given a major refurbishment with improvements made to the fountain and new railings fitted. Author T.S. Eliot worked for nearly forty years for publishers Faber and Faber in Russell Square. In the mid 1930s his wife Vivien, from whom he had separated, paraded outside the office with a sandwich board saying 'I am the wife that T.S. Eliot abandoned'. These days the square is more famous for being a location for the BBC's *Sherlock* series.

Gardens & Squares

St Alphage Gardens, EC2V 7WS
Travel: Mansion House LU
This was once a churchyard and is now a public garden with the added attraction of a large chunk of the Roman City Wall as a feature. The garden is a relatively narrow strip, built on two levels. The grass areas are lined with flower beds and benches with wooden steps leading to a lower garden and further on a small herb garden.

St James's Square, SW1Y 4JU
Travel: Piccadilly Circus LU
Laid out in the 1670s, this is one of London's oldest squares. It is small but well maintained and ideal for escaping the noise and traffic of Piccadilly. The square contains an imposing statue of William III astride a horse.

Soho Square, W1D 3AP
Travel: Tottenham Court Road LU
Soho Square is a popular green space with the office and shop workers of the area. On summer days it is often hard to find space to sit. The square has stayed pretty much the same since the 1920s, with the paths and grass plots arranged around a central area where a statue of Charles II stands. The singer Kirsty MacColl wrote a song about the square and a bench has been placed here in her memory.

Tavistock Square, WC1H 9BQ
Travel: Russell Square LU
This fine square was built by James Burton and Thomas Cubitt between 1803-26. Since those times the park's trees have reached maturity providing the contemporary visitor with plenty of shade. The square is associated with pacifism with a monument to Mahatma Ghandi and a large stone commemorating conscientious objectors.

Gardens & Squares

Tate Modern Garden, SE1 9JE
Travel: Blackfriars Rail
Close to the Tate Modern, this garden on the south bank of the Thames has a central plaza, a lawn with birch trees and terraces surrounded by hedges.

Torrington Square, WC1E 7JL
Travel: Russell Square & Euston LU
Another square owned by the University of London, Torrington is essentially an elongated space with gravel paths broken up by plots of grass and ivy. Edged by Birkbeck College and the Student Union, it also has the large Art Deco style School of African and Oriental Studies building in the distance. There's a café kiosk at the Byng Place end, and every Thursday a farmer's market pitches up on the square from 9am-2pm.

Trafalgar Square, WC2N 5DN
Travel: Charing Cross LU & Rail
This square was laid out by John Nash in the 1820s and named to commemorate Nelson's victory at the Battle of Trafalgar (1805). Since that time the square has become a national meeting place where crowds gather to celebrate or protest. The area is dominated by Nelson's Column but there are many other monuments, mainly to commemorate great military men such as Sir Henry Havelock. Relatively new developments to the north side of the area feature a large piazza in front of the National Gallery, replacing a busy road. Traffic is still very heavy around the square but it remains a pleasant place to visit if only to have a look at the monuments. In the north-west corner, the fourth plinth stood empty from 1841 to 1999. It is now a dedicated site for showing contemporary works of art by national and international artists. Big names whose work has been featured include Antony Gormley, Yinka Shonibare, Thomas Schütte and Marc Quinn.

Gardens & Squares

The Tradescant Garden at the Garden Museum, SE1 7LB
Transport: Vauxhall or Lambeth North LU

The long disused Lambeth church that holds the grave of Captain Bligh has a garden at the back dedicated to the 17th-century father and son gardening duo (both called John Tradescant). The garden is laid out in geometric style with plants of that period and contains the tomb of the Tradescent family. The Garden Museum (www.gardenmuseum.org.uk) is a fascinating place for the green fingered with regular exhibitions and one of London's best cafés.

Victoria Tower Gardens, SW1P 3SF
Travel: Westminster LU

This large public garden stands between the Houses of Parliament and Lambeth Bridge. It contains a number of fine statues including a cast of Rodin's *Burghers of Calais*. It is a great place to enjoy some peace from the traffic and crowds of Whitehall. Although interrupted by Parliament, Tower Gardens can be considered a continuation of the Embankment Gardens which extend along the Thames to the east (see page 239).

Waterloo Millennium Green, SE1 7AA
Travel: Waterloo LU & Rail

This inner city green sits opposite the Old Vic Theatre in Waterloo, at the corner of Waterloo Road and Baylis Road. Once a run-down adventure playground, it was redesigned for the millennium and has become a firm favourite with office workers and locals when the weather is fine. It now features a fountain, wildflower and marsh gardens as well as a children's playground. The area is surrounded by mature trees which helps visitors forget the surrounding busy roads. This popular green space was given a Green Flag award in 2020-1.

Westminster Abbey College Gardens, SW1P 3PA
Travel: St James's Park or Westminster LU
The garden of the famous medieval monastery was historically used to grow food and medicinal plants, also providing a peaceful place for the monks. Today's garden has a 17th-century style knot garden, a fig and mulberry tree and four statues of the Apostles which date from 1686.

Wilmington Square, WC1X 0EB
Travel: Angel LU
A garden square with rose bushes, a 19th-century pavilion, a bird feeding station and an annual bedding display.

Woburn Square, WC1H 0AA
Travelt: Russell Square & Euston LU
Opposite Gordon Square and parallel with Torrington Square, the smaller Woburn Square is a lush little enclave with a summer house, children's playground, mature plane trees, shrubbery and a lawn.

SACRED TO THE MEMORY
OF M. ELIZABETH WRIGHT, THE WIFE OF REAR ADMIRAL PUGH
WHO DIED APRIL 12 1818 IN THE 30 YEAR OF HER AGE

HER SPIRIT SOAR'D TO HEAVEN, THAT BLEST DOMAIN
WHERE VIRTUE ONLY CAN ITS MEED OBTAIN
ALL THE GREAT DUTIES SHE PERFORM'D THRO LIFE
THOSE OF A CHILD, A PARENT AND A WIFE

The Tradescant Garden at the Garden Museum

Gardens & Squares

NORTH

Culpeper Community Garden, N1 0EG
Travel: Angel LU

Named after the 17th century botanist, herbalist and astrologer Nicholas Culpeper, this is a green oasis in the heart of Islington. Formerly a derelict site, it was developed in 1982 by the local community. It is now an organic garden with numerous plots, a pond, lawn, rose pergola and wildlife area.

Gardens & Squares

WEST

Cadogan Place Gardens, SW1X 1PQ
Travel: Sloane Square LU
This fine garden dates from the 18th century and still has some of its original trees including mulberry trees. The garden is private but participates in the London Open Gardens Weekend (see page 231).

Cleveland Gardens, W2 6DE
Travel: Bayswater LU
A quiet public garden surrounded by Bayswater's grand white stucco houses. Inside is a Japanese garden and children's play area, which springs into activity during the summer. Plum, plane and cherry trees are found within the garden.

Courtfield Gardens East, SW5 0LZ
Travel: Earl's Court LU
A deep sunken garden with a miniature bog, vibrant ornamental flowerbeds and an adjoining garden area to the west. The garden is private but participates in the London Open Gardens Weekend (see page 231).

Ennismore Gardens, SW7 1JA
Travel: Knightsbridge LU
A short walk from Hyde Park and Kensington Gardens, this is a pleasant little green space. It contains an ornamental urn to commemorate Hollywood icon Ava Gardner, who lived for a time in nearby Ennismore Square.

Gardens & Squares

Ladbroke Square, W11 3LX
Travel: Notting Hill Gate LU
The rectangular garden between Ladbroke Grove and Kensington Park Road is the largest of a series of tucked away green squares in the W11 area. It was the original site of the 19th-century Hippodrome Racecourse, which is now commemorated in nearby Hippodrome Place. The garden is private but participates in the London Open Gardens Weekend (see page 231).

Queen's Gate Gardens, SW7 4PB
Travel: Gloucester Road LU
This fine Victorian garden is not far from the Natural History Museum. There are visible circles in the lawn that mark the site of underground bomb shelters from WW2. The garden is private but participates in the Open Gardens Weekend (see page 231).

Rembrandt Gardens, W2 1XB
Travel: Warwick Avenue LU
A well-tended little garden that overlooks the Regent's Canal at Little Venice. The garden has plenty of picnic tables from where you can enjoy the slow procession of narrow boats.

John Madejski Garden at the Victoria and Albert Museum, SW7 2RL
Travel: South Kensington LU
What was once the Pirelli Garden at the V&A Museum was revamped as the John Madejski Garden in 2005. The title is in honour of the English businessman who gave £2 million to the V&A. Located at the heart of this grand museum it is essentially an Italianate-style courtyard with grass lawns, stone paving, water jets, lemon trees and excellent night lighting created by Patrick Woodroffe. The garden offers a welcome escape from the crowds of the V&A.

John Madejski Garden

Gardens & Squares

South

Bonnington Square, SW8 1TE
Travel: Vauxhall LU/Rail
More a garden than a square, this quirky re-claimed bombsite was created by garden designers Dan Pearson and James Fraser in 1994, along with other local residents. It includes a 30-foot water wheel planted with wisteria, a boat, a walnut tree and tropical plant beds. It's known locally as the 'Pleasure Garden'.

Harleyford Road Community Garden, SW8 1TF
Travel: Vauxhall LU/Rail
Close to the Oval cricket ground, these gardens sprang up in 1984, when local residents started growing vegetables on the one and a half acres of wasteland. The garden now has a wildlife area, pond and children's play area. You can take a short cut from here through to Bonnington Square.

Southwark Cathedral Churchyard, SE1 9DA
Travel: London Bridge LU/Rail
This garden is to the east of Southward Cathedral and is open to the public during the day but closes in the evenings. It contains a sunken lawn, liquid amber trees, and shrubs. The herb garden is often used by the cathedral's education centre and local schools visit to study the use of plants in medicine. The Cathedral has emphasised its connection with William Shakespeare in recent years and in 2020 a statue of the Bard by Raphael Maklouf was erected here. The garden backs on to Borough Market, the most popular food market in London.

Bonnington Square

Museum of the Home Herb Garden

Gardens & Squares

EAST

Museum of the Home Gardens, E2 8EA
Travel: Hoxton LO

The Museum of the Home is one of east London's hidden gems. Dedicated to English interior design, the museum occupies the almshouse established in the will of Sir Robert Geffrye in the early 18th century. There are lawns in front of the Museum, but one of the main attractions is the walled and gated herb garden. This was opened in 1992, having been created on a formerly derelict site next to the museum. It now boasts a central bronze fountain and twelve beds filled with plants for cosmetic, medicinal, household or kitchen use with over 170 types of herbs as well as roses, honeysuckles and lilies. In addition, there is a sequence of small period gardens, arranged chronologically, which reflect the museum's historic interiors. If you need refreshment after your exertions there is a good café and restaurant within the museum.

Ropemakers' Field, E14 8BX
Travel: Limehouse DLR

At the eastern end of the Regent's Canal, within a minute's walk of Limehouse Basin, lies this green space. The area was for centuries associated with London's maritime trade and its name derives from the many rope making workshops that existed here. The space is well designed with plenty of park benches and a children's playground. It's a great place to catch your breath after a walk along the canal.

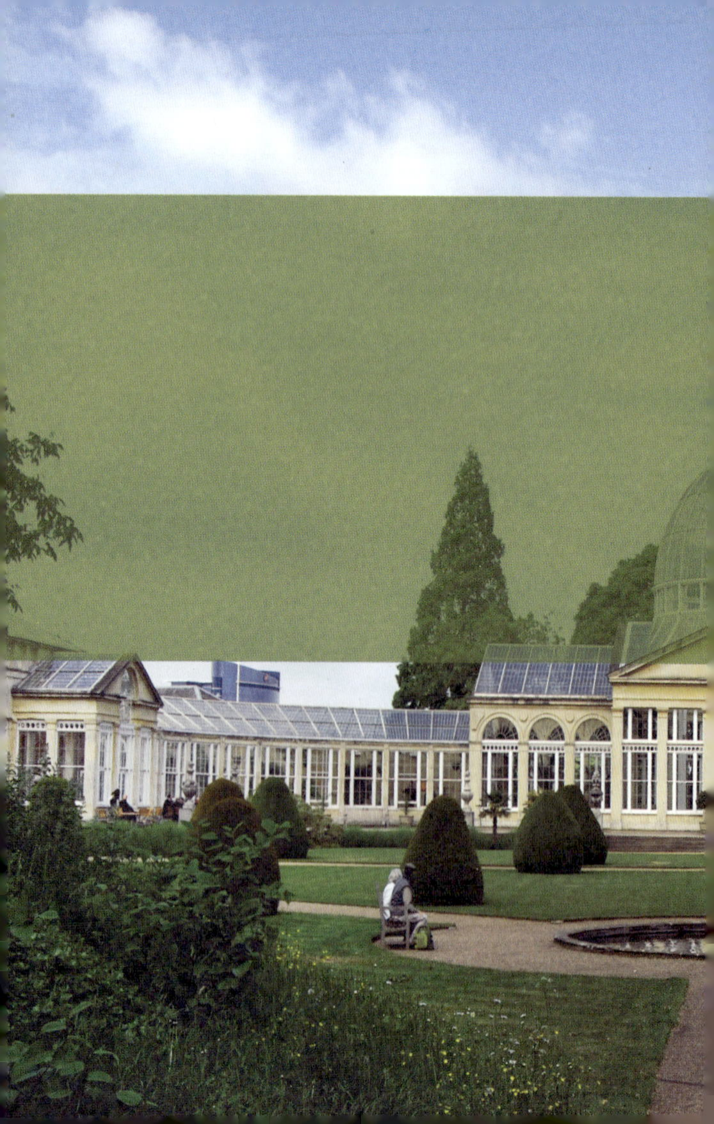

OTHER GREEN SPACES
- Gated Parks & Gardens
- Commons
- Roof Gardens

Syon Park

GATED PARKS & GARDENS

Chelsea Physic Garden.................. 267
Hampton Court Gardens................ 269
London Wetland Centre............... 273
Royal Botanic Gardens, Kew........... 275
Syon Park and Gardens 280

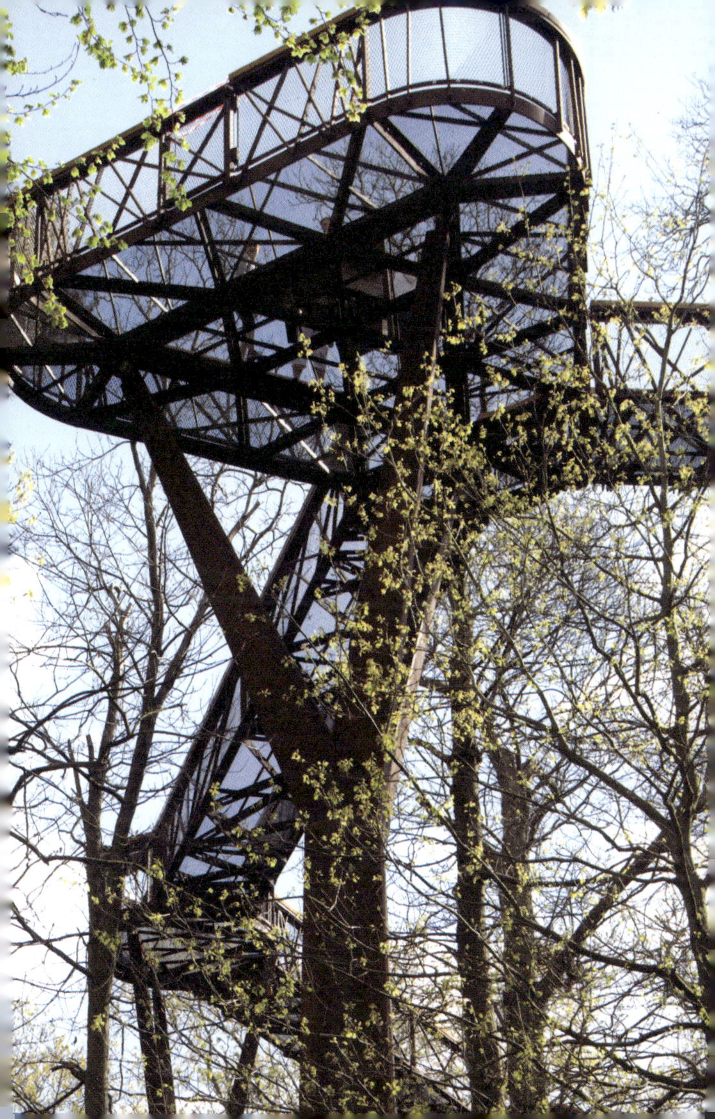

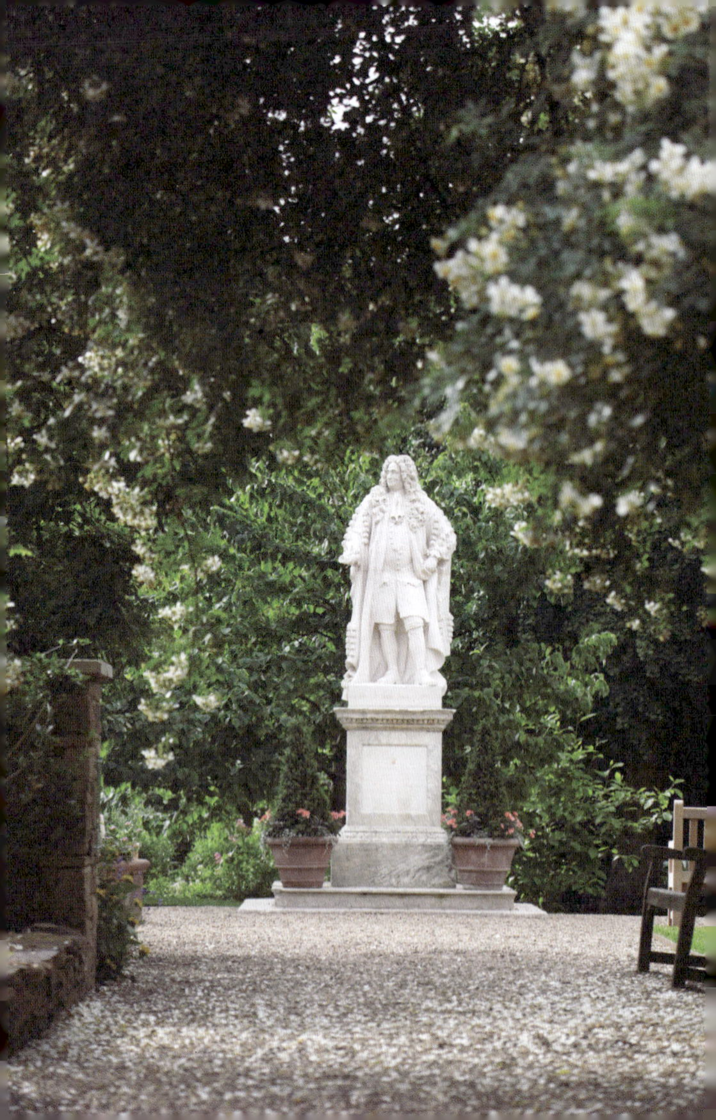

Gated Parks & Gardens

Chelsea Physic Garden

66 Royal Hospital Road, SW3 4HS
Sun-Fri 11:00-17:00
020 7352 5646
www.chelseaphysicgarden.co.uk
Travel: Sloane Square LU
Area: 4 acres
Admission: £12.50

Established in 1673, the Chelsea Physic Garden is the second oldest botanical garden in the UK (the University of Oxford Botanical Garden beats it by half a century). The garden was founded by the Apothecaries' Company as a place for training their apprentices. Cotton seeds grown on the grounds were shipped to Georgia in 1732 for use in America's cotton industry.

Today this botanical garden also offers regular walks, dance and story-telling sessions for children, resident poets, a teahouse café and lawns for relaxing or picnicking. Wonderfully knowledgeable staff conduct tours of the garden, revealing uses of plants for medicine, digestion and perfumes. Another option is to listen to plant information via the garden's audio system.

The garden holds a broad collection of medicinal plants from the tropical and sub-tropical Mediterranean regions and the Canary Islands. The newly created ethnobotanical garden of world medicine shows how different peoples around the world use plants for healing and therapeutic purposes, from Traditional Chinese Medicine to the Aboriginal medicine of Australia.

The garden's south-facing riverside position creates a warm micro-climate that allows the largest outdoor fruiting olive tree in Britain to thrive here. Another claim to fame is the 1817 discovery of forced rhubarb at the site – when rhubarb plants left covered in a bucket developed tender stems and curling yellow leaves, which inspired a legion of copycat gardeners. The statue of botanist and inventor of chocolate, Hans Sloane, takes pride of place in this remarkable garden.

Gated Parks & Gardens

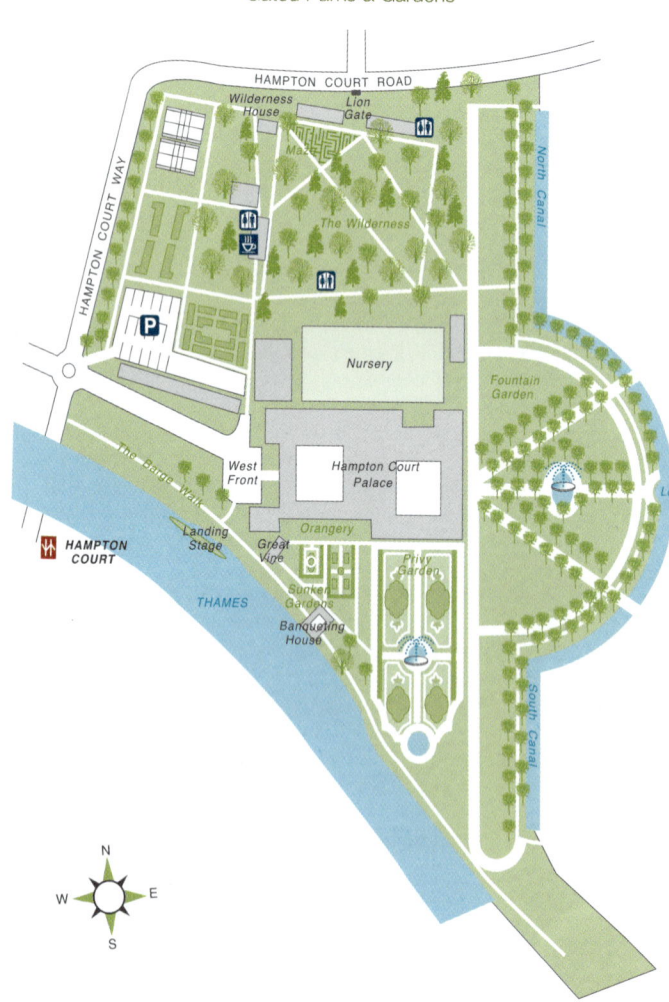

Gated Parks & Gardens

Hampton Court Gardens

East Molesey, Surrey, KT8 9AU
Daily dusk until dawn
020 7352 5646
www.hrp.org.uk
Travel: Hampton Wick Rail
Area: 810 acres

The exceptionally well-coiffured 60 acres of Hampton Court Gardens, with its pristine gardens, arbours, tree-lined walks and woodland areas, surrounds the famous royal palace. With over 500 years of royal history behind it, this is a far more genteel affair than the unkempt expanse of nearby Bushy Park (see page 212).

Displaying a heady mix of Dutch, Italian and French design influences, the gardens date from the 17th century. The riverside gardens include the famous maze with its half a mile of paths and a soundscape, which was installed in spring 2005 – perhaps to calm any visitors who get lost within the surprisingly complex series of hedges. Established in c.1700, this was Britain's first hedge-planted maze and was so well loved that by the time royal gardener Capability Brown came to the palace in the 18th century he was expressly forbidden from making any changes to it. This must have been a frustrating state of affairs given his anti-formal design style and the fact that he lived next to the maze for twenty years. These days the maze attracts somewhere in the region of 300,000 visitors a year who generally take about half an hour to negotiate the labyrinth – although there are a few lost sheep that take a lot longer.

Costumed guides offer free tours of the palace, and there are talks during the summer given by gardeners, housekeepers, flower arrangers and the vine keeper. The latter has a busy time tending the palace's Great Vine, which was planted in 1769, and is the largest in the world at over 120 feet long. It is capable of producing a bumper 600 pounds of black grapes a year, which are sold to visitors. This enterprising spirit is nothing new. Hampton Court has a tradition of grape trading that goes back nearly one hundred

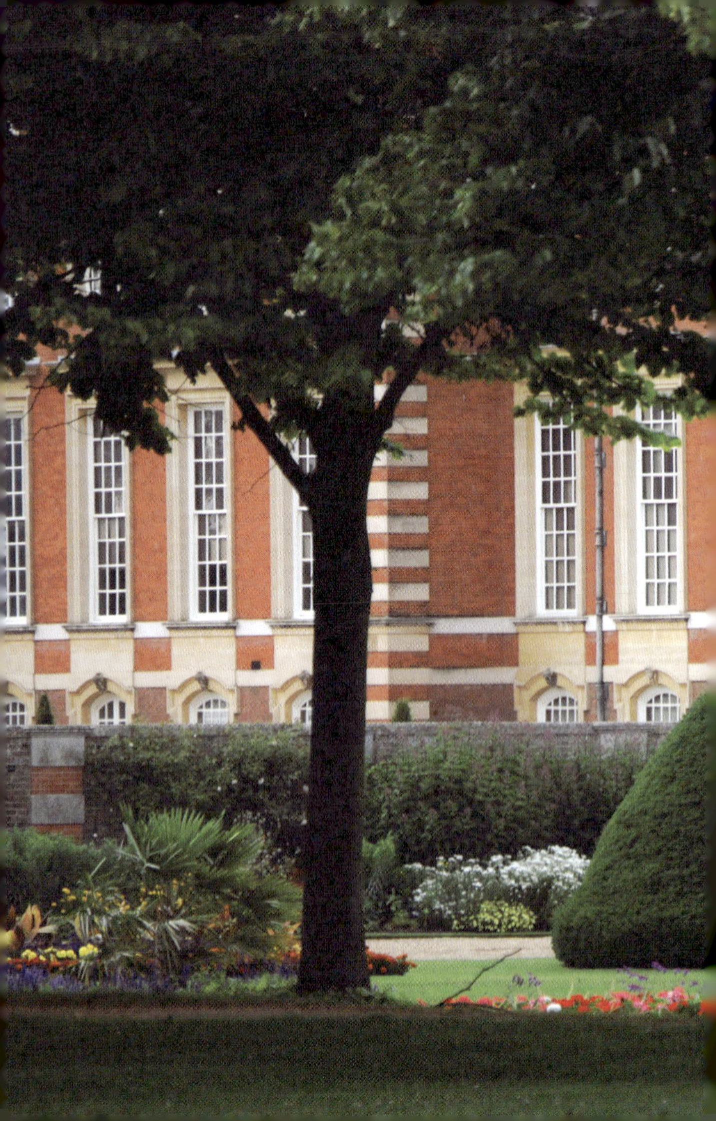

Hampton Court Park

years to King George V's reign. He started sending grapes to hospitals before eventually selling them to palace visitors.

Avenues of lime trees, lakes and a sunken water garden, dating back to Henry VIII's residency, keep up the park's regal appearance. Further attractions include the Fountain Garden, with its neat lines of umbrella-shaped yews and the Long Water – the artificial lake that runs parallel to the Thames. This area forms one of several gardens around the palace. The others include the less formal Northern gardens with mixed hedges and herbaceous borders, the Wilderness and the much-visited Maze, and then there's the South gardens with a series of sunken pond areas, the Knot Garden and the famous Privy Garden. The Privy Garden was completed for William III in 1702 and restored in 1991-1995, using the same varieties of plants that were originally grown there. Beyond the formal gardens lies the extensive parkland, known as Home Park, which is an open area of 750 acres where the royal herd of fallow deer roam.

At one time, entrance to the park and gardens was free. Now that Hampton Court Palace is run as a charity, a fee has been introduced to fund the maintenance necessary to keep the place open to the public. Palace tickets include automatic access to the gardens and maze, although it is still free for those visiting the park areas, but not the palace and the gardens.

Gated Parks & Gardens

London Wetland Centre

Queen Elizabeth Walk, SW13 9WT
020 8409 4400
wwt.org.uk/wetlandcentres/london
Travel: Barnes Rail
Area: 105 acres
Admission: £10-15

One of nine UK conservation centres run by the Wildfowl & Wetland Trust, the London Wetland Centre opened in May 2000, and earned itself a Site of Special Scientific Interest (SSSI) award by 2002. The first project of its kind in the world, its 105 acres have been carved out in an area that's just four miles from central London, and gives its many visitors a chance to observe the growing populations of rare or threatened wildlife that thrive on the site's open water, lakes, mudflats and reedbeds.

The whole area is dotted with various indoor and outdoor features including a function room for corporate events, and a state-of-the-art 3-screen cinema which shows short films about the London Wetland Centre and the work of the WWT. The art gallery is another of the centre's indoor options, displaying work by wildlife and landscape artists with about seven exhibitions a year. Other activities include tours and workshops from bird feeding with a warden to wildlife photography.

Near the edge of the lakes the three-storey Peacock Tower provides a panoramic view of the reserve and the expanse of marshland where wildfowl like wigeon, lapwing and snipe regularly gather. There's also a pristine split-level heated bird airport (or observatory), that gives an excellent view of the main lake and London skyline. The whole area is great for children to run around in but there's also a dedicated playground towards the east of the centre, with underground tunnels to explore.

N
E
S
W
RIVER THAMES
Brentford Ferry Gate
P
Kew Palace
Queen's Garden
Main Entrance
Orangery
Kew Gardens Gallery
Alpine House
Princess of Wales Conservatory
Broad Walk
KEW BRIDGE
Cumberland Gate
KEW GARDENS
Palm House Pond
Palm House
Victoria Gate
Azalea Garden
Rhododendron Dell
Bamboo Garden
Lake
King William's Temple
Temple of Bellona
KEW ROAD
Evolution House
Temperate House
Marianne North Gallery
Woodland Glade
Queen Charlotte's Cottage
Japanese Gateway & Landscape
Pavillion Restaurant
Pagoda
Lion Gate

Gated Parks & Gardens

Royal Botanic Gardens, Kew

Kew, Richmond, TW9 3AB
Opening hours change seasonally (check website)
020 8332 5655
www.kew.org
Travel: Kew Gardens LU & LO
Area: 300 acres
Admission: £14-24

For the last two centuries, gardeners and researchers have converged on this green oasis on the south-west bank of the Thames. The botanical garden was declared a World Heritage Site by Unesco in 2003. Combined with this international reputation, Kew is also a major visitor attraction with artspaces, educational resources and access to the gardens. In addition it offers a year-round programme of festivals and other live events.

The garden's most famous attractions are the Amazonian water lilies, and the plants in the steamy Palm House. This includes the Chilean vine palm, raised from a seed collected in Chile in 1846, and the world's tallest indoor plant. A giant bamboo is said to grow up to a metre a day, and then there's the strychnos tree, which produces a deadly poison used in hospitals to paralyse patients' muscles during surgery. The Temperate House plays host to the world's largest permanent orchid display, with one resident's petals growing to an impressive three feet in length.

The Kew Gardens experience can involve hanging out in a rainforest, strolling down huge tree-lined avenues, stepping through a desert-like landscape or picking your way through student allotments. Containing around ten percent of the world's flowering plant species, it even has its own police force – perhaps as a warning to any light-fingered visitors who are after some cuttings.

There's a lot to see here, which can be a bit daunting if you're considering where to start. Unless you've got something specific that you want to see, it's probably best not to plan, and to stumble across the different features and hidden-away areas as you find them.

Recently, an Opium Poppy field was planted at the Thames end of the gardens – permission was given by the Home Office – and other features include a series of modern gardens created by horticultural students. Kew's educational role is channelled through a varied programme that includes teacher guidance, available through www.kew.org.

The Pagoda is another popular landmark within the grounds. Built in 1762, the building has approximately 253 steps to the top of its 10-storeys. For years the structure has been too shaky to allow entry, but during special festivals like the annual Plantasia, there is limited access. It's a great way to see panoramic views of the park and beyond. Just west of the Pagoda the aerial tree walk offers another high-level vantage point from where you can survey the lush forest canopy of the gardens.

Festivals that take place on the grounds include Kew The Music, a summer event that has featured acts including Simple Minds, Jules Holland and His Rhythm & Blues Orchestra and Elvis Costello. In the garden area surrounding Kew Palace, the annual Kew the Movies festival offers open-air cinema and usually takes place during the August Bank Holiday.

The Marianne North Gallery is located at the eastern border of the gardens. It looks a bit like a red-brick community centre, but inside the rooms are packed with over 800 lively paintings by Marianne North, a 19th-century traveller with a passion for painting plants. She presented her artwork to Kew and had this gallery built for the purpose, while she hot-footed it off to South Africa, the Seychelles and Chile to continue her passion for painting exotic fauna.

There's a huge amount of ground to cover, from the elaborate glass houses to the herbaceous gardens. If you're not up to walking your way around, you can book a ticket on the Kew Explorer. An eco-friendly gas-powered road train, it runs from the garden's Victoria Gate, and provides a laid back 35-minute tour of the site, allowing passengers to jump on and off when they like.

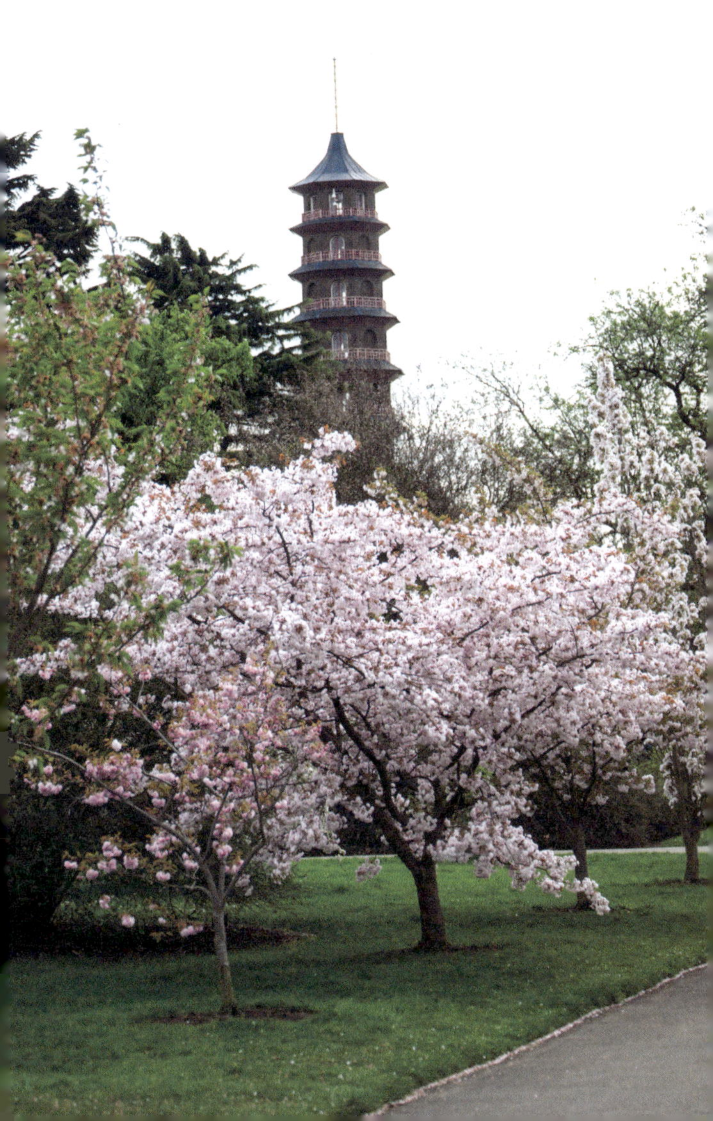

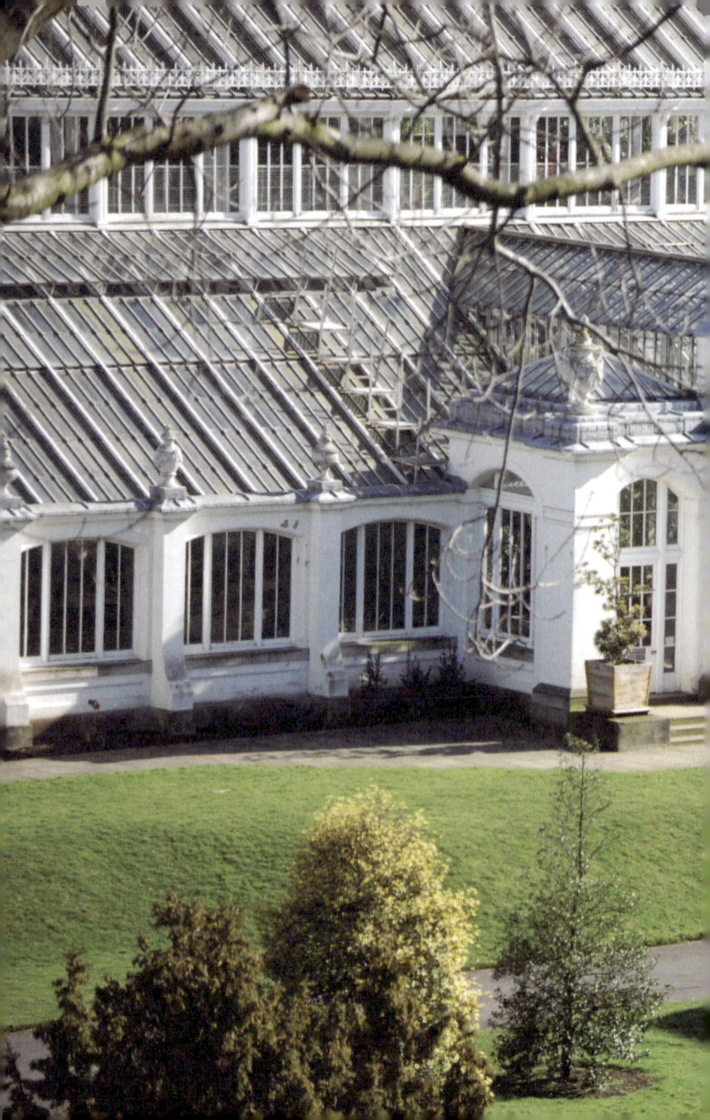

Royal Botanic Gardens, Kew

Gated Parks & Gardens

Syon Park and Gardens

Syon Park, Brentford, Middlesex, TW8 8JF
Wed-Sun 10:30-16:30
020 8560 0882
www.syonpark.co.uk
Travel: Syon Lane Rail
Area: 200 acres
Admission: £7-14

The well-manicured lawns and neatly-trimmed hedges within the walled grounds of Syon Gardens give a definite sense of being in an exclusive setting. The park's trees include Champions – the largest in the country – and rare types such as wingnuts from Asia and Zelkovas from southern Europe. A central lake framed by willows, peacocks and snoozing ducks; all add to the pleasure of visiting this historic house about ten miles from central London with its landscaped gardens beside the Thames.

Home to the Duke of Northumberland's family for over 400 years, Syon is named after Syon Abbey, which was founded in 1415 and stood on the northern bank of the River Thames before being demolished by Henry VIII. This wasn't a popular move at the time, but he perhaps received his comeuppance in 1547, when his coffin was brought to Syon on its way to Windsor for burial. It is said that the box burst open during the night, and in the morning dogs were found licking up the king's remains.

The 200 acre park has all kinds of appealing features. The garden area was first established in the mid-16th century and occupies about thirty acres. It was re-landscaped in the 18th century by royal gardener Capability Brown, who introduced two lakes, one of which is now used for trout fishing.

The Syon Park rose garden that once stood at the front of the house no longer exists, although the Rose Garden Gate still stands in the south of the grounds as you drive up the road towards Syon Park proper. It's a shame not to see the vibrant shrubs that once punctuated the grounds, however you can find over 200 varieties of roses on offer at the Syon Park Garden Centre.

The park's centrepiece is the Great Conservatory. A real eye-catcher, it was commissioned by the 3rd Duke of Northumberland in 1826, and was the first of its type to be built out of gunmetal, Bath stone and glass. It was a fancy bauble where the Duke could show off his exotic plants, and served as an inspiration for English gardener and architect Joseph Paxton when he was preparing his own designs for the Crystal Palace.

Wedding receptions, TV, magazine and film shoots regularly use the Syon landscape, with Gosford Park (2001), Emma (1996) The Madness of King George (1994) and Belle (2013) being some of the better-known period movies to have filmed here.

Where a butterfly house once stood, the Aquatic Centre now takes pride of place. It is an attraction that's popular with families and is essentially a seven day a week show-and-sell store that houses a wide range of marine and fresh water species and other goods and equipment relating to fishkeeping. The centre also offers regular opportunities for children to feed the large koi carp that swim in open tanks as well as observe other rare species including the sharks, stingrays and puffer fish.

COMMONS

Barnes Common............................. 283
Clapham Common 285
Peckham Rye Common 286
Streatham Common 288
Tooting Commons.......................... 289
Wandsworth Common 290
Wimbledon Common..................... 293

Commons

Barnes Common

Vine Road, SW13 0NE
Area: 120 acres
020 8891 1411
www.barnescommon.org.uk
Travel: Barnes Rail
Facilities: Cricket pitch and football pitch, nature trail

This green area is close to the starting point of the annual Oxford and Cambridge boat race at Mortlake. It covers around 120 acres, which in the 16th century were shared between the villages of Barnes and Putney. This happy state of affairs continued until 1589, when a dispute broke out between the two communities, which led to Putney residents being barred from the common. By the second half of the 19th century the common, a huge expanse of marshland, was being used for research by naturalists. Nowadays, it's separated from Lower Putney Common by Common Road, but its cricket and football grounds are still well-used.

Barnes Common has a place in the annals of rock, being the site of pop star Marc Bolan's fatal car crash in 1977. Flowers and ribbons still mark the spot to this day, and to commemorate the twenty-fifth anniversary of the musician's death, a bronze bust was unveiled beside the site by his son Rolan Bolan.

Designated as a local nature reserve in 1992, the common is great for spotting green woodpeckers and rare flowers. On the first Sunday of every month the Friends of Barnes Common (www.barnescommon.org.uk) run nature sessions for children of all ages (with a guardian). These usually start at 10.30am and involve hunting for signs of wildlife and insects, putting up bird and bat boxes and taking part in quizzes.

Clapham Common

Commons

Clapham Common

Clapham High Street, SW4 9DE
Daily 24 hours
020 7926 9000
www.lambeth.gov.uk
Travel: Clapham South LU
Area: 220 acres
Facilities: Rugby pitch, football pitch, grass athletics sprint track, tennis courts, netball & basketball court, skatepark, fishing ponds, playgrounds, paddling pool, cafés

Right up until the 20th century Clapham Common was a peaceful pasture where animals grazed. In earlier days it was also a hangout for 17th-century highwaymen, including the 'notorious sinner' Robert Forrester. He dressed in ladies' clothes to fool those travelling in passing stagecoaches.

The origins of the common date back to Saxon times, when the land contained a small settlement known as Osgod Clapha, which remained an isolated hamlet for many centuries. The name indicates that the common may have had ownership links with a Saxon nobleman Osgod (or Osgot) who died in 1054. It wasn't until the end of the 17th century, when the Fire of London made many Londoners homeless, that the south-west of the city became a popular place to live. At times the wildlife of the common encroached on the human dwellings and rewards of ten shillings were paid for all those who could kill a decent number of hedgehogs or polecats.

By the 18th and 19th centuries the common was surrounded by grand houses belonging to City merchants, philanthropists, and the likes of diarist Samuel Pepys who lived here from 1700 to 1703.

Today, bars, shops and restaurants surround the west and south sides of the common. The common now features open grassland areas, woodlands, tree-lined paths, three ponds (including one for model boats) and the oldest and largest bandstand in London. There are also areas for rugby, tennis, basketball and football, and regular concerts and live events.

Peckham Rye Common

Peckham Rye, SE15 & SE22
Daily 7:30 until dusk
020 7525 2000
www.southwark.gov.uk
Travel: Peckham Rye LO & Rail
Area: 64 acres
Facilities: Adventure play area, football pitches, skatepark, nature garden, outdoor gym, bowling green, café

Angels and chocolate have an indelible link with this area of common land. It's where Elizabeth Cadbury, the Quaker wife of the chocolate manufacturer, once lived, and is also the site where the poet William Blake claimed to have seen a vision of angels in an oak tree on the rye. The common surrounds the 49-acre Peckham Rye Park (see page 161), which opened to the public in 1894. Not as intricately designed as the inner park, which has undergone significant restoration in recent years, the wider green area does have children's playgrounds, leafy glades and a stream running along its edge.

One of the main attractions of the common is its café, situated at the boundary of the enclosed park. The food and coffee is excellent and they also offer a range of delicious Italian ice creams.

Peckham Rye Common

Streatham Common

SW16 3BX
Daily 24 hours
020 7926 9000
www.streathamcommon.org
Travel: Streatham Rail
Area: 36 acres
Facilities: Children's play area, seasonal paddling pool, tennis courts, football pitch, cricket field, café

Streatham Common's 36 acres lie on the southern edge of Streatham, and stretch up towards Norwood from the High Road. Tucked within it is the four-acre walled Streatham Rookery (see page 106) with its themed gardens.

The common was once part of a large swathe of land stretching from Norbury to Tulse Hill, with a scattering of ponds, which were fed by a series of springs from Norwood via Beulah Spa, near Crystal Palace. The area had a tradition of cricket matches during the 18th and 19th centuries, with those who were grand enough to have their houses situated around the edges of the land, having private access gates to the sports fields. There's still plenty of room for sports, but no particular activity takes precedence. There's a playground and a seasonal paddling pool, which now works pretty well as a place for small children to practice their bike skills. During the summer paddlers do get to use an alternative shallow pool near the car park at the top of the common, and the nearby café serves excellent food.

Events take place throughout the year, and these are usually organised by the Friends of Streatham Common, who arrange regular funfairs. The annual Kite Day lifts off every April and is open to flyers of all manner of kites from sello-taped bin bags to well-crafted aerodynamic constructions. The annual butterfly walk takes place every July and is a great way to find out more about the butterflies that populate this unspoilt green oasis. As the nights draw in the Friends also arrange an evening bat walk to discover more about these nocturnal creatures.

Tooting Commons

Tooting Bec Road, SW16 & SW17
Daily 24 hours
0203 959 0015
www.wandsworth.gov.uk
Travel: Tooting Bec LU
Area: 221 acres
Facilities: Athletics track, fishing, horse riding, lido, tennis courts, sports pitches, café

This 221 acre green expanse is the remnant of a piece of open land that once stretched as far as Mitcham. Dr Johnson Avenue divides the larger Tooting Bec from the smaller Tooting Graveney Common. Thanks to their preservation by the Metropolitan Board of Works in the late 19th century, both commons can now be enjoyed as one single expanse of green space amid the urban sprawl of Tooting.

One of the biggest draws is the art deco Lido – the largest in Europe – that was first built in 1906. Every summer, crowds flock to this swimming pool, which has a paddling area and café. The lido's annual opening times are from late May to the end of September, although it also opens every Christmas Day to allow local masochists the chance to swim in arctic conditions.

The rest of the landscape is made up of woodland, open grassland and sports areas. Dr Johnson Avenue is lined with fine oaks that were planted in the late 16th century to commemorate a visit by Elizabeth I. The avenue was later named after the 18th-century writer and lexicographer Samuel Johnson, who regularly visited his friend Henry Thrale, whose house overlooked the common. The old Keeper's Lodge was built in 1879 and can still be seen today.

Not far from the junction of Tooting Bec Road and Elmbourne Road at the far south western edge of Tooting Graveney, there's an old boating pond. Close by are a series of sculptures that were carved out of trees damaged in the great storm of 1987.

Wandsworth Common

Trinity Road, SW11 & SW18
Daily 24 hours
020 8874 7530
www.wandsworth.gov.uk
Travel: Wandsworth Common Rail
Area: 175 acres
Facilities: Sports pitches, tennis courts, bowling green, fishing, trim trail, children's playground, café

Both Wandsworth and Clapham Common are often referred to by locals as 'Nappy Valley' as they both seem to be magnets for young families. Wandsworth Common's 175 acres stretch from the edges of Balham to Battersea Rise, with a history that goes right back to the 11th century. In those days there were public rights on the common to cut wood, graze animals and cultivate the land. This changed as London expanded westward and pressure grew to develop the area. Gradually large chunks of the common passed into private hands, and the area was divided by new road and rail links. By 1887 the common was a muddy, treeless expanse that needed public attention.

Today, it's a different story. Edged by 19th-century and Edwardian houses, the common is as it should be – a sprawling green space with sports pitches, tennis courts, bowling greens and ornamental areas. On Windmill Road, there's a wind pump, which was built in 1840 to revive the common's water supply. It's been redundant since 1870, and is now Grade II listed.

The Scope is a 25-acre section of the common that's specifically managed for wildlife with oaks, silver birch, woodland and grassland found here. It's also home to the Nature Scope Centre that offers various nature and wildlife activities, community projects and walks for visitors of all ages (www.naturescope.co.uk).

The common has two lakes with one for fishing (seasonal membership required) and there's also a popular café.

Wandsworth Common

Wimbledon Common

Commons

Wimbledon Common

Windmill Road, SW19 5NR
Daily 24 hours
www.wpcc.org.uk
Travel: Southfields LU & Wimbledon Rail
Area: 1,140 acres
Facilities: Cricket pitch, football and rugby pitches, golf course, horse riding, walking trail, museum, café

This common is huge, comprising around 1,140 acres, divided by the busy A3 and bounded on the east side by Wimbledon Park. The common peters out where Wimbledon Common joins Richmond Park, making it almost twice the size of Hampstead Heath. The sprawling acres of Wimbledon Common include both Putney Heath and Putney Lower Common.

Facilities include playing fields, cottages, two golf courses, gravel pits, woodlands, sixteen miles of horse rides, warrens, camp areas, lakes and ravines. Two thirds of the common have been designated as a Site of Special Scientific Interest (SSSI) as well as a Special Area of Conservation (SAC). There's plenty to see, with a landscape that features unenclosed and unspoilt grassland areas.

Towards Putney Heath at Windmill Road, the old windmill has been standing here since 1817. Built by a carpenter, Charles March, it was working until 1865, before eventually becoming a residential property. By 1975, it had been restored and now operates as the *Windmill Museum, where milling and other activities are demonstrated and tours are offered by the local volunteers who run the place.

The size of Wimbledon Common and its miles of track make it one of the best places around London to mountain bike. This is also the only way to cover the vast acreage of the common unless you have access to a horse.

*The Windmill Museum Windmill Road, SW19
(www.wimbledonwindmill.org.uk)
Open: March to October Sat 2pm-5pm, Sun & Bank Hols 11am-5pm

ROOF GARDENS

Barbican Conservatory.................. 295
Beech Gardens 295
Crossrail Place Roof Gardens...... 297
Culpeper Rooftop Garden............ 297
Garden at 120.................................. 298
Sky Garden 298

Barbican Conservatory

Silk Street, EC2Y 8DS
Check website for opening hours
www.barbican.org.uk
Travel: Barbican LU
Admission: Free

The Barbican Conservatory is the second largest of its kind in London after Kew. An idiosyncratic afterthought, it was built around the fly tower of the Arts Centre theatre and opened in 1984, with a cacti-filled Arid House being added two years later. Within this concrete jungle you'll find three pools with of cold-water fish such as koi carp. roach and tench. In recent years it has been the site of art installations such as the Indian sculptor Ranjani Shettar's work. The Conservatory opening hours change each week and are ticketed, with slots for the following week released on Fridays at 10am. One of the capital's gems with over 2,000 species of tropical and sub-tropical plants, plus resident terrapins and an aviary.

Beech Gardens

Beech Street, EC2Y 8DE
Daily 24 hours
www.cityoflondon.gov.uk/things-to-do/city-gardens/find-a-garden/beech-gardens-the-barbican-estate
Travel: Barbican LU
Admission: Free

Beech Garden, found within Barbican Estate, is a container roof garden on a large scale, made up of formal beds sunk into the tiled surface of the Barbican's 'podium' level. It was planted by ecological plant expert Nigel Dunnett with a beautiful palette of sustainable and wildlife-friendly plants that can cope with the three distinct micro-climates within the site and its scanty three feet planting depth. Fourteen newly planted tree specimens add height and interest, and include multi-stem amelanchier and black elder. Dunnett's new scheme is designed to be low maintenance and require minimal watering.

Crossrail Place Roof Gardens

Crossrail Place Roof Gardens

Crossrail Place, E14 5AB
Daily 9:00-21:00 or sunset in summer
canarywharf.com/open-spaces/crossrail-place-roof-garden/
Travel: West India Quay DLR, Canary Wharf LU
Admission: Free

Located amid the skyscrapers in Canary Wharf. This garden sits on the Meridian line and has been uniquely conceived so plants are placed according to the hemisphere of origin, with Asian flora like bamboos to the east, and plants such as ferns from the Americas to the west. In the 19th century, trading ships from around the world would dock in this area, and the planting reflects this melting pot of cultures with species drawn from across the globe. If you're still not sold, within the space you'll also find an amphitheatre that hosts performance and music events in the summer months.

Culpeper Rooftop Garden

40 Commercial Street, E1 6LP
Mon-Thu 12:00-0:00, Fri-Sat 12:00-1:00, Sun 12:00-21:00
www.theculpeper.com/rooftop
Travel: Aldgate East LU

Whilst this roof garden is only open to diners of The Culpeper, it has the unique feature of producing the food you eat from the very garden you sit within. The pub isn't entirely self-sufficient, but their allotment goes a long way. Their vision is for similar spaces to pop up with associated pubs. On the seasonal menu, expect to see courgettes, aubergines, herbs and chillies hiding in the foliage. The lunchtime set menu is £35 and includes a starter, main course, sides and a pudding. In the evenings it becomes a predominantly drinking space with a dedicated cocktail bar that sits under a glass atrium at the entrance and churns out unique beverages. These include virgin cocktails for those who want to match the wholesomeness of the setting, as well as the alcoholic variety, serving as a good pre-drinking spot to begin your Shoreditch night out.

Roof Gardens

Garden at 120

120 Fenchurch Street, EC3M 5BA
Mon-Fri 10:00-21:00, Sat & Sun 10:00-17:00 (Apr-Sep), Mon-Fri 10:00-18:30, Sat & Sun 10:00-17:00 (Oct-Mar)
www.thegardenat120.com
Travel: Fenchurch Street Rail
Admission: Free

Situated on the 15th floor of a fairly non-descript office block, you'll find a little patch of green with unbeatable views, and what's more, it's completely free. Designed by landscape architects Latz+Partner, the roof garden boasts a mixture of manicured mazes and wild walls with climbing plants, including vibrant wisteria. Without a café, copy the office workers and bring a picnic in tow. On warm days be weary that it is accessed on a first-come-first-served basis so there will sometimes be a short wait, which will be duly rewarded with remarkable views across the capital's skyline.

Sky Garden

1, Sky Garden Walk, EC3M 8AF
Mon-Thu 8:00-0:00, Fri-Sat 8:00-1:00 & Sun 8:00-0:00
www.skygarden.london
Travel: Monument LU
Admission: Free

With the claim to fame of being London's highest public garden, Sky Garden is one of the capital's most popular tourist attractions and you can see why. Free to enter, it ticks all the boxes. Experience the glitz and glamour of this central location while being surrounded by jungle-like foliage, not to mention the 360-degree views of the skyline. Starting on the 35th floor of the iconic Walkie Talkie building, it features three storeys of landscaped gardens lush with South African and Mediterranean plants, observation decks, an open-air terrace, two restaurants and a bar. Whilst entry is free, you must book your 90-minute timeslot in advance on the website with tickets are released every Monday.

Sky Garden

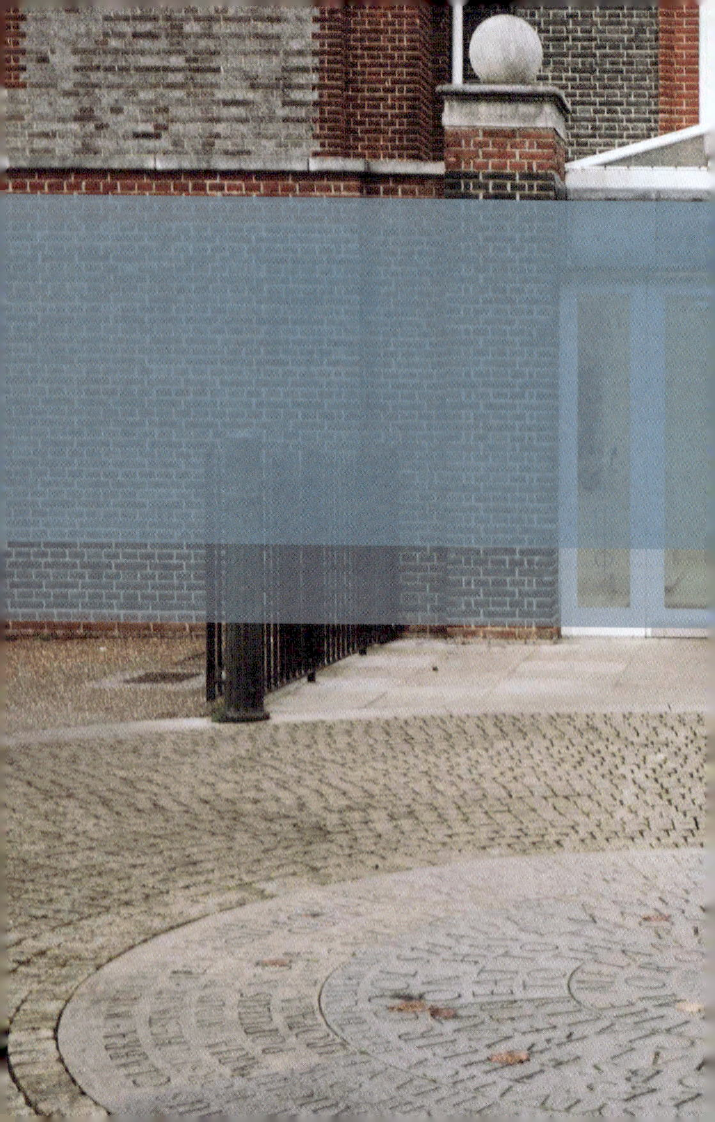

LANDMARKS

Serpentine Gallery

NORTH
Alexandra Palace 304
London Zoo **304**
Regent's Park Open Air Theatre 305

WEST
Fulham Palace **305**
Holland House 306
Serpentine Gallery **306**
Speakers' Corner 307

SOUTH
Crystal Palace Museum **307**
National Maritime Museum 310
Queen's House **310**
The Royal Observatory & Planetarium ... 311
The Thames Barrier **311**

EAST
Hackney City Farm 312
Ragged School Museum **312**

The Thames Barrier

NORTH

Alexandra Palace

Alexandra Palace Way, N22 7AY
Daily 9:00-17:00
020 8365 2121
www.alexandrapalace.com
Travel: Alexandra Palace Rail
Admission: Free

Triumphantly labelled as 'the people's palace' when it opened in 1873, Alexandra Palace was built within its parkland setting to provide Victorian London with a spectacular leisure centre. These days, the Guy Fawke's night fireworks display is the biggest annual draw, although the Palace is regularly used for exhibitions and conferences. Features include an indoor ice-skating rink and the boating lake and pitch and putt course in the summer. The Palace received Grade II listed status from English Heritage in 1996.

London Zoo

Outer Circle, Regent's Park, NW1 4RY
Opens 10:00 daily, closing times vary
www.londonzoo.org
Travel: Mornington Crescent LU
Admission: £20-30

London Zoo gives visitors the chance to observe over 650 species that live here, which include a varied range of reptiles, fish, invertebrates, birds and mammals, with around 112 of these listed as threatened species. Extending over 36 acres, it's difficult to know where to start, but a guidebook and map is available at the entrance for £6.

Regent's Park Open Air Theatre

Inner Circle, Regent's Park, NW1 4NU
0333 400 3562
www.openairtheatre.com/
Travel: Regent Park LU

There's always a summer season of (mainly Shakespearean) plays at Regent's Park's (see page 33) famous theatre, which opens every year from the end of May to the beginning of September. First established in 1932, when thespian Sydney Carroll put on four matinées of *Twelfth Night*. The theatre was transformed in the 1960s and is now one of London's largest, with a 1,200 seating capacity. The present auditorium was built in 1975. An online heritage project documents the theatre's production history since its inception.

WEST

Fulham Palace

Bishop's Avenue, SW6 6EA
Daily 10:30-16:00
020 7736 3233
www.fulhampalace.org
Travel: Putney Bridge LU

This ancient palace has been rebuilt several times, and remained the main residence of every Bishop of London up until 1973. Today's mixed styles are the result of constant re-structuring, and the Grade I listed building has a red brick Tudor courtyard and a Georgian façade on the east front. Tours of the interior and grounds of the palace cost £8 for adults with children allowed in for free. The tours take in the Great Hall, Victorian Chapel, Bishop Terrick Rooms and garden walks can also be booked on the first and third Sunday of each month. Fulham Palace Gardens (see page 85) and Bishop's Park (see page 81) are also well worth visiting.

Holland House

Holland Walk, W8 7QU
020 7937 0748
Travel: High Street Kensington LU

The remains of Holland House take centre stage inside Holland Park (see page 90). What exists today is essentially the shell of the Jacobean mansion that survived the Blitz with a restored east wing which houses the Holland Park Youth Hostel. In the 1960s the house's Garden Ballroom was converted into a Café. During the summer there's a 10-week run of open-air theatre and ballet performances in the canopied Opera Holland Park (www.operahollandpark.com) at the front of the house.

Serpentine Gallery

Kensington Gardens, W2 3XA
Tue-Sun 10:00-18:00
020 7402 6075
www.serpentinegalleries.org
Travel: Lancaster Gate LU or South Kensington LU
Facilities: Shop, bookshop, café
Admission: Free

Originally built as a tearoom in the 1930s, the Grade II listed building was converted to a gallery in 1970. Since that time the gallery has acquired an impressive back list of high profile exhibitors. Over 500,000 visitors each year visit the sleek exhibition spaces which include the recently built Serpentine Sackler Gallery designed by Zaha Hadid. Every year a contemporary architect or artist has been commissioned to design an outdoor pavilion beside the gallery. The space is used for a programme of open air events that run from June to September. Past pavilion designers have included Oscar Niemeyer, Frank Gehry and Ai Weiwei. The art bookshop at the entrance is also well worth a browse.

Speakers' Corner

Hyde Park, W2 2UH
Sun from midday
www.speakerscorner.net
Travel: Hyde Park Corner LU

For over 150 years, Speakers' Corner at the Marble Arch end of Hyde Park (see p.19) has given many mouthy Londoners the chance to express their views to a public audience who can listen, heckle or move on to another speaker on a soap-box. It is a type of verbal street theatre which draws crowds every Sunday come rain or shine. Historical figures who have spoken here include William Morris, George Orwell, Emmeline Pankhurst, Marcus Garvey and CLR James. It is worth remembering that in less liberal and democratic times this area was a site for public execution known as Tyburn.

SOUTH-EAST

Crystal Palace Museum

Anerley Hill, SE19 2BA
Sun 11:00-15:00
07434 975 582
www.crystalpalacemuseum.org.uk
Travel: Crystal Palace LO & Rail
Admission: Free

The Crystal Palace Museum is housed in a one room, former engineering school at the Anerley Hill edge of the **Crystal Palace Park** (see page 134). Run by volunteers from the Crystal Palace Foundation, the museum's displays include videos and audio presentations, as well as artefacts from the original Crystal Palace exhibition. It's well worth visiting if you want to put the park's remaining ruins into historical context. The curators know their stuff and are happy to chat if you have any questions.

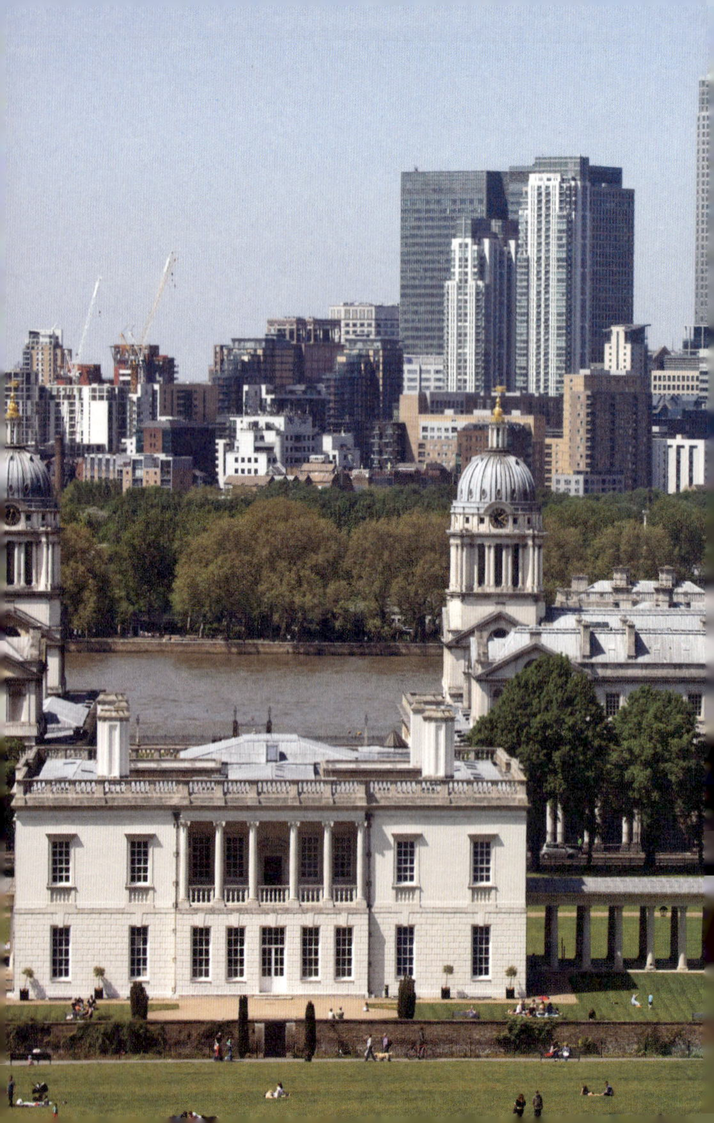

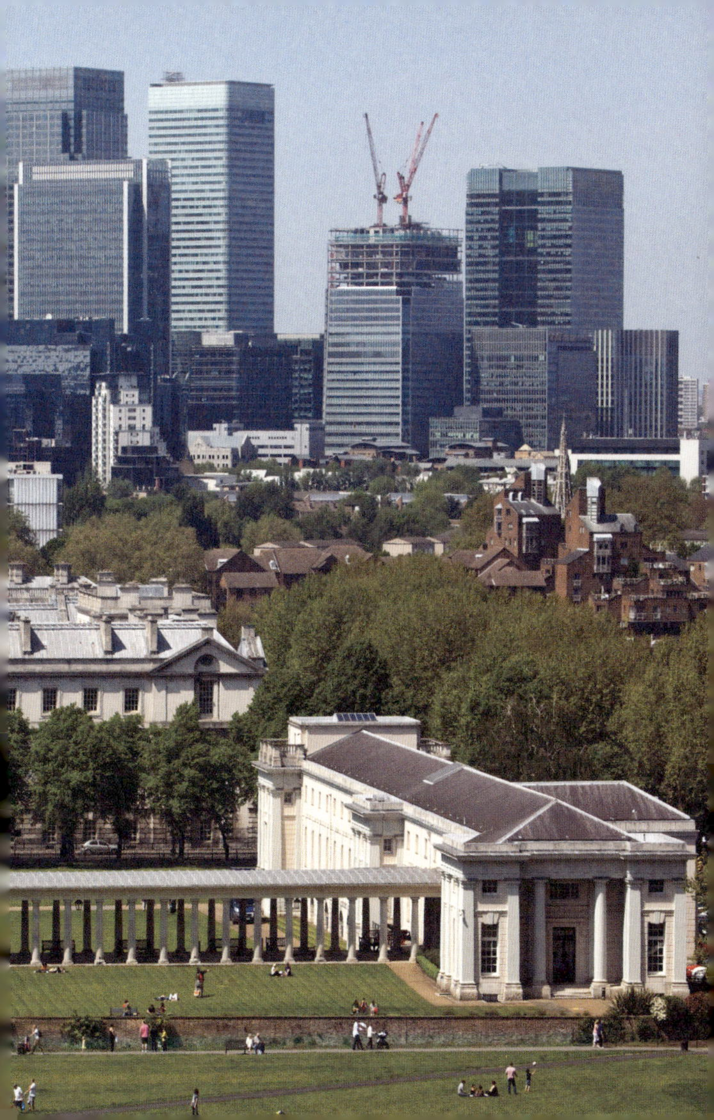

National Maritime Museum

Romney Road, SE10 9NF
Daily 10:00-17:00
020 8858 4422
www.rmg.co.uk
Travel: Cutty Sark DLR
Admission: Free

The National Maritime Museum is one of a cluster of historic buildings beside Greenwich Park (see page 147). An impressive lawn-fronted entrance on Romney Road leads to a bright and airy lobby and a series of galleries offering permanent and temporary exhibitions on all things related to maritime history from Morse Code to trade and expeditions. Three floors open up a world of seafaring delights, with galleries dedicated to Explorers, Passengers and Maritime London among other nautical themes. Sculptor and artist Yinka Shonibare's 'Nelson's Ship in a Bottle' also has a permanent space in the museum grounds.

Queen's House

Park Row, SE10 9NF
Daily 10:00-17:00
020 8858 4422
www.rmg.co.uk
Travel: Greenwich DLR & Rail
Admission: Free

This elegant Inigo Jones designed building was commissioned for Anne of Denmark in 1616 and was one of the first classical buildings in England. Queen's House sits next door to the National Maritime Museum and its grand interiors provide a fitting environment for the Museum's art collection. The Tulip Staircase was the first cantilevered staircase to be built in this country and worth visiting in its own right. The staff are friendly, well informed and always willing to share their knowledge with visitors. A great place to visit in conjunction with Greenwich Park (see page 147).

Landmarks

Royal Observatory & Planetarium

Blackheath Avenue, SE10 8XJ
Daily 10:00-17:00
020 8858 4422
www.rmg.co.uk
Travel: Greenwich DLR & Rail
Admission: Free

Part of the National Maritime Museum, the Royal Observatory sits in the centre of **Greenwich Park** (see p.145) and offers visitors the chance to explore the official home of Greenwich Mean Time. The Observatory is the official starting point for each new day, year and millennium, with the Meridian Line cutting through its courtyard. This enables visitors to place their feet on either side of it and to straddle two hemispheres. Time, space and cosmology are also explored through gallery exhibitions and in the domed Planetarium.

The Thames Barrier

1 Unity Way, Woolwich, SE18 5NJ
Sat 10:30-15:30
020 8305 4188
www.gov.uk/guidance/the-thames-barrier
Travel: Woolwich Dockyard Rail
Admission: £6.50-£12

Described as the eighth wonder of the modern world, the Thames Barrier remains an awesome example of design and engineering. It sits across the river from the **Thames Barrier Park** (see page 198), with its 10 steel gates forming an impregnable wall that has prevented the flooding of central London at dangerous times of heavy river discharge and high tide. The Learning and Information Centre on the south bank will tell you all you need to know about the history of the Barrier and how it works. If you are interested in seeing the Barrier in operation, take a look at the main website which gives details of the planned closure of the gates in the coming months.

EAST

Hackney City Farm
1A Goldsmith's Row, E2 8QA
Tue-Sun 10:00-16:30
020 7729 6381
www.hackneycityfarm.co.uk
Travel: Hoxton LO
Admission: Free

Just on the edge of Haggerston Park (see p. 182), Hackney City Farm is home to geese, pigs, chicken, sheep and cattle, all living within urban E2. Visitors can get touchy-feely with the lambs in spring, when bottle-feeding sessions sometimes take place. Other activities including story-telling, circus skills, textile-making and throughout the year there are special events such as bike workshops, clothes swaps and jumble sales. The organic garden is open for community planting or simply enjoying the scent of its aromatic herbs. The farm's organic Frizzante Café is a real treat that should not be missed.

Ragged School Museum
46-50 Copperfield Road, E3 4RR
Wed-Sun: 10:00-17:00
020 8980 6405
www.raggedschoolmuseum.org.uk
Travel: Mile End LU
Admission: Free

What started life as a canalside warehouse before becoming a school for local poor children is now a fascinating museum dedicated to the history of Victorian education. The staff are wonderfully adept at recreating the life of a Victorian classroom and there is even a kitchen where children can try chores like rug beating and pegging washing on a line.

Hackney City Farm

Hampton Court Flower Show

PARK LIFE
- Cafés
- Park events

Allium

'Ambassador'

CAFÉS

Napoleon talked of an army 'marching on its stomach' and the same can be said of those trekking through London's parks and gardens – without the guns and needless slaughter. Just occasionally friends persuade me to visit the countryside and trudge through furrowed fields without an herbaceous border in sight and, worst of all, no convenient place to sit and have a cappuccino. Acknowledging my love of the urban green space (where nature has been tamed), I include here some of the best cafés to be found in London's parks.

The Brew House

Kenwood House, Hampstead Lane, NW3 7JR
Daily 9:00-18:00
020 8341 5384
Travel: Highgate LU
It gets very busy at this café, which is housed in what was once the servant's wing next to Kenwood House. Breakfasts are served from 9am, while the lunch menu is available from 12 noon and changes daily. During the summer the terrace area has an ice cream and Pimms stand.

The Broad Walk Café

Kensington Gardens, W2 2UH
Opens at 8:00, closing times change seasonally
020 7034 0722
Travel: Regents Park LU
These two cafés are next to the Diana Memorial Playground and serve freshly cooked meals, salads, sandwiches and fair trade tea and coffee. There's a specific children's menu at the Playcafé and outdoor seating.

Brown & Green Life

Crystal Palace Park, Thicket Road, SE20 8DS
Daily 8:30-17:30
020 8653 3799
www.brownandgreencafe.com/brownandgreenlife
Travel: Crystal Palace Rail
Situated in the main car park at the Thicket Road entrance, this no frills café serves chips, big mugs of tea, cakes, fry-ups and other snacks to those exploring the grounds of Crystal Palace.

Cafés

Brockwell Park Café

Brockwell Park, SE24 0PA
Daily 9:00-17:30
020 8671 5217
Travel: Herne Hill Rail

A Grade II listed building, this once grand Regency mansion is today a popular café. The outdoor table areas are always crowded in the summer and the place is well loved for its all day breakfasts, Italian ice creams, hot drinks, cakes and no-nonsense staff.

Collici Serpentine Lido

Hyde Park, W2 3XA
Opens at 8:00, closing times change monthly
020 7706 7098
www.colicci.co.uk/locations/hyde-park
Travel: Hyde Park Corner LU

This café offers great views across the Serpentine, alfresco eating or indoor dining and a selection of newspapers to read if the views of the Serpentine aren't enough.

The Dulwich Clock Café

Dulwich Park, College Road, SE21 7BQ
Mon-Fri 8:00-17:30, Sat & Sun 8:00-18:00
020 8299 0643
colicci.co.uk
Travel: West Dulwich Rail

All-day breakfasts, own-brand coffee and locally bought meat and fish make this café a fine pit stop after a long stroll around Dulwich Park. The interior is stylishly designed with colourful modern tiles and they also now make their own pizza, if you fancy something more substantial.

Cafés

Golders Hill Park Café

North End Way, NW3 7HD
Daily 9:00-18:00
020 8455 8010
Travel: Golders Green LU

This family-run café offers pasta meals and salads as well as its famous Italian ice creams. The place is very popular so expect big queues in the summer.

Horniman Café

100 London Road, SE22 0RS
Daily 9:00-17:30
020 8699 4666
Travel: Forest Hill Rail

This Victorian conservatory is now the home of this funky international café attached to the equally marvellous Horniman Museum. The café offers hearty favourites such as lasagne and the full English Breakfast along side more healthy Mediterranean options and a selection of kids' meals. The outdoor seating is very popular in the summer months.

Kensington Palace Pavilion

Kensington Palace, Kensington Gardens, W8 4PX
Daily 10:00-18:00
020 3166 6113
www.orangerykensingtonpalace.co.uk
Travel: Queensway LU

Advance reservations are recommended at this grand café just outside Kensington Palace. Freshly baked cakes are also on offer, as well as hot meals at lunchtimes. All this can be enjoyed within sumptuous architectural surroundings, which include Corinthian columns and eighteenth-century wood carvings. The restaurant also serves alcohol if you fancy pushing the boat out.

Cafés

Lauderdale House Café

Waterlow Park, Highgate Hill, N6 5HG
Mon-Fri 10:00-18:00
020 8348 8716
Travel: Archway LU

Lauderdale House café serves delicious food to those exploring Waterlow Park with anything from a hot meals to delicious cakes on the menu. The terrace garden seating provides great views of the surrounding park, but be prepared to queue at the weekend as this place is very popular.

Lido Café at Brockwell Park

Dulwich Road, Brockwell Lido, SE24 0PA
Tue-Sat 8:30-21:00, Sun-Mon 8:30-18:00
020 7737 8183
Travel: Herne Hill Rail

In addition to the Brockwell Park Café at the top of the park, the Lido Café sits next to the pool and does a roaring trade in the summer. Unlike the lido, it is open all year round and transforms into a restaurant in the evenings offering a good wine list and craft beers.

Pavilion Café

West Boating Lake, Victoria Park, E9 7DE
Mon-Fri 7:00-17:00, Sat & Sun 8:00-18:00

In the last 15 years this café has been transformed from an uninspiring caff into this fashionable, organic eatery offering a seasonal menu. It's a case of 'farewell fried egg sarny, hello Eggs Benedict', but the food is excellent and the place is always busy. The outdoor seating offers a great view of the boating lake and the barista coffee and fine teas are delicious.

Cafés

Pavilion Tea House

Charlton Way, SE10 8QY
Mon-Fri 8:30-16:30, Sat & Sun 8:30-16:00
020 8305 2896
www.royalparks.org.uk
Travel: Greenwich DLR

A fine octagonal art deco style building near the Greenwich Park's Royal Observatory. Here traditional breakfasts, snacks, soups and gorgeous meals such as grilled salmon or stone baked pizza are served. From May to August there are jazz and barbeque evenings.

Pear Tree Café

Battersea Park, SW11 4NJ
Mon-Sat 8:00-22:00, Sun 8:00-20:00
020 7978 1655
www.peartreecafe.co.uk
Travel: Battersea Park LU

Designed like a 1930s rotunda and in a perfect location next to the boating lake, this café offers an extensive menu all freshly made and with quality ingredients. Unusually for a park café, Pear Tree serves throughout the day and into the evening.

Pembroke Lodge

Richmond Park, Richmond, Surrey, TW10 5HX
Daily 9:30 until 15 minutes before dusk
020 8940 8207
www.pembroke-lodge.co.uk
Travel: Richmond LU & LO

This Georgian mansion was once the home of philosopher Bertrand Russell. It now houses a café with extensive park views and a grand banqueting room. Warm scones with jam and clotted cream are a popular option and available after 3pm.

Cafés

Regent's Bar & Kitchen

Queen Mary's Garden, Inner Circle, Regent's Park, NW1 4NU
Daily 8:00-20:00
020 7935 5729
www.royalparks.org.uk
Travel: Baker Street LU

You'll pay a bit more for a meal or a sandwich here, but there's no arguing with the top-notch location next to the rose gardens and close to the park's Open Air Theatre. There is a takeaway counter packed with goodies for picnics, and a smart indoor dining area. The garden terrace has seating for 150 and table service where you can enjoy the all-day menu and they also serve alcohol which is rare for a park café.

Riverside Café

Morden Hall Park, Morden Hall Road, Morden, SM4 5JD
Mon-Fri 6:30-16:00, Sat 7:30-15:30
020 8685 9462
Travel: Morden LU

Overlooking the River Wandle, the café serves coffee, lunches and teas, and also has a gift shop. It is situated inside the large walled kitchen garden, from where they source many of their fresh vegetables.

Serpentine Bar & Kitchen

Eastern side of the Serpentine, W2 2UH
Daily 8:00-20:00
020 7706 0464
Travel: Hyde Park Corner LU

Park-side dining at its best, this café (formerly known as the Dell) has a large outdoor seating area (terrace and garden) and serves a wide selection of food and drink. It has the added advantage of being housed in a building by the modernist architect Patrick Gwynne on a site overlooking the Serpentine.

Springfield Park Café

Springfield Park, Springfield Lane, Upper Clapton, E5 9EF
Daily 10:00-16:00
www.springfieldparkcafe.co.uk
Travel: Clapton LO

This café is found inside the White Lodge mansion at Springfield Park. It's best enjoyed in the summer when the house opens its huge French windows leading out into the garden. Staff are friendly and the menu features organic juices, all-day breakfasts, children's meals and generous salads.

Stables Café

The Stables Courtyard, Gladstone Park, Dollis Hill Lane, NW2 6HT
Wed-Sun 9:00-16:00
Travel: Dollis Hill LU

This lovely café, inside the walled garden at the top of Gladstone Park, is a great place to while away a sunny afternoon with treats such as freshly-made ciabatta sandwiches, fresh cakes, pressed juices, and hot soup in the winter. It's located next door to the Stables Gallery, which shows work by local artists.

St James's Café

St James's Park, SW1A 2BJ
Opening times change seasonally
020 7839 1149
royalparksorg.uk
Travel: St James's Park LU

Outside seating gives you a fine view of the lake at this park café. The food is very good, but expensive with little change from £7 for tea and a slice of cake. There's a self-service buffet as well as table service.

Cafés

Stables Tea Room
Isleworth, Middlesex, TW7 4RB
Daily 10:00-17:00
020 8232 5057
www.nationaltrust.org.uk
Travel: Osterley LU
This tearoom in Osterley Park's stable yard offers coffee, tea, lunches and snacks. The menu uses vegetables from the park's farm and there are children's lunchboxes with homemade cakes or biscuits.

Timber Lodge Café
1A Honour Lea Avenue, Queen Elizabeth Olympic Park, E20 1DY
Daily 9:30-17:00
020 7241 9076
www.queenelizabetholympicpark.co.uk
Travel: Hackney Wick LO
Situated in the North Park section, this bright, high-ceilinged and airy café serves weekend brunches using fresh, seasonal produce. There are also sweet treats, natural juices and hot drinks and plenty of seating outside when the weather is fine.

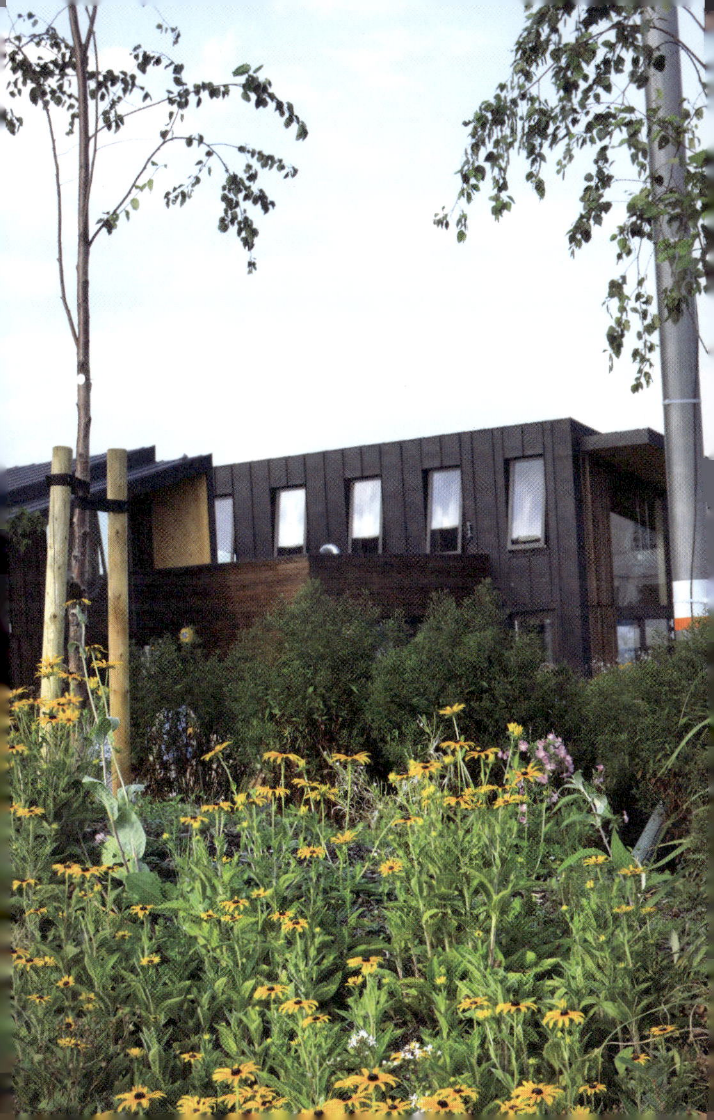

PARK EVENTS

Many of London's parks often confirm their activities pretty close to the day, so it's always best to check the website whether expected events – particularly non-corporate ones – are taking place. Annual treats come in the form of live music or drama performances in some of the larger spaces like Regent's Park or Holland Park, which have created institutions out of their respective theatre and music shows. Privately organised events are very much down to individual organisers, and are therefore not the responsibility of the park itself.

Public firework displays in London's Parks have rather fallen out of fashion, partly because of environmental concerns but more usually because of the decline in local government funding. Ally Pally, Battersea Park and Wimbledon are still going strong and we include them all here.

For sporty types there are too many local park events to mention here but the weekly Parkrun events take place across London (and the country) every Saturday morning and are a great way to get your 5k under your belt with a friendly crowd of like-minded runners. Details of Parkrun can be found on their website www.parkrun.org.uk.

May-September

Regent's Park Open Air Theatre

Inner Circle, Regent's Park, NW1 4NU
www.openairtheatre.com
0333 400 3562

You know that summer's officially started when the Regent's Park Open Air Theatre gets going. Running since 1932, the theatre is an institution, with a programme of plays running from May to September. The repertoire embraces anything from contemporary comedies to Shakespearean classics. There's seating capacity for 1,200.

June-August

London Open Gardens

londongardenstrust.org.uk
Mid-June annually

Mid-June is when this two-day, annual event rolls into town. Run by the London Parks and Gardens Trust, the weekend sees around 200 of London's private gardens open their gates to the public. A number of special activities also take place in selected public gardens in 25 London boroughs.

Opera Holland Park

Ilchester Place, W8 6LU
0300 999 1000
www.operahollandpark.com

The Holland Park opera season has included performances of Verdi's *Macbeth*, *Madame Butterfly* by Puccini and *Eugene Onegin* by Tchaikovsky. The company runs a 'free tickets for young people' scheme. Check the website for dates and times.

Hampton Court Palace Flower Show

East Molesey, Surrey, KT8 9AU
0333 320 6000
www.rhs.org.uk/hamptoncourtflowershow
Travel: Hampton Court Rail

Show gardens, budget gardens, experimental spaces – the Hampton Court Palace Flower Show has all of these as well as cookery demonstrations and workshops. The second largest horticultural show in the UK (after the Chelsea Flower Show), it takes place in early July each year.

Kew the Music

Kew, Richmond, TW9 3AB
www.kewthemusic.org
Travel: Kew Gardens LU & LO

An annual open-air concert set against a beautiful botanical backdrop. The event caters for all kinds of musical taste from jazz to Motown, hip-hop to classical. Elvis Costello, Simple Minds, Jools Holland and others have all headlined here.

Lambeth Country Show

Brockwell Park, SE24 0PA
020 7926 1000
www.lambethcountryshow.co.uk

The annual Lambeth Country Show celebrated its 40th anniversary in 2014. It takes place on the third weekend of July. Upwards of 150,000 people attend each year for the chance to see livestock on display, as well enjoy the craft stalls, live bands, art exhibitions, organic food and children's activities.

July-Aug

Carnaval Del Pueblo

Burgess Park, Albany Road, SE5 7QH
www.carnavaldelpueblo.co.uk
This is the largest Latin American festival in the UK, with an audience of around 80,000 people. It starts with over 15 carnival floats that travel through Peckham before arriving at Burgess Park. On the main stage there are headline artists from Brazil, Mexico and the Andean countries. There's also a funfair, salsa show, competitions and dance classes.

November

Alexandra Palace

www.fireworks.london
The Ally Pally fireworks display has evolved over the years into a massive one-night festival with cinema screenings, ice skating and German beir festival all among the offerings around a central firework and lazer show. Tickets need to be bought in advance and it does sell out so be sure to book in advance of the big night.

Battersea Park Fireworks

www.batterseaparkfireworks.com
This display extends over two days with two firework displays and a bier tent for the grown ups. Tickets are available from the website.

Wimbledon Park & Morden Fireworks

www.merton.gov.uk
One of London's best firework displays with two displays on the night, the earlier one designed for children and an accompanying funfair.

Hampton Court

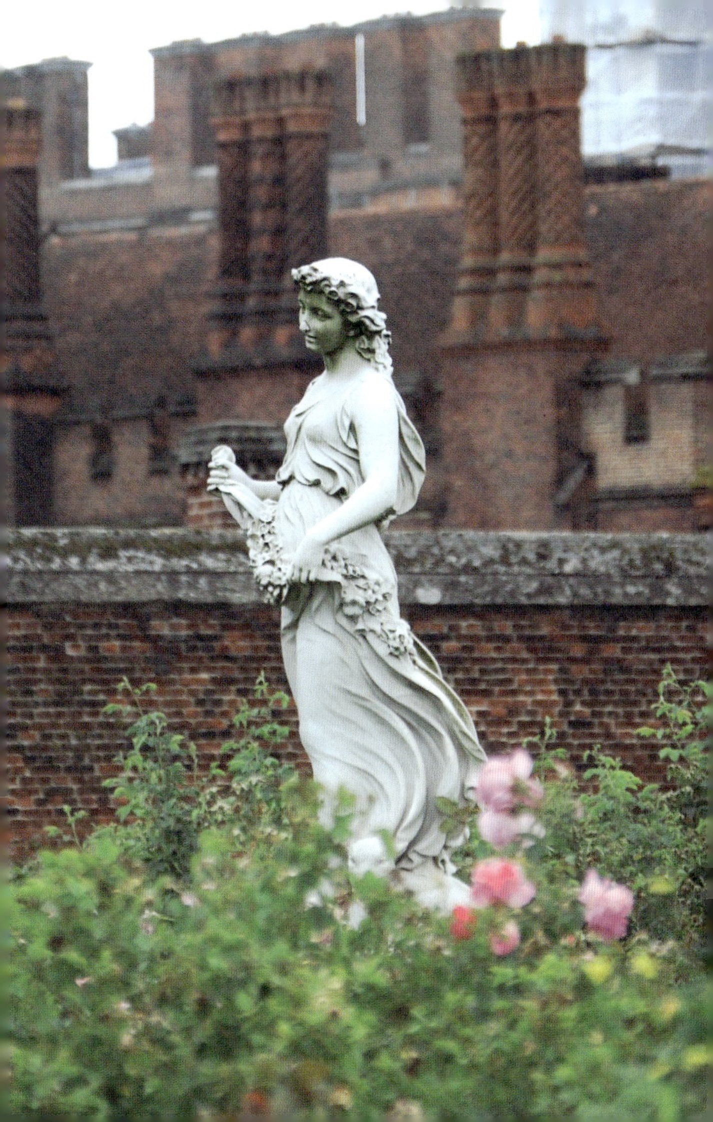

Additional Picture Credits

p.74, p.83, p.108, p.169, p.236, p.261, p.293 © Natalie Pecht / p.30, p.43, p.86 © Stephen Millar/ p.146 © Royal Observatory/ p.152 © Horniman Museum, p.200
© Valentine's Park, p.236 © Brunei Gallery, p.263 © Syon Park, p.266 © Charlie Hopkins, p.294 © Serpentine Gallery

Bibliography

Bygone Pleasures of London, W.S Scott (London 1948)
Exploring London's Gardens, Lorna Lister (Lorna Lister 2001)
London Parks and Gardens, M. Brace & E. Frankel (Pevensey P 1986)
London's Parks and Gardens, J. Billington & S. Lousada (Frances Lincoln Publishers Ltd 2003)
The Royal Parks of London, Guy Williams (Academy Chicago Pub 1985)
Walking London's Parks and Gardens, G. Young (New Holland 1998)
London and Its People, John Richardson (Ebury Press 1995)
The London Encyclopedia (Ben Weinreb, Christopher Hibbert) 2011
Oxford Dictionary of London Place Names, A. D. Mills (Oxford University Press 2004)
A Literary Guide to London, Ed Glinert (Penguin Books Ltd 2000)
A Taxi Driver's Guide to London, S Raingold (Foulsham 1973)
Walking Notorious London, Andrew Duncan (New Holland UK 2004
The Green London Way, Bob Gilbert (Lawrence & Wishart Ltd 1991)
Terence Conran on London, Terence Conran (Conran Octopus 2004)
Georgian London, John Summerson (Yale University Press 2003)
The Lost Rivers of London, Nicholas Barton (Historical Publications 1992)
Blue Guide London, Roger Woodley (A & C Black 2002)
London's Secret History, Peter Bushell (Constable 1983)
The Open Spaces of London, A. Forshaw & L. Bergstrom (Allison & Busby 1986)
The Annals of London, J.Richardson

(Weidenfeld Nicolson Illustrated 2001)
A Walk Round London's Parks, Hunter Davies (H Hamilton 1983)
American Walks in London, R. Tames (Weidenfeld Nicolson 1996)
Underground London, Stephen Smith (Abacus 2005)
London (The Biography), Peter Ackroyd (Vintage 2001)
London: A Short History, A N Wilson (Phoenix 2005)
The Worldwide Guide to Movie Locations Presents: London, Tony Reeves (Titan Books 2003)
The Peopling of London (Fifteen Thousand Years of Settlement from Overseas), Nick Merriman (Museum of London 1993)

Index

A
Abney Park Cemetery & Nature Reserve 44
Alexandra Palace 304
Alexandra Palace Park 47
Argyle Square 234

B
Barnes Common 283
Barbican Conservatory 295
Barnsbury Wood 48
Battersea Park 98, 101, **102**
Beech Gardens 295
Belair Park 142
Belgrave Square Garden 228, **234**
Bermondsey Spa Gardens 123
Bishop's Park 81
Bloomsbury Square 228, **235**
Bonnington Square 258
The Brew House Café 317
British Medical Association Council Garden 235
Broad Walk Café 317
Brockwell Park **125**, 318, 320
Bruce Castle Park 49
Brunei Gallery SOAS Roof Gardens **237**
Burgess Park **131**, 329
Bushy Park 212

C
Cadogan Place Gardens 255
Calthorpe Community Garden 228, 237
Camley Street Natural Park 50
Carnaval Del Pueblo 329
Cavendish Square 228, **237**
Charterhouse Square 228, **238**
Chelsea Physic Garden 267
Clapham Common 285
Cleveland Gardens 255
Clissold Park 53
Coram's Fields 13
Courtfield Gardens East 255
Crossrail Place Roof Garden 297
Crystal Palace Museum 307
Crystal Palace Park **134**, 317
Culpeper Community Garden 254
Culpeper Rooftop Garden 297

D
Devonshire Square 228, 238
Drapers' Hall Garden 238
Dulwich Park **140**, 318

E
Eardley Road Sidings 107
Embankment Gardens 228, **239**
Emslie Horniman Pleasance 82
Ennismore Gardens 255
Epping Forest 215

F
Finsbury Circus Garden 228, **239**
Finsbury Park 54

Index

Finsbury Square 228, **239**
Fulham Palace 81, 85, **305**
Fulham Palace Gardens 85

G

Garden at 120 298
Geraldine Mary Harmsworth Park 144
Gladstone Park **56**, 323
Golden Square **228**, 242
Golders Hill Park Café 319
Gordon Square 228, **242**
Gray's Inn Gardens 242
Green Park 15
Greenwich Park **147**, 310-11, 321
Greenwich Peninsular Ecology Park 153
Grosvenor Square 229, **243**
Gunnersbury Park 86

H

Hackney City Farm 182, **312**
Hackney Marshes 179
Haggerston Park **182**, 312
Hammersmith Park **89**
Hampstead Heath 63
Hampton Court Gardens 269
Hampton Court Palace Flower Show 328
Hanover Square 229, **243**
Harleyford Road Community Garden 258
Highgate Wood & Queen's Wood 67
Holland House 306

Holland Park 76-77, **90**, 327
Horniman Gardens 154
Horniman Café 319
Hyde Park **19**, 318

I

Inner Temple Garden 240-1, **243**
Island Gardens Park 178

J

John Madejski Garden at the V &A Museum 256
Jubilee Gardens 229, **244**

K

Kennington Park 156
Kensington Gardens 11, **18**, 317, 319
Kensington Palace Pavilion 319
Kentish Town City Farm 70
Kew the Music 328
Kyoto Garden 79, 91-3

L

Ladbroke Square 256
Lambeth Country Show 328
Lauderdale House Café 73, **320**
Leathermarket Gardens 157
Leicester Square 229, **244**
Lido Café at Brockwell Park 320
Lincoln's Inn Fields 27
London Fields 185
London Open Gardens 231
London Wetland Centre 273
London Zoo 304

Index

M

Mary Harmsworth Park 144
Meanwhile Gardens 94
Mile End Park 186
Morden Hall Park **217**, 322
Mount Street Gardens 229, **244**
Myatt's Fields Park 158
Myddelton Square 245
Museum of the Home Gardens 261

N

National Maritime Museum 310
Norwood Grove 107

O

Open Gardens Weekend 230-1
Opera Holland Park 306, 327
Osterley Park 211, **219**, 324
Oxleas Woods 160

P

Paradise Park 70
Pasley Park 171
Pavilion Tea House 321
Pear Tree Café 321
Peckham Rye Park & Common 161, 286
Pembroke Lodge 321
Phoenix Gardens 28
Pimlico Gardens 245
Portman Square 229, **245**
Postman's Park 8-9, 31
Primrose Hill 33
Priory Park 71

Q

Queen Elizabeth Olympic Park **189**, 324
Queen's Gate Gardens 256
Queen's House 310
Queen's Park 75
Queen's Wood 67

R

Ragged School Museum 186, 312
Ravenscourt Park **96**
Red Lion Square 229, **247**
Regent's Park **33**, 305, 322, 327
Regent's Park Open Air Theatre 327
Rembrandt Gardens 256
Richmond Park **222**, 321
Riverside Café 322
Riverside Walk Gardens 247
Ropemakers' Field 261
Royal Botanic Gardens 275
The Royal Observatory & Planetarium 147, **311**, 321
Ruskin Park 164
Russell Square 229, **247**

S

Serpentine Bar & Kitchen 322
Serpentine Gallery 306
Sky Garden 298
Slade Gardens 165
Soho Square 229, **248**
Southwark Cathedral Churchyard 258
Southwark Park 166

Index

Speakers' Corner 307
Springfield Park **194**, 323
Stables Tea Room 324
St Alphage Gardens 229, **248**
St James's Café 323
St James's Park **37**, 323
St James's Square 229, **248**
Streatham Common 288
Streatham Rookery 106
Sunray Gardens 167
Sydenham Hill Woods 142
Sydenham Wells Park 168
Syon Park and Gardens 280

T

Tabard Gardens 169
Tate Modern Garden 249
Tavistock Square 229, **248**
The Thames Barrier 311
Thames Barrier Park 198
The Tradescant Garden at the Garden Museum 229, 250
Tooting Commons 289
Torrington Square 229, **249**
Trafalgar Square 229, **249**

U

Unigate Wood 107

V

Valentine's Park 201
Vauxhall City Farm 111
Vauxhall Park 112
Vauxhall Pleasure Gardens 114
Victoria Park 202
Victoria Tower Gardens 229, **250**

W

Walworth Garden Farm 171
Wandsworth Common 290
Wanstead Flats 206
Waterloo Millennium Green 250
Waterlow Park 43, **72**, 320
West Ham Park 207
Westminster Abbey College Gardens 251
West Square Gardens 172
Wilmington Square 251
Wimbledon Common 293
Windmill Gardens 117
Woburn Square 251
Wormwood Scrubs 97

Subject Index

Animal enclosures
Alexandra Palace Park 304
Battersea Park 102
Clissold Park 53
Coram's Field 13
Crystal Palace Park 134
Horniman Gardens 154
Kentish Town City Farm 70
Regent's Park 33
Vauxhall City Farm 111
Victoria Park 202

Athletic tracks
Clapham Common 285
Crystal Palace Park 134
Finsbury Park 54
Haggerston Park 182
Hampstead Heath 63
Kennington Park 156
Mile End Park 186
Queen Elizabeth Olympic Park 189
Regent's Park 33
Ruskin Park 164
Springfield Park 194
Tooting Commons 289
Victoria Park 202

Bathing ponds/Lidos
Brockwell Park 125
Hampstead Heath 63
Hyde Park 19
London Fields 185
Tooting Commons 289

Boating lakes
Alexandra Palace Park 47
Dulwich Park 140
Finsbury Park 54
Greenwich Park 147
Gunnersbury Park 86
Hampstead Heath 63
Hyde Park 19
Regent's Park 33
Victoria Park 202

Bowling greens
Bishop's Park 81
Brockwell Park 125
Bruce Castle Park 49
Bushy Park 212
Clapham Common 285
Dulwich Park 140
Finsbury Circus Garden 239
Gladstone Park 56
Gunnersbury Park 86
Hammersmith Park 89
Hampstead Heath 63
Hyde Park 19
Peckham Rye Park 161
Ravenscourt Park 96
Southwark Park 166
Springfield Park 194
Valentine's Park 201
Vauxhall Park 112
Victoria Park 202
Wandsworth Common 290

Cafés

Alexandra Palace Park 47
Barbican Conservatory 295
Battersea Park 102
Beech Gardens 295
Birdsong Café 144
Bishop's Park 81
Brew House 317
Broad Walk Café 317
Chelsea Physic Gardens 267
Clapham Common 285
Clissold Park 53
Coram's Fields 13
Crossrail Place Roof Garden 297
Culpeper Rooftop Garden 297
Dulwich Park 140
Embankment Gardens 239
Epping Forest 215
Finsbury Park 54
Garden at 120 298
Gladstone Park 56
Golders Hill Park Café 319
Green Park 15
Greenwich Park 147
Gunnersbury Park 86
Hackney City Farm 312
Hampstead Heath 63
Hampton Court Gardens 269
Highgate Wood and Queen's Wood 67
Holland Park 90
Horniman Café 319
Hyde Park 19
Island Gardens Park 178
Kennington Park 156
Kensington Gardens 18
Kennington Palace Pavilion 319
Lauderdale House Café 320
Leathermarket Gardens 157
Lido Café at Brockwell Park 320
Momo's Garden Café 242
Morden Hall Park 217
Oxleas Woods 160
Pavilion Café 320
Pavilion Tea House 321
Pembroke Lodge 321
Queen Elizabeth Olympic Park 189
Queen's Park 75
Regent's Park 33
Richmond Park 222
Riverside Café 322
Royal Botanic Gardens 275
Russell Square 247
Serpentine Bar & Kitchen 322
Sky Garden 298
Southwark Park 166
Springfield Park Café 323
Stables Café 323
Stables Tea Room 324
Streatham Rookery 106
Thames Barrier Park 198
Tooting Commons 289
Victoria Park 202

Cricket Pitches
Barnes Common 283
Burgess Park 131
Bushy Park 212
Clissold Park 53
Crystal Palace Park 134
Dulwich Park 140
Epping Forest 215
Finsbury Park 54
Greenwich Park 147
Hackney Marshes 179
Hampstead Heath 63
Highgate Wood and Queen's Wood 67
Holland Park 90
London Fields 185
Regent's Park 33
Springfield Park 194
Valentine's Park 201
Victoria Park 202
West Ham Park 207
Wimbledon Common 293

Farms
Coram's Fields 13
Crystal Palace Park 134
Hackney City Farm 312
Haggerston Park 182
Osterley Park 219
Queens Park 75
Vauxhall City Farm 111

Fishing
Battersea Park 102
Burgess Park 131
Bushy Park 212
Clapham Common 285
Crystal Palace Park 134
Gunnersbury Park 86
Hampstead Heath 63
Osterley Park 219
Richmond Park 222
Syon Park and Gardens 280
Tooting Commons 289
Victoria Park 202
Wandsworth Common 290

Horse riding
Bushy Park 212
Dulwich Park 140
Epping Forest 215
Hampstead Heath 63
Hyde Park 19
Richmond Park 222
Tooting Commons 289
Vauxhall City Farm 111
Vauxhall Pleasure Gardens 114
Wimbledon Common 293

Nature Reserves/ Wildlife areas
Abney Park Cemetery & Nature Reserve 44
Barnes Common 283
Battersea Park 102
Bushy Park 212
Camley Street Natural Park 50
Eardley Road Sidings 107

Index

Epping Forest 215
Greenwich Peninsular Ecology Park 153
Haggerston Park 182
Highgate Wood and Queen's Wood 67
Holland Park 90
London Wetland Centre 273
Norwood Grove 107
Peckham Rye Park 161
Richmond Park 222
Southwark Park 166
Sydenham Hill Woods 142
Unigate Wood 107
Wandsworth Common 290

Tennis Courts

Battersea Park 102
Bishop's Park 81
Brockwell Park 125
Bruce Castle Park 49
Burgess Park 131
Bushy Park 212
Clapham Common 285
Clissold Park 53
Dulwich Park 140
Finsbury Park 54
Gladstone Park 56
Greenwich Park 147
Gunnersbury Park 86
Hackney Marshes 179
Hammersmith Park 89
Hampstead Heath 63
Hyde Park 19
Lincoln's Inn Field 27
London Fields 185
Myatt's Fields 158
Priory Park 71
Queen Elizabeth Olympic Park 189
Queens Park 75
Ravenscourt Park 96
Regent's Park 33
Ruskin Park 164
Southwark Park 166
Springfield Park 194
Streatham Rookery 106
Sydenham Wells Park 168
Tooting Commons 289
Valentine's Park 201
Vauxhall Park 112
Victoria Park 202
Wandsworth Common 290
Waterlow Park 72
West Ham Park 207

About us:

Based in London, Metro is a small independent publishing company with a reputation for producing well-researched and beautifully-designed guides.

London's Hidden Walks Series

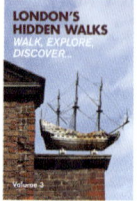

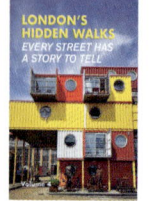

A wonderful way to explore this sometimes secretive city." Robert Elms, BBC London 94.9FM

To find out more about Metro and order our guides, take a look at our website:

www.metropublications.com

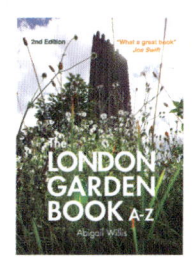

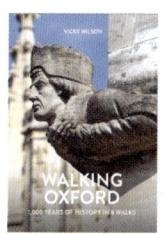

THE LONDON GARDEN BOOK A–Z
2nd Edition
"What a great book" Joe Swift
Abigail Willis

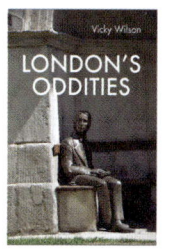

LONDON'S ODDITIES
Vicky Wilson

LONDON ARCHITECTURE
Marianne Butler

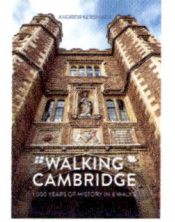

WALKING CAMBRIDGE
ANDREW KERSHMAN 
1,000 YEARS OF HISTORY IN 6 WALKS

WALKING BRIGHTON & HOVE
ANDREW KERSHMAN
1,000 YEARS OF HISTORY IN 8 WALKS

WALKING OXFORD
VICKY WILSON
1,000 YEARS OF HISTORY IN 8 WALKS

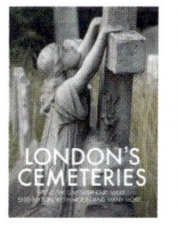

LONDON'S CEMETERIES
VISIT THE CAPITAL'S MAGNIFICENT SEVEN, STOKE NEWINGTON AND MANY MORE

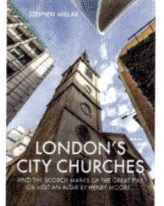

LONDON'S CITY CHURCHES
STEPHEN MILLAR
FIND THE SCORCH MARKS OF THE GREAT FIRE OR VISIT AN ALTAR BY HENRY MOORE

VEGGIE & VEGAN LONDON
ROWAN PRZENGYWEJE

LONDON'S HOUSES
FROM WORKHOUSE TO ROYAL PALACE, COME IN, CLOSE THE DOOR AND STEP BACK IN TIME

LONDON'S MONUMENTS
FROM BOUDICCA AND BYRON TO GUY THE GORILLA

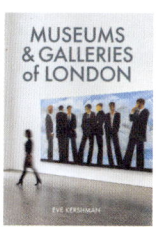

MUSEUMS & GALLERIES of LONDON
EVE KERSHMAN

GREEN LONDON
Written by Nana Ocran
Photography by Metro
(other photo credits – see p.337)
Edited by Abigail Willis
Design by Susi Koch & Lesley Gilmour
Illustrations by Lesley Gilmour

All rights reserved. No part of this publication may be reproduced, stored in a retrieval system or transmitted in any form or by any means electronic, mechanical, photocopying, recording or otherwise without the prior consent of the publishers and copyright owners. Every effort has been made to ensure the accuracy of this book; however, due to the nature of the subject the publishers cannot accept responsibility for any errors which occur, or their consequences.

Published in 2023 by Metro Publications Ltd
www.metropublications.com

Metro® is a registered trade mark of Associated Newspapers Limited. The METRO mark is under licence from Associated Newspapers Limited.

Printed and bound in China
© Metro Publications Ltd 2023
British Library Cataloguing in Publication Data.
A catalogue record for this book is available from the British Library.

ISBN 978-1-902910-75-8

MIX
Paper | Supporting responsible forestry
FSC® C016973